In Search of Truth

For my Teacher

In Search of Truth
Faith and Modern Science

C.W. Adams

Readworthy
New Delhi

First published in 2008 by

Readworthy Publications (P) Ltd.

Regd. Off.: A-18, Mohan Garden
Near Nawada Metro Station
New Delhi – 110 059 (India)
Phone: 011-2537 1324

Branch: 4662/21, Ansari Road
Daryaganj
New Delhi – 110 002
Phone: 011-43549197

Fax: +91-11-2537 1323
Email: info@readworthypub.com
Web: www.readworthypub.com

In conjunction with

Sacred Earth Publishing
Wilmington, Delaware (USA)
www.sacredearthpublishers.com

Cataloging in Publication Data–DK

Courtesy: D.K. Agencies (P) Ltd. <docinfo@dkagencies.com>

Adams, C. W., 1958-

In search of truth : faith and modern science / by C.W. Adams.

p. cm.

Includes bibliographical references (p.)

Includes Index

ISBN India : 978-81-89973-60-5 (PBK) US : 978-0-9816045-0-3
ISBN India : 978-81-89973-61-2 (HBD) US : 978-0-9816045-4-1

1. Truth. 2. Faith. 3. Philosophy and science. 4. Religion and science. I. Title.

DDC 121 22 Library of Congress Control Number: 2008902201

Printed at D.K. Fine Art Press, Delhi - 52

Contents

Introduction *vii*

1: The Search for Truth 1

2: True Identity 13

3: The Science of Faith 49

4: The Intentional Creation 105

5: Evolution of the Living 157

6: The Personal Universe 215

References and Bibliography 269

Index 291

Introduction

Each of us persistently seeks fulfillment. This is because we experience an emptiness that cannot seem to be filled with the various physical things we try to consume. No matter how wealthy, famous or surrounded with people we might be, our emptiness within persists.

This constant emptiness indicates we have a deeper need beyond this physical existence. Many of us, after realizing material consumption does not fulfill us, will begin a search for the Truth. During this search, we may approach modern science for objective answers. Unfortunately, most of us find that modern science does not seem to objectively explore the Truth. Instead, we often find various science journals and publications pushing a particular agenda. We often find our modern scientists stuck in the paradigm of having to satisfy financially-driven scientific institutions, scientific publications, peers and educational institutions, all of which often seem to have particular agendas related to profits and/or reputation.

As a result, we unfortunately find that much of the institution of modern science comes up short on its obligation to help us find the Truth. This is not to say, however, that there is a lack of modern research pointing the way towards the Truth. Many of our modern researchers have made honest attempts to provide us with information indicating at least in some small way, where the Truth may lie. After even a lifetime of research and exploration through modern science, however, many of us find modern science presents very little Truth that can be applied to life in a practical manner.

Many turn to organized religion to satisfy our quest for the Truth. As we do, we are often faced again with various agendas of those who dictate the terms of faith. Though we may find honorable teachers who pass wisdom with integrity, we may also find many institutions teaching dogma emphasizing interpretations that satisfy specific agendas. We may also find religious institutions focused on the sectarian differences with other institutions rather than the science of their teachings. The conclusion of many in our society is that the teachings of some of these institutions are not practical when viewed from a perspective of science.

Continuing our pursuit, we may also come upon various philosophical teachings that partially appeal to our sense of Truth, but do not seem to answer our practical questions. Some of the newer philosophical teachings may also come with agendas and broad scientific theorization. While some are blended with the newest theories of physics and chemistry, many of these also include strong profit incentives. We might find some of these philosophies butter us up with flowery language, yet come up short on substance and practicality.

Why should the Truth not make practical sense to us? Why should we not be able to clearly understand and apply the Truth in our everyday lives? Why should we not be able to apply the Truth to scientific data and our hearts, minds and faith all at the same time?

Conversely, why should science and philosophy not answer the basic questions we have concerning the world around us, and our basic needs to understand ourselves?

The *Search for Truth* is an attempt to reveal Truth in real terms: it is Truth applied to real life. Real science is Truth applied because everything in existence conforms to the Truth. The Truth can be observed within all things, once our vision is cleared of the fog of speculation and desire. Nature does not conflict with the Truth because nature fits inside the Truth. Since nature conforms to the Truth, its application and evidence is apparent in science.

Unlike blind faith, Truth exposes the lies and deceptions brought forth by those who seek their own gain. Truth sheds a light on the unseen parts of our lives and uncurls the mysteries of the universe. Truth shines a beam into our heart, squelching the shadows of doubt and judgment.

As it is often said, nothing of value comes easily. Finding the Truth in this lifetime undoubtedly requires diligence. It requires a serious questioning of everything around us: a doubting of everything we are taught and everything we see. It requires study and contemplation. It requires self-doubt and inner work. It requires a humble and persistent quest, without any proud stance of:

"I have found it."

Finding the actual meaning to our existence requires sincerity and humility. It requires an honest look at ourselves and an assessment of our intentions. Are we looking for the actual Truth or are we simply trying to *fit in?* Are we searching for real Truth or are we trying to appear religious or philosophical in order to gain the respect of others? Are we following someone's teachings just because *others* accept them or because their teachings truly make sense to us?

Indeed, during our search for Truth we must not let those who have not found the actual meaning of life convince us that it is not there. After all, if life had no meaning, why would we constantly search for it?

These are the hard questions we must ask ourselves throughout our search for Truth. It is not easy to doubt our own intentions and the intentions of others, but it is necessary. It is easy to assume that we have the best of intentions, and that what we know is all there is to know. It is harder to accept that there is a lot out there we do not know. Yet it is this very acknowledgement that is necessary to enable learning.

Knowledge is inseparable from action: To truly know something is to live within that reality—understanding it through personal application. Personal application also requires humility. The moment we become proud of what we think we know Truth will slip away from us. Within Truth, pride has no place. Real Truth in action will continually humble us, its light fading should we try to proudly claim it: Just as water will seep through our hands should we try to grasp it.

We must take comfort in knowing that ultimately the search for the actuality of our existence, as long as it is done earnestly, honestly and with integrity, will never be a waste of time. The beautiful thing about the Truth is that even a small sliver of it can shine the brightest of lights upon our lives. Like walking with a lantern in the wilderness, even one small light can light an entire path as we walk down it.

During our search for the meaning of life, we come upon so many obstacles. These obstacles are put there for a reason. We must consider the possibility that our own personal search for Truth at this moment may or may not be the search for the actual Truth. A saying that might describe this is:

"You can't handle the truth."

If we are truly looking for the Truth about life and who we truly are, we must be prepared for the Truth possibly destroying our misconceptions and expectations. We must therefore be ready to give up our ideas and speculations.

Although even a little Truth is satisfying, it is endless, and our hunger for it will never cease. As opposed to material facts, which eventually lead to satiation and boredom, Truth feeds our inner being. Truth satisfies us while keeping us humbly yearning for more. This is because actual Truth is expansive, and humility is its companion.

The information provided in this book relate to the modern culture we live in today. With information swirling around us at incredible speeds, we have more opportunity than ever to access information. In receiving information however, we must be careful to consider the source. We should consider that many media sources pad, filter, or distort information for purposes of profit and market dominance. Through satellite television and the internet, we can now potentially know more about other cultures and peoples than ever before. We can also be bombarded by images and ideas that seek to color our vision of reality and distract our attention. Skeptics of the Truth might even say:

"If it is too good to be true it probably isn't."

Often it is assumed that the theories and speculations supported by educational institutions are scientific fact. These scientific postulations, though presented through seemingly credible media by professional researchers with advanced degrees, are still at the end of the day, speculative guesses.

In this writing, we offer the reader logical explanations of the world around us together with common occurrences, everyday observations, documented scientific data and ancient wisdom. People who keep up with basic news media, access the internet, have had a basic science course or two and live in the modern world should be familiar with some of these points. Some of the points made and examples given may irritate those in the scientific community, as they may not be *controlled* observations nor referenced adequately. As we will illustrate, true *control,* obtained by eliminating all known and unknown variables while isolating outside influences, is virtually impossible to achieve by humans. We just do not have that sort of authority over nature. As such, we may stumble upon the realization that:

"The more we know,
the more we know we don't know."

In an effort to illustrate some of the points advanced here, some of the observations, experiments, and theories published by scientists over the past few centuries are presented. While providing reference and illustration from documented reports, this is by no means an attempt to render a complete picture of that particular scientist, theory, observation, or experiment in this context. While an attempt to illustrate and review the science as documented in available references is being made, there is an understanding that there are often many sides and views to every subject. As discovered during the completion of the author's doctoral degree, reviews and criticisms of peers and professors can provide substance and reference for further inquiry. While one might construe unfairness with critique, we must also recognize that one of the basic tenets of modern science is to provide a forum for review and appraisal. If a particular scientist is not accepting of any such review and appraisal, then we should hardly consider that scientist part of a peer-reviewed forum.

If we accept peer-review as part of science's model, then we must be ready to also review and appraise the entire process and the fundamental assumptions that provide the foundation for further assumption. As any builder will tell us, the need for a strong foundation for any large building is essential. Therefore the fundamental assumptions used by modern science should be considered rather carefully and even skeptically prior to building further assumptions upon them. If modern science cannot openly consider such skeptical reviews and appraisals of its assumptions, then we can hardly call this institution science.

This said, we offer our fellow scientists respect and appreciation for their attempts to find the Truth. Whether their search comes with ulterior motive or complete integrity, we thank them for their efforts. While this book may question and identify incongruities within the institutions, assumptions and logic of many modern scientific conclusions, it also in many cases utilizes this very same institution and research to establish or illustrate its evidence. Either way, we respect the attempt to provide an objective basis for establishing Truth, and hope that those scientists who read this will also respect the need to provide possible alternatives to current assumptions and conclusions.

There are a number of allegorical stories and analogies used to clarify and illustrate certain points. Most of these are presented for easy distinction. It is hoped the reader will ponder these with an eye towards the effect Truth has upon the universe: Truth must beam into the largest and smallest: into the simple and the complex—all simultaneously.

Forgive us for repetition of some points. These points may either be more complex or be key issues or evidence. Sometimes we will address these from various vantages to provide better perspective.

Appreciation is given to the author's mentors, professors, and teachers who encouraged a thorough study of the facts over the years. In addition, humble acknowledgement is given to an ancient and confidential knowledge, lovingly passed down through many generations of devoted teachers. We give thanks to these devoted teachers, and hope this work fairly passes this information to another generation. Furthermore, we hope this work may somehow inspire the sincere searcher to make progress on the path towards the Ultimate Truth.

C.W. Adams, 2008, info@actualtruth.org

1

The Search for Truth

A man walking down the street came upon a dog. The big dog with thick golden hair weaved about the road, sniffing at the ground anxiously. Its eyes darted from one side of the road to another as it paced back and forth. The man approached the dog to check its collar. The collar had no tag. The dog appeared anxious and desperate. The dog directed his wet nose up and down the man's body, sniffing the man's feet and hands thoroughly, as if they might provide some solution. The dog then returned to sniffing along the ground. The anxious and purposeful behavior of the dog told the man the dog was looking for someone. The man concluded the dog must be lost and looking for its owner. As the man walked on, he kept an eye out for a man looking for a dog.

Why search for something that does not exist?

Because the dog was searching anxiously, intent on finding something or someone, the logical assessment would be that the dog was lost and looking for its owner. Why would the dog search for someone or something that did not exist?

If the man had observed the dog strolling around sniffing trees and digging up bones without any urgency, the man would probably assume the dog was not lost. He might assume it was taking a short walk away from home, combing its neighborhood for new scents, and buried treasure. He would not make any effort to locate its owner in that case because there was no problem.

If we examine human behavior, we notice a pattern similar to the lost dog. Most of us spend our lives in perpetual search. Our search typically focuses on looking for that *something or someone* to bring us fulfillment. Then, as we remain unfulfilled, the probe may turn inward. This is only logical because in order to know what will fulfill us, we must first know *who we are.* Thus we often hear people say:

"I need to find myself."

Most of us at one time or another has asked the critical questions *who am I? Why am I here?* Our search for answers to these will take a number of forms. For some it may become the search for our ancestry. We might search through our family tree for the *roots* of our family genealogy. For an astronomer it may become a lifetime of search for life on other planets. For a psychologist it may become a search for a better understanding for what makes people *tick.* For an archeologist it may become a search for what happened to our ancestors. For a physicist it may become a search for the structure of the universe. For others it may become philosophical or religious study.

Most of us focus our search for fulfillment upon finding that special someone who will make us happy. From a very young age, we begin our search for a mate. We assume there is someone special out there intended just for us. Should we believe we have found that person, we may marry them. Then for a while, we may settle down. It is assumed that once we have found that special someone, our search is over and we can settle down. This concept assumes that we have *settled* for someone, almost as though we know the person we settled for is not necessarily the person we were searching *for.*

While some may successfully settle down the urge for someone of the opposite sex after marriage, this rarely stops our quest for fulfillment. We find this in our observations of couples the world over. Once they have found each other, we see couples urgently directing their search at establishing a family. We see couples change their focus from each other to having children. We see couples focus their attention on buying a home or homestead. We find couples focusing their attention on establishing the means to provide for this home: a good career and income.

Once the homestead is established, the kids have come, and career and income is set; we do not see an end to the seeking of the individuals within the family. Rather, we see the search continue in so many other forms, as these individuals reach out for other hobbies, groups, and activities in their search for fulfillment.

Simple observation reveals that in one way or another, we are all *struggling* in our attempts to accomplish fulfillment. On a daily basis, we toil, engaging in competitive activities to achieve particular goals and objectives. When we get frustrated with these attempts, some may for a moment ask *why or what am I searching for*, but for many, the conveyor belt of modern society redirects our search towards physical acquisition.

We can observe our redirected search for Truth in our media. In television, investigative journalism and mysteries of the unknown are very popular. The facts surrounding a missing child, or whether a man killed his wife intrigue most of us. Also popular are science fiction dramas that explore outer-world alien scenarios. 'Reality shows' are also quite popular, though many are far from real. In these 'reality shows', there is usually some suspense added in terms of an unknown factor: Who will win, or who will pick whom. In literature, true mystery stories or realistic fictional works are very popular. The fantasy novels popular among children are not so attractive to adults. Adults tend to have a fascination with true stories with mysterious details, or fictional works of mystery and suspense. The urge to obtain more information is why newspapers and news magazines are so popular. Finding the facts and uncovering the mystery of an event draws the readers. All of these forms of media reflect a commonality among every individual in our society: Our incessant search for Truth.

We can also see tremendous energies being focused upon scientific discovery in modern society. Billions are spent every month in efforts to peer further into outer space or see smaller units of microphysical matter. Our urge for scientific discovery has evolved into a frenzied outreach into every nook and cranny of our physical dimension. The amount of money spent by governments on scientific discovery is astounding when one considers the alternate uses of such funds. One might consider space flight and other scientific exploration a waste of money when poverty and starvation are so rampant around the world. This simply illustrates the urgency our society has for finding Truth. The search for answers regarding our existence is apparently more important than the survival or health of our society or other human beings.

Where is my home?

At one time or another, we all search for a good place to live and *belong*. Depending upon our financial condition, we may look for that special place to call *home*. Our idea of *home* is typically a mix of being close to our job, being close with our family and friends, and being in a comfortable or convenient location: A place where we feel we *belong*. Often climate or convenience will be sacrificed for the ability to be close to our family. In the context of priorities, most of us rate our family ahead of physical comforts. Where we *settle* is usually determined by changing factors. Then after the hassle of finding a place to call home, as soon as we settle in, many of us will continue to look for a better place. Or we may spend years renovating our current house in an attempt to feel that we belong here.

Outside of the raw nature of our house, we look to belong within a family and community. When we are younger, we strive to belong with our family. As we grow we seek to belong with the people around us—our schoolmates and later our workmates. Later we may seek to form a new family to belong to as we become old enough to marry and have children. Then we may search for that right town or neighborhood to belong to. When we find an area we are comfortable with, we may seek a position and role to play within that community—all in an effort to belong to a community. Our role is critical to us, as we often relate our role within one or more of these communities or groups as defining ourselves. In these various ways, we look to find ourselves by locating that place and role where we *belong.*

We search for the perfect situation.

These are only a few of the forms our search takes on. In reality, most of us are searching for *something* at every moment. If it is not one thing, it is another. At some point in time we'll search for that successful job or career, pondering the purpose of our existence in relationship with our career choices. At another point we might search for that perfect partner to settle down with. At still another point we will look for the right college or school. Many of us will endeavor for many years in order to accomplish a professional career, only to later change careers; being unfulfilled with our previous choice. We will also search for friends and associates to share and exchange ideas with—typically those on the same *wavelength.* Some of us will also spend considerable time searching for more mundane items. We might search for the right car, the right clothes, or the right furniture. While many of us might believe these items will provide some sense of fulfillment directly, many of us might also believe that if we possess the right material objects, others will love us.

We are thus searching for the perfect mix in life—the perfect scenario. From our partner to our job, house, friends, and car, we endeavor to put together the perfect combination. For this reason, people in modern society are constantly on the go. We are rushing to achieve that perfect mix, moving and changing constantly in various attempts to rearrange things. To get things arranged *just so,* we might change jobs or careers, move to a new location, or buy a new car when these all may work just fine. In these ways, we continue to look for the perfect scenario.

Vacations are a good example of our search for the perfect scenario. During two or three weeks out of every year, many of us endeavor to accomplish the ultimate vacation. Rather than using those weeks to relax and rest, we prefer to endeavor with much difficulty and expense to travel to a remote location, only to lie down or run around in another place. Our hope is that by going to this remote place we will find, at least for a few days, that perfect scenario. This is why we typically vacation in tropical locations. We imagine the comfortable weather and beauty of the tropics will create that perfection for which we are searching.

We seek to find it.

The perfect scenario is typically so vague that we may refer to our goal as *"finding it."* We may look for *it* through various sensual activities—seeking fulfillment within eating, sex, music, visual entertainment and other objects of the senses. Frustrated by these, we may seek to find *it* within our relationships, searching for that perfect partner. We may take a vacation, find a new house, change jobs, or create new goals in hopes of finding *it.* We may fantasize about achieving whatever *it* we are anticipating. This increases our hopes that *it* will give us happiness. We may work hard for many years to accomplish *it,* saving up our money to buy *it.* Our dreams of finding *it* are usually accompanied by *its* perceived rewards or results. We may visualize our accomplishing *it* with people cheering us or looking up to us with envy—wishing they had *it.* These types of visualizations serve to create the illusion of future happiness. This is not what happens however. The illusion of *it* bringing us happiness becomes obvious when—once we reach *it*—we immediately begin to search for the next *it.* The fulfilling of *it* must just be around the corner, we assume.

Worldly frustration deepens the search.

At some point or another—often after a number of failed attempts at happiness—the conscious human may embark on a quest for some hard truth about existence. This may come at a young age, when we are curious about life and want to know *why* things are the way they are. Our western culture can unfortunately squelch the early search: The early search can easily be overrun by our society's persistent messages that physical things will fulfill us.

Should our earlier inquisitiveness be ignored or overrun, most of us will eventually come to a point in our lives where we urgently question everything. This might follow a trauma such as a death in the family, a serious injury, or the loss of a job. It might simply result from not being fulfilled after achieving physical success. Sometimes this is referred to as a *mid-life crisis,* because it often occurs after a person has had enough time to accomplish career, financial or family goals once imagined as being fulfilling. This might appear to others as an attempt to be young again, as youth is often connected with learning, exploration and starting over. Actually, it is a renewed search *"to find myself."*

Sometimes a person might—after becoming completely exhausted with the stress and uncertainty of the physical world—undergo what is commonly termed a *nervous breakdown.* Although often we may think of the nervous breakdown as a negative and uncomfortable event, it can also lead to a serious intent to truly *find ourselves.*

Would we search for something that did not exist?

Our incessant searching tells us that we know deep inside there is a reason for existence. Our search for the perfect scenario tells us that the perfect scenario exists. Like the lost dog, our very search implies its existence.

Every one of us asks the same questions at one time or another during our lifetime:

Who am I?

Where do I come from?

What is my purpose for existing?

The quest to know these answers is the common thread among every human society. Every nationality, every sect, every tribe, and all humans search for the answers to these questions. These questions pervade the richest and poorest societies. They concern the young and the old. They are pondered by the most and least educated of us. They are asked among various media ranging from the oldest manuscripts and cave drawings to the latest movies, web pages and modern music lyrics.

This isn't to say that no one finds answers. As in most things, results are relative to the effort made. A diligent effort to ponder the questions and find the answers will result in greater opportunities to obtain those answers. Good, complete answers typically require a persistent quest from the right sources. A half-hearted attempt at finding anything will typically result in half-completed discovery.

Speculation does not satisfy our search.

Speculation does not satisfy our search because speculation comes from the mind. If a person says "I think….." it is usually followed by "I really don't know—I could be wrong." Speculation does not qualify as Truth because it is tainted by the contents of the mind. The mind, like a tape recorder, records, and catalogs input from the senses. Therefore, the mind is limited by sensory input. If the input is faulty, the speculation will be faulty. A person who speculates and claims "this is fact" is only being deceptive to themselves and others.

Speculation requires no evidence. Speculation requires no observation. Speculation may follow an observation but will have no assurance that the interpretations of the observation were factual. Thus, speculation has no real scientific rigor.

Virtually anyone can speculate on any matter. A person with no formal education can speculate just as well as a person with an advanced degree. We typically give more credibility to speculators with advanced degrees though. We assume they are basing their speculations on more information. We assume the advanced degree indicates more knowledge on that subject matter. The uneducated man also may speculate on the same subjects, coming to similar conclusions. At the very least, since speculation does not require solid evidence, there is no assurance that either the educated or the non-educated speculator is correct in their postulations.

Most double blind, randomized and controlled clinical studies are concluded with speculation. The interpretation of the observations will be subject to the speculation of the researcher concluding the results. This conclusion will be based on the researcher's opinions, based on his or her background and history of sense perception. In this way modern science is highly speculative, and thus cannot satisfy our search for Truth.

A knowledgeable resource is more reliable than a speculative one. A person who receives information from a knowledgeable source becomes a knowledgeable resource as well. Should a person receive a fact and add speculation to it, the fact must be separated from the speculation to be considered fact again. Once facts are tainted with speculation, separating them can be quite a challenge. A conclusion drawn by a speculative interpretation of the facts is still in the end, speculation.

Consider the source and its practical application.

Truth, or reliable information, must come from a reliable source. The messenger of the information must also be reliable.

One must therefore determine whether the source and the messenger are both reliable. Fortunately, Truth can be confirmed from within as well as from without. "Truths" which do not make practical sense as they are applied to reality cannot be confirmed. If it does not make practical sense it must be questioned.

We have lost the Truth.

Our persistent searching tells us that Truth has been a part of us in the past. We have obviously become separated from it. This is why we search for it now. Something lost and searched for was previously possessed.

At the end of the day, it is logical that Truth *must* exist if we are, to varying degrees, each searching for it. Since we are seeking the Truth about our identity and the purpose for our existence, we must *have* an identity and *have* an ultimate purpose for existence. Again like the lost dog, we wouldn't know we were missing something unless we had a prior experience of its existence.

If we consider the intensity of our various individual searches and our probing for answers in every nook and cranny of existence, it is obvious that the answers to these questions are critical to us. The answers are the key to our very reason to live. Not knowing *who we are* or *why we are here* makes us undeniably *lost:*

> *A man arrives at an international airport on a plane from a foreign country. The first things customs agents ask the man as he gets off the plane are: "Show me your passport," and "what is the purpose of your stay?" In other words,* who are you? *and* why are you here? *If the man had no passport, did not remember his name, and could not state why he came into the country, the customs agents will surely identify him as being* lost *(and probably even crazy).*

Knowing *who we are* and *why we are here* are most certainly the most vital pieces of information we can and should know. Conversely, not knowing the answers to these questions puts us in the precarious situation of not only being lost, but also puts us in a situation where we do not know what we should be living for, and what we should be doing with our lives. Functioning in such a way leaves us in the uncomfortable position of acting somewhat crazy, as we anxiously look for what we have lost—much as a lost dog might sniff around—hoping to find something we are missing.

***

Conclusion: *As we become frustrated in our persistent search for fulfillment within the physical world, we may begin a search for the Truth regarding our existence. Since we search for this Truth, it must exist. Understanding our identity and origin will lead us to our purpose for existence and ultimately what will make us happy.*

2

True Identity

The car raced down the open freeway, hurtling its driver towards the man's office. Just as the driver thought he was going to be on time that morning, traffic started backing up. Slowing down with the traffic, the car was rear-ended by oncoming cars. The collision from the rear forced the car to crash into the next car in front. A number of cars piled up as a result. The driver was fortunately unhurt, but his car was crushed. The driver struggled to get out of the car, but unfortunately, the car door was stuck. He was pinned under the steering wheel. Emergency vehicles were onto the scene quickly. Tow trucks began hauling away the piled-up cars one at a time. The driver was relieved when they pulled away the other cars and got to his car. Something was very wrong, however. The tow truck operators hooked his car up and began hauling the car away to the wrecking yard without pulling him out first! The man screamed to be let out as they drove away with the car in tow, but they did not hear him. Arriving at wrecking yard, they began the automated process of dumping the car into the compactor. Incredibly, they had forgotten the driver inside the car.

Who am I?

If we ask someone their identity they will most likely describe either their body's physical features or their body's country of origin. They might say "I am American" or "I am black" or "I am five feet tall, weigh 125 lbs, and female with brown eyes." The logical question is: Am I really this physical body? If so, what happens if our body gains 100 lbs of weight? Does our identity change?

Most of us have a hint that our identity runs deeper than our physical body. A person with a black body wants equality with a person with a white body because that person considers that beneath the skin, we are equal. Similarly, an obese person wants to be treated equally with someone of a more slender stature. Why would we request equality unless we are assuming we have deeper identities?

As modern science has debated this topic, there have been two general views: The first a general machine-like information-processing generating system with various modules of activity, all competing for control. This "chaos-machine" theoretically builds upon a system of learning and evolution without any central person or actor. The other, more prevalent view, portrays each of us as an individual living being, central and governing to the body's existence.

Among proponents of the spirit-driven nature, there is also some debate regarding the characteristics of the spirit. Some suggest it is a portion of the living organism (e.g., *"body, mind and spirit"*). To others it is the morality or "soul" of a person. While debate on this topic continues among researchers searching for the right model of life, there are a number of observational and scientific considerations to consider before we settle our conclusions.

How much do I weigh?

By any physical observation made in the death of any living being, something living leaves the body at death. When we see a living body full of life, movement, energy, personality, and purpose, we understand these symptoms of life are still within the body. When death arrives, suddenly the symptoms of life leave: There is no movement, no energy, and no personality existing within the dead body. The body becomes lifeless.

After thousands of years of scientific observation and research on cadavers no one—not even our modern researchers with seemingly advanced medical instruments—has been able to find any chemical or physical element existing within the body when it is alive, missing when it is dead. The dead body has every physical and material component the living body had. All of the cells are still there. The DNA is still there. All of the nerves, the organs, the brain and central nervous system—every physical element—is still resident in the cadaver.

The claim of the soul weighing 21-grams probably best lies in the urban legend category. In 1907, family physician Dr. Duncan MacDougall attempted an experiment where six patients were monitored as they died upon a table rigged with a scale. Of these six patients, two results had to be eliminated. Two subjects showed minute weight loss upon death, which increased with time with no net loss. Only one result gave an immediate weight loss upon death, yet even that loss reversed itself. In the final analysis, one subject out of six showed a net loss estimated at 2/3 ounce (converted later to a theoretical 21.3 grams). The others showed mixed and inconsistent results. Furthermore, the patient with the 2/3 ounce loss had tuberculosis. Dr. MacDougall also added that the patient was losing about one ounce of water weight per hour due to sweating and respiration prior to death.

A fellow doctor in Massachusetts, Dr. A. Clarke, immediately debated this single finding, arguing the typical sudden rise in body temperature before and subsequent cooling without circulation upon death could account for slight weight changes due to evaporation. Especially noting the patient had lethal tuberculosis.

Until his own death in 1920, Dr. MacDougall tried to repeat the results without success. In one test, he cruelly killed fifteen dogs while weighing them, and found no consensus of weight loss.

No other study has corroborated such a theory of weight loss upon death.

Over thousands of years of intense cadaver research and autopsy, nothing has substantiated any gross difference between the live and dead body. Organs, bones, nerves, brains, blood, neurochemistry, DNA and so many other physical aspects of the live and dead body have been analyzed. Nothing physical has been found to be missing after death.

Quite obviously, the dead body is missing the immeasurable element of *life.* This element drove the living body. This element gave the body personality. This element gave the body energy. This element gave the body the desire to survive. This element gave the body the factors that drove the healing processes, the digestive processes, the sensual processes, the circulatory processes, and so many other biological and biochemical processes. This element of life is definite. It is not imaginary. Seeing a dead body formerly living will clearly illustrate that this key element is real.

The life force has never been seen under a microscope, a CT scan, an MRI, or by any other physical piece of equipment. Furthermore, since this living force separates from the body at death, yet is not evident in physical elements of living or dead bodies, we can scientifically conclude that the life force is not a physical part of the living body.

Since the personality is also gone when this life is gone from the body, it would only be logical to conclude that each of us 'personalities' *is* this life force, and not the physical body: Just as the car driver is not the car. The car driver can and needs to get out of the car at some point. Therefore, the car driver has a separate identity from the car. For this same reasoning, when Socrates' students asked him how he wanted to be buried, Socrates' reply was that they can do whatever they want with his body after death, because he will already have gone by then.

Who is lost during amputation?

If a person were to have an arm amputated because of an infection or other injury, no one considers this person any less of a person. This logic can be extended to even severe cases such as the loss of both arms and legs. An explosion or other traumatic accident might leave ones torso intact while amputating ones arms and legs. Regardless of losing these appendages, the person is still perceived as a whole person, even though their body cannot function in certain ways. The person who operates the body still contains the same conscious being with the same ability to think and reason. This is why paraplegic and quadriplegic rights are protected by law, and why quadriplegic Steven Hawking is considered one of the today's foremost theoretical physicists. Physically disabled people are given equal rights because society considers them equal in all respects despite their physical handicap.

The physical organs can be considered using the same logic. It is now commonplace in medicine to surgically remove replace organs such as kidneys, livers, hearts, hips and other parts in order to preserve the healthy functioning of the body. Some parts—like hearts and hip sockets—are now replaced with artificial versions. Modern medicine has illustrated through many years of organ transplants that a person's identity does not travel with their organ. Otherwise, we might have—as a few comedic theatrical performances have suggested—people whose personalities reflect their organ donors' personality. Imagine: A person receiving another person's heart assuming an aspect of the personality of the dead donor?

We might compare this to an auto accident: Let's say a car is brought into a repair shop after a collision: The shop determines the car needs the tires changed, the engine rebuilt and various other parts of the car replaced before the car can be put back on the road. These changes and new car parts do not affect the driver of the car. The driver will still be the same person no matter how many new parts are put on the car. After the engine is rebuilt, the new tires are installed and the other parts are replace, the unchanged driver gets back into the car and drives it away.

Life is distinct from matter.

The difference between our physical body and our self requires a clear differentiation between matter and life. This investigation has been captured under the term *autopoiesis.* Autopoiesis is the study of the characterization of a complete living system as it compares to either a part of another living system or non-living matter.

To investigate this we could first analyze the difference between a living organism and a chunk of matter without the component of life. An easy comparison would be between single-celled bacteria and a dead cell separated from a living body. A single-cell bacterium is a complete living organism. Studies have shown bacteria indeed respond to stimuli, avoid death, and avert pain. As we know from fighting diseases, bacteria will intelligently mutate and adapt to antibiotics. The new antibiotic-resistant "superbugs" are examples of bacteria who have intelligently navigated and overcome challenges. Living bacteria also conduct the other activities required for independent survival: eating, digesting, reproduction, movement, response to stimuli, sense perception, the intention to survive, and self-organization.

Non-living objects display none of these characteristics independently. While a machine may digest and respond to stimuli, it will not have sense perception and self-organization. It relies upon a living person to organize its tasking. Once a cell has been disconnected from a living organism like a human body, the cell ceases functioning. A single cell can be put into a Petri dish however and kept alive through incubation (this is called *in vitro).* However, this cell's functioning is now dependent upon the stimulation of the lab equipment driven by living lab operators. It is no longer displaying sense perception, the desire to survive or independent organization. It has simply become a surrogate of the lab scientists.

Over many years of cruel animal research, test results have revealed that animals have the same *'self-concept'* awareness as humans. This 'self-concept' is evident by their responses to various environmental challenges. The functions of their mechanical physiology has also confirmed that this *self-concept* pervades through all living tissues, reflected by the display of episodic memory—remembering specifics about the past events and others. For this reason, we see animals learning quickly which activities result in pain, and which activities result in pleasure (Dere *et al.* 2006). They respond simply because every living being seeks pleasure.

Within the laboratory, science has blurred the distinction between living and non-living matter. Bitbol and Luisi (2004), confirmed by Bourgine and Stewart (2004) and others, sums up the distinction between living organisms and non-living matter to be founded upon on the principle of *cognition.* As stated clearly by Bourqine and Stewart, *"A system is cognitive if and only if sensory inputs serve to trigger actions in a specific way, so as to satisfy a viability constraint."* Bourqine and Stewart also contend *"A system that is both autopoietic and cognitive is a living system."* Bitbol and Luisi add to this by saying *"the very lowest level of cognition is the condition for life,"* and *"the lowest level of cognition does not reduce to the lowest level of autopoiesis."*

When we consider the element of cognition, we bring into focus the nature of awareness. Cognition is the awareness of "self" and "non-self." The awareness of "self" and "non-self" are required for a living organism to consider survival important. Without an awareness of "self" and "non-self" there is no intention for fulfillment. Without intention and the awareness of self, there is no consciousness. Without consciousness, there is no life.

The body recycles itself every five years.

Throughout its physical lifetime, our body is continually changing, yet we continue to maintain our core identity and consciousness. Research has shown all living cells in the body have a finite lifespan, ranging from minutes to days to years. It is thought a few cells of the body—such as certain bone marrow stem cells and brain cells—may exist through the duration of the body. Still there are only a handful of these cells compared to the estimated 200 trillion cells making up the body. By far the vast majority of cells in the body will participate in cell division, with the older cells becoming broken down and replaced by the newly divided cells. Thus, we see a constant sloughing off of dead cells from the body and a constant breakdown and wasting of cell parts through the liver and out the body. We might consider these facts:

> *Surface gastric cells are replaced about every five minutes. All stomach-lining cells are replaced within a week. Skin cells are all replaced within about a month and a half. The entire liver is regenerated within two months. The bone cells will all be replaced within a year.*

Furthermore, the composition of every cell—its atoms and molecules—undergo an even faster turnover. Every cell in the body, including even the stem cells, is made up of molecular combinations of atomic waves. Molecular cell wave-parts make up the nucleus complete DNA, RNA, cytoplasm, various organelles, a cell membrane. Each of these components is made of molecules, and each molecule is made up of various atomic standing waves. These atomic and molecular cell units are constantly being replaced by the minute with fresh atomic wave rhythms.

Each of our body's cell membranes allow for diffusion, osmosis and ionic channel movement, giving each cell a constant exchange of molecules, atoms and ions.

Active cells will replace molecules quite rapidly. Brain cells will recycle all their molecules within three days. In fact, 98% of all the atoms and molecules in the body are replaced within a year, and most biologists agree all the atoms and molecules within the body are replaced by new ones within five years.

Noting our physical bodies change nearly every cell within days or a few years and within five years, every atom and molecule is replaced from the food we eat, the water we drink and the air we breathe, *the body we were wearing five years ago is not the same body* we are *wearing today.* We are wearing a completely different body. In effect, we have each *changed bodies.* Every rhythmic element of matter—every vibrating atom—is new. This might well be compared to a waterfall. The water within a waterfall is always changing. From moment to moment, the waterfall will be made up of different water. Therefore, the waterfall we see today is not the same waterfall we saw yesterday.

Since each of us is the same person from moment to moment and year to year within an ever-changing body, logically we each have an identity separate from this temporary vehicle. We cannot be the body, since the body has been replaced while we are still here. Should we look at our photograph taken five years ago, we will be looking at *a completely different body* from the one we are wearing today. The eyes looking at the eyes in the picture will be different eyes.

Could I be the brain?

One might propose that since we have yet to transplant someone's brain maybe we are the brain. Most of us have heard of or seen the famous neurosurgical experiments first documented by Dr. Wilder Penfield, wherein stimulation of the temporal cortex stimulates particular memories. These experiments or their successors might leave us with an impression we are the brain since we feel so close to our memories and emotions.

This assumption is disputed by brain research over the past fifty years on both humans and animals. In many cases various brain parts have been removed, leaving memory and emotion intact. Mishkin (1978) documented the removal of either the amygdala or the hippocampus did not severely impair memory. Mumby *et al.* (1992) determined that memory was only mildly affected in rats with hippocampus and amygdala lesions. According to a substantial review done by Vargha-Khadem and Polkey (1992), the past twenty years of surgical documentation revealed numerous hemidecortication operations—the removal of half the brain. In a majority of these cases, a cognition and brain function continued. A few cases even documented an improvement in cognition! Additionally, in numerous cases of intractable seizures, where substantial parts of brain have been damaged, substantial cognitive recovery results in 80 to 90% of the cases.

These and numerous other studies illustrate that the person is not reduced by brain damage or removal. They are still the same person. They still have the same personality. Many retain all their memories. The majority of stroke patients go about living normal lives afterward. While sometimes we see memory and some cognitive and motor skills affected by cerebrovascular stroke, the person within is unaffected by physical changes in the brain.

There are many organisms who have memory and sense functions without even having a brain. Bacteria, for example, do not have brains, yet they can memorize a wide variety of skills and events, including what damaged or helped them in the past. Other organisms such as plants, nematodes and others are living replete with memory and recall without having brains.

MRI and CT brain scans on patients with various brain injuries or stroke have shown particular functions will often move functions from one part of the brain to another after the original area was damaged. We must therefore ask: Who is it that moves these physical functions from one part of the brain to another? Is the damaged brain area making this decision? That would not make sense. Are the brain neurons making the decision? How would the new brain neurons know what functions the old neurons had if those neurons are now damaged?

The retention of memory, emotion, and the moving of brain function from one part of the brain to another is evidence there is a deeper mechanism or *operator* within the body who is *utilizing* the brain, rather than the person *being* the brain. The person *operating* the body is the continuing element. The physical structures continually undergo change while the operator remains, adapting to those changes.

How old am I?

Consider how most of us perceive the aging of our body with respect to our identity. Most of us try to deny the age of our body in one respect or another. While younger people want to pretend their body is older, older people want to pretend it is younger. Most adults refuse to accept getting old. As any birthday party will illustrate, adults are surprised at the body's age as it gets older. We try to disconnect ourselves from the physical age of our body somehow. This denial is often joked about, but to most of us—as we are faced with an ever-wrinkling body—it is no laughing matter. We are often embarrassed by our body's age as we get older. For this reason, many older adults do not want to state their age. They are embarrassed by it. Furthermore, many dress the body with make-up, hair dyes and/or trendy clothes in an attempt to hide its age.

For this same reason, many in our society undergo extreme forms of surgery in order to achieve a younger-looking body. In these cases, the self is in conflict with the images left by the body. Plastic surgery, hair-removal, hair transplantation, breast enhancement, and various other medical interventions are all extraordinary attempts to desperately reconcile our true selves with the temporary physical body.

In recent years, this struggle for self-identification has become more desperate in some cases, with people undergoing drastic surgery to attempt to change their body's gender. Grotesque procedures such as sex organ replacement, combined with hormone injections, are sadly becoming commonplace in medical centers. Gender change is another stark example of how the self feels incompatible with the physical body.

Sexual preference has become a hot topic relating to identity. Our society's tolerance of homosexuality and cross-dressing has led to gender confusion among many in our society, including children. One recent report estimated as many as three million children in the U.S. suffer from gender confusion. Many are given hormone blockers—preventing their body's puberty development—in a misguided attempt to facilitate their clarification of their gender.

Same-sex attraction and gender confusion is the result of identifying the body with the self. Homosexuals illustrate this when they feel the only way to alleviate their inner struggle and confusion about their real identity is to *'come out,'* and declare being *'gay'* to others. This perceived self-identification has nothing to do with ones actual identity however. For this reason the *'coming out'* does not alleviate the core issue causing confusion. Its declaration to the world merely serves to distract the person from understanding their real identity as nonphysical.

Am I biochemical?

Over recent years, various researchers have proposed from one basis or another that our identities are chemical. They have proposed emotions and personality are seated within chemical combinations such as hormones and neurotransmitters—which flow through the bloodstream and the synapses of our nervous systems. Could our identities be a mixture of complex chemicals? A logical review of the scientific evidence would indicate otherwise.

Emotional responses to environmental stimuli will initiate any number of biochemical *cascades* to occur within the body. A cascade occurs when one chemical release stimulates the release of another biochemical and that biochemical in turn stimulates the release of another, which in the end stimulates a particular tissue or organ response. With each cascade, there is a particular set of end responses from various tissues and nerves. For example, when we receive an indication of possible danger, our body will respond by activating the hypothalamus to send hypothalamic hormones to the pituitary gland. In response, the pituitary gland releases ACTH (adrenocorticotropic hormone), which in turn induces the adrenal cortex to secrete glucocorticoid hormones such as cortisol. These two hormones in turn encourage the release of biochemicals epinephrine and norepinephrine, which work with the glucocorticoids to stimulate muscle response. The lungs, the heart and the pancreas are stimulated into action by these and other biochemicals. They stimulate an increased utilization of oxygen and glucose by the muscles for their proper functioning. This entire cascade of chemical release is designed to aid the body in evasion or defense against the impending danger.

Because neurologists and other researchers have seen these neurological biochemicals at locations connected to response to emotional states, the assumption is that these biochemicals somehow contain the emotion. They propose that chemicals such as endorphins, dopamine, serotonin, epinephrine, or acetylcholine each contain particular emotions, and are thus the elements of emotion or life within the body. While these signaling biochemicals connect with receptors positioned at the surface of particular cells, the response by the cell is due to the emotion somehow being released from the chemical. An example is the famed *opiate receptor,* which has been linked with the cell's reception of morphine or endorphins and feelings of euphoria.

One basic problem with this speculation is that no two organisms respond identically to the same chemical. With opiates for example, some may hallucinate while others may only respond casually. On the other hand, some may have nightmarish experiences. If these structurally identical neurochemicals *contained* the emotion, why would each person respond differently to the same chemical and dose?

The major question this brings to bear is: *Who* is observing these euphoric feelings or hallucinations? *Who* observes these positive or negative sensations?

The perception of pain may offer some clarity. In 2005 Dr. Ronald Melzack, a co-author of the famous *gate control theory* of pain transmission, updated his theory of pain from a simple gateway effect to one of a multidimensional experience of *'neurosignatures'*. His new theory—which he calls the *"body-self neuromatrix"*—explains that the consensus of clinical research on acute pain, behavior and chronic pain indicates an independent perceptual state, observing and exchanging feedback and response with the locations of injury. Because doctors and researchers have found a good portion of the pain response is unrelated to specific injury but rather a modification of sensory experience, this *neuromatrix* indicates an interaction between the nervous system and what Melzack calls the *"self."*

Elaborating, pain requires two components: 1) The sensory transmission of pain and 2) the observer or experiencer of that pain. Now once that pain is experienced, there may also be a feedback response from the experiencer. This feedback may either be 1) take action to remove the cause of the pain, or 2) if there is no apparent cause then be extra-sensitive to the pain (Baranauskas and Nistri 1998) until the cause is determined. This increased sensory elevation may lead to what is called *noiceptic pain*, or pain not appearing to have a direct physical cause. Some might also refer to this type of pain as being *psychosomatic,* although psychosomatic pain is often thought of as not real. Noiceptic pain is considered real, but its cause is not physically apparent.

Regardless of the name, this type of pain is very difficult to understand and manage, especially for doctors and patients dealing with chronic pain appearing unrelated to trauma or inflammation. Because the self naturally seeks pleasure, we would propose the current cause of that pain is always real, from either a gross physical level or a more subtle level. Regardless of the level the self experiencing that pain would certainly be considered separate from it (why else would the self want to escape it?) and any biochemical messengers assisting in its transmission.

The discoveries of new biochemical *ligands* observed during cognitive events have unveiled yet another chemical-identity-based theory, suggesting these biochemicals are the source of memories, and together they form the basis of our personality. The proposals surmise that when certain biochemicals tie with particular synaptic (nerve) cells, the emotional response produces a memory response. They propose since these certain biochemicals are present in larger volumes during memory recall, memories must be contained within them.

Since these biochemicals are present during certain responses or memories, it may make sense that these chemicals have a *role* in physical responses to emotions or memories. However, the proposal of memory and emotions existing *within* the chemicals is not supported by logic or observation. If the chemicals contained memory or emotion, these characteristics should exist in the chemicals both inside and outside of the living mechanics of the body. Researchers often will remove biochemicals from bodies, putting them into beakers as they draw blood or other body fluids. This theory is tested thousands of times a day by hospitals who transfuse blood from one subject to another. In none of these cases are emotions or feelings being transferred from one person to another. Once drawn, the biochemicals contained in the blood do not display any sort of memory or emotion consistent with the emotions displayed by the previous host.

This is not to say injected biochemicals do not elicit a physical response. The organism receiving epinephrine or another neurochemical may incur have a physical response consistent with the cascade related to that biochemical. Injected adrenaline may produce a physical reaction of increased heart rate, for example. But adrenaline drawn from one person during a fearful response will not induce a recall of that specific fear in the person it is injected into.

We must therefore conclude there is someone inside who is either—directly or indirectly—initiating or responding to the body's neurochemicals. In all cases, in order to stimulate any emotional response, there must be an conscious stimulant. Fuel may ignite a spark in the cylinder of an automobile engine causing combustion, which will push the rods into motion, exerting force on the axel cranks. Fuel is not the driver though. Nor does fuel contain directions for the destination. The driver of the car consciously turns the key and determines its direction using a steering wheel, accelerator, and brakes.

When the living being leaves the body at death there are no emotions exhibited in the dead body. While all the neurochemicals and cells—all the ligands and receptors—are still contained within the body, the body supports no memory or emotional response because there is no longer a conscious driver present. The conscious driver ultimately initiates as well as responds to the neurochemistry of the body.

Emotions elicited from a response to an observation or other sensual stimuli would logically come from someone who separate from those stimuli. Because emotion is integral with interpreting stimuli, an observer would be necessary for that interpretation. Without an observer, there could be no decision-making: No optional behavior. We would essentially all be robots.

This does not mean that all physiological responses require interpretation and decision. For example should we touch the burner of a stove there is programming in place within the neural network to instantly react by pulling the hand away. This will happen often before the self has a chance to make a decision. However, it does not mean the self cannot decide to resist that reaction of pulling away. A firewalker may intentionally walk on the coals despite his autonomic system screaming to jump away onto the cool sand. These observations lead us to understand the self can be involved in almost any autonomic system should there be such an intention.

Other stimuli may require the emotional self to respond. Otherwise, no action will take place. Upon hearing the alarm in the morning, the self could choose to do nothing—lying in bed for the rest of the day. The self could also intend to accomplish something that day, and rise to begin the day's activities.

Once sensual stimuli are pulsed to the neural network after being received by one or many of the biochemical receptors, the body forms specific information waves. These waves have been studied over the past fifty years using an apparatus called the *electroencephalograph* (also referred to as EEG). EEG studies have confirmed that the brain's neurons, in response to signals from either the sensory nerves or incoming responses around the body, produce various brainwave patterns. While there are numerous specific wave patterns, they are generally categorized by their frequency range. The main frequency ranges of brainwaves include *Gamma, Alpha, Beta, Theta and Delta waves: Gamma waves* are high-frequency waves that range from between thirty and sixty cycles per second. *Alpha waves* have a range of between eight to thirteen cycles per second. *Beta waves* have a range of fourteen to thirty cycles per second. *Theta waves* have a range of four to seven cycles per second. *Delta waves* have a range of from less than one cycle per second to about three cycles per second. While the higher frequency waves are prominent during periods of higher stress or problem solving, the slower, lower-frequency waves tend to be dominant during periods of relaxation, meditation, or sleep. Still, all of these types of waveforms are typically present.

At any particular point in time, there are billions of brainwaves of various specific frequencies moving around the brain. As the different waves collide—or interfere—they create different types of interference patterns. As confirmed by neurological research headed up by Dr. Robert Knight (Sanders *et al.* 2006) at the University of California/Berkeley and UC/San Francisco, the interaction of these interference patterns together formulate a type of mapping system. This mapping system forms a type of screen, upon which the self can view sensory information coming in from the eyes, ears and other sense organs, together with the feedback from the body.

As the self views the waveform image patterns, it can respond with intention. Intention from the self is typically translated through the pre-frontal cortex and medial cortex to create response brainwave patterns, although other cortices are also sometimes used. These response brainwave patterns are translated through the hypothalamus and pituitary gland to produce master hormones such as growth hormone, adrenocorticotropic hormone, follicle-stimulating hormone, oxytocin, luteinizing hormone, and others, stimulating the cascade of physical response as mentioned above. For example, waves in the delta frequency range tend to stimulate the production of growth hormone. One of growth hormone's more versatile effects is its ability to advance the healing and regeneration process.

Researchers have observed during feelings of love or compassion an increase in biochemicals like dopamine, serotonin, and various endorphins in the bloodstream. Did the emotions stimulate the biochemicals or did the biochemicals stimulate the emotions? While considered somewhat radical, there is a growing contingency of research scientists proposing the emotion is stimulated (or even created) by the biochemicals. This would be equivalent to saying love comes from biochemicals and our personalities are chemical.

We must question the logic of this proposal, however. While dopamine, serotonin, and endorphins are circulating at heightened levels following activities such as laughing eating, sex and post-traumatic stress, these biochemicals are also circulating at other times, albeit at different levels. If they were creating the emotion, they would be present only in and prior to specific emotions. Instead, they are present during a variety of emotions. We also are not seeing different molecular structures between the biochemicals in different moods.

On the other hand, we could logically conclude that the body produces positive (or negative) feedback neurotransmitter or hormonal messengers, which could well stimulate an emotional *response* to those messengers. Considering that these biochemicals increase to different levels depending upon the condition of the body, it would seem appropriate that the self would be able to respond to this condition. It would also be logical that once the self did respond to a particular sensory stimulation or physical feedback messenger, that emotional response would also stimulate particular biochemicals. In other words, these biochemicals are messengers. Like current in an electric wire, the process can move in either direction. Biochemicals can be stimulated by emotional decisions as well as potentially stimulate an emotional response. This would reveal these biochemicals as parts of a cyclic balancing process, while the self is the observer and driver of the cycle.

To suggest any one of these biochemicals is responsible for a particular emotion would be to ignore its physiological relationship with the rest of the body's biochemistry. Almost every biochemical process in the body is cyclic, with various operational conclusions. 'Biochemical emotion' would also ignore the presence of an intentional observer—responsible for responding to the body's balance as well as driving its balance towards particular objectives.

We can illustrate this process on another level. Hearing that a friend was hurt will cause an emotional reaction. The emotion was experienced following the aural reception. Upon hearing this and reacting emotionally, a physical response might follow, such as tears or a rush to the hospital. These physical responses were stimulated by the emotion. The initial emotion was stimulated from hearing. This emotion was felt by the self and the self initiated a physical response to those emotions. It would be nonsensical to say that the biochemicals in the tears caused the emotional response.

The self controls the body during biofeedback.

Consider biofeedback. Sensors are attached to various parts of the body to monitor physical responses like heart rate, breathing, brainwaves, muscle activity, etc. These sensors are connected to a computer, which displays the various response levels onto a monitor for the subject to see. The heart rate amplitude and frequency readings will be displayed on the monitor in waves, bars, and/or numbers. With a little practice, most people—once they see their heart rate with graphics clearly on the monitor—can consciously lower their heart rate with intention. Biofeedback has thus been used successfully to teach a person to alter various other functions such as muscle tension, hunger, stress, etc. Biofeedback training gives people the ability to directly control a variety of physical responses including stomach cramps, muscle spasms, headaches, and other occurrences—many known to be part of a biochemical cascade.

The reason why a person can learn to control certain biochemically-driven autonomic functions is that the self ultimately exists outside the biochemistry of the body. It is the self who can decide to influence physical functions. Once the person intends to make a change, the mind will facilitate the stimulation of the biochemicals by the appropriate glands to produce a physiological response. Even without biofeedback, a person can initiate various autonomic responses. Most of us have experienced how a physiological fear response may be initiated by simply imagining a dangerous event or situation. This happens every day in the professional world, where executives stress over events that have not happened nor may never happen. This stress increases the heart rate and stimulates stress biochemical release. Most of us have experienced being worried about an event that may never happen. The resulting increase in our heart rate indicates our body's autonomic response to the anxious self.

If the self can affect the body's biochemistry with anxiousness, the self is separate from the biochemistry. Furthermore, if the self can affect the body's biochemistry intentionally, there is no question of the self's ability to direct the body through intention.

This neurochemical process would be analogous to a computer operator operating a computer. A computer will tabulate, calculate, and memorize data. It will display various graphics and perform various functions, based upon the input of the operator. The software and hardware are set up in such a way to coordinate computer functions very quickly and automatically. However, these functions require human initiation. A computer operator must turn on the computer and input into the machine certain intentional commands in order to initiate and maintain the computer's functions.

In the same way the physical body, with all of its functional chemistry and various physical responses going on, is ultimately being steered by a personality within: this is the self, the living being—the operator of the body.

It is difficult sometimes to separate the living being inside the body from the various physical and biochemical operations. This is because the feedback-response system is bridging the self with the physical body. For example breast-feeding is now being rediscovered. Researchers have discovered breast-feeding not only gives the child better nourishment and a stronger immune system, but also renders a better temperament and brain development due to some of the biochemistry of breast milk.

This notion is consistent with the observation of various nutrients or drugs altering moods and behavior.

Chemicals influence behavior because they not only stimulate physical tissue response, but they also give feedback to the self about what is going on in the body. For example, the feeling of thirst is nerve electro-chemical signal to the self that the body needs water. A combination of hormonal, osmotic, ionic and nerve signaling all integrate to stimulate *osmoreceptors* located among brain tissue (such as the anteroventral third ventricle wall). Once stimulated, these receptors initiate waveform signaling through the hypothalamus, which converts into the more subtle waveforms of the mind. Through the reciprocation of the mind, the self observes this feedback, and responds by initiating action to find some water.

A computer will also feed back to its operator in the same way. The computer is not only designed to perform operations based upon the input of the operator, but it is designed to feed back to the operator the results of those operations, signaling a need for new responses from the operator.

This process is called a feedback loop. The body's feedback system is designed to respond to environmental and physical changes around the anatomy. The system is designed to signal to the self on how the body is functioning. This is one of the purposes for serotonin release in the body: To feed back the presence of a body in balance. A diet balanced in proteins, carbohydrates, and fats, along with physiological activities that stimulate the conversation of tryptophan to serotonin such as relaxation, laughter, and exercise. This combined state of balance results in a normal flow of serotonin, which feeds back to the self the presence of a healthy balance.

Pain, on the other hand, indicates quite the opposite: Some imbalance exists somewhere and the pain feeds back to the operator the need for an adjustment somewhere. This adjustment could be the diet, fluid intake, a sitting posture, lack of or the wrong type of exercise or an infection of some sort. Chronic pain indicates a continuing lack of balance in the body.

Just as an instrument panel on an automobile tells us the running condition of car, we can monitor the condition of our body through these and other neurochemical feedback mechanisms. Just as the car driver slows down when the speedometer shows the car is over the speed limit, the self makes the needed adjustment when the body's feedback systems indicate those needs.

Should we misidentify ourselves as the body, we might confuse the body's positive feedback mechanisms as pleasurable. This misconception leads us to attempt to manipulate our body's biofeedback mechanisms. Eating, for example, will stimulate positive feedback neurochemicals such as serotonin and dopamine when there is a balance of nutrition and satiation. Our taste buds feed back positive neural signals when we eat something sweet or fatty (food providing energy). In an effort to gain pleasure from these positive responses, many of us continue to eat long after the body has enough for its fuel. An ongoing attempt to become fulfilled through eating often results in obesity, frustration, and even depression. In the same way, the car driver does not get full when he fills the car's fuel tank.

Our identity emerges in clinical death research.

Evidence concluding our identity as nonphysical has been presented by a number of respected researchers over the past four decades. With the advent of resuscitation and medical life-support technologies has come a proliferation of patients whose bodies have clinically died prior to resuscitation. Author and researcher Dr. Raymond Moody pioneered this research in the 1960s, and thus introduced us to the *Near Death Experience* (or NDE). Dr. Moody presented hundreds of cases documenting common experiences among patients declared clinically dead in a clinical setting. Dr. Moody's research reviewed a cross-section of thousands of cases of patients with a variety of religious and socio-economic backgrounds. Dr. Moody discovered a common experience: After separating from the body, the self floats above it, viewing the various resuscitation efforts taking place on the body. This if often followed by the self remotely traveling to and viewing loved ones. Often traveling at the speed of thought to their homes or locations, the self often tried in vain to communicate with their loved one. Afterward, many subjects detailed being drawn into a darkened tunnel with a bright light at the end. At the end of the tunnel, many either entered or saw a dazzling light or personality. Many reviewed their lives in an instant. Many went on to meet with this personality. In many cases the personality indicated it was not "their time yet." Following this, many instantly returned to their body. This usually coincided with the revival of the body. While specific experiences were often different, most NDE subjects experienced separation from their physical body and felt, at the very least, peaceful (Moody 1975).

Naturally, this research had its skeptics. A few questioned Dr. Moody's protocols, which included patient selection and interview techniques. This gap was quickly filled by Kenneth Ring, Ph.D. In a well-received peer-reviewed book published in 1985, Dr. Ring randomly selected 101 patients who had experienced an NDE. Dr. Moody's patients were collected as their data were presented to him. This offered some but not complete randomness. By contrast, the 101 patients studied by Dr. Ring were chosen randomly to eliminate any bias, imagination, hallucination, inconsistency, and other elements possibly affecting the objectivity of their after-death experience. Of the 101 subjects, a third reported out-of-body experiences, and a quarter reported entering the darkness or tunnel with the light at the end. About 60% reported at least a positive, peaceful experience. Those NDE subjects whose death was the result of a suicide attempt experienced no tunnel with light. The suicide

NDEs in this study experienced a "murky darkness," after feeling separated from their body, but they did not proceed any further (Ring 1985).

Ring's findings—though not in the exact same percentages—were substantiated by professor of medicine and cardiologist Michael Sabom, M.D. in a 1982 work called Recollections of Death: A Medical Investigation. There have been other investigations confirming these experiences (Blackmore 1996). Dr. Elisabeth Kubler-Ross documents researching some twenty thousand cases of near-death in her 1991 book On Life After Death, confirming the same primary conclusions of the research done by Sabom, Moody and Ring.

Upon review of the other various explanations, it appears unlikely any of the possible physical causes could suitably explain the NDE—except that the self is not the body. The sheer cross-section of people with this same experience provides too much variance to provide any other rational explanation. The common NDE experiences regardless of the level of religious reverence, expectation levels, drug-administration, knowledge of NDE and brain or biochemical stimulation certainly provides few alternatives.

Additionally, when both Moody and Sabom tested the observations of NDE out-of-body observations with hospital staff, they almost without exception confirmed the observations the NDE subjects made from outside of a body clinically unconscious. While unconscious and with eyes closed the patient could hardly be expected to observe those events—even if by subconscious hearing—due to the detail of the NDE subject descriptions. To this, skeptical researchers have suggested some sort of paranormal experience. We must ask those skeptics how rational it is to accept the notion of a paranormal experience but not accept an out-of-body observation?

Again by far the most logical and scientific approach to this topic is the self is truly a separate entity from the body and after the body dies, the self departs.

Remote viewing indicates a deeper seer.

For twenty-three years, the Stanford University Research Institute studied *parapsychological phenomena* (commonly termed psi—after the Greek letter *psi,* or *psyche*) and *remote viewing* with a grant from the United States government. Two physicists named Dr. Russel Targ and Dr. Harold Puthoff teamed up for much of this research, and they conducted controlled experiments under the watchful eye of the CIA. Much of this top-secret research was not released to the scientific community due to it sensitivity to international security. Part of the research consisted of sealing especially talented subjects into guarded rooms with observers. From the sealed rooms, the subjects remotely viewed and described in detail events and locations thousands of miles away. Their viewing documented minute details of the location down to the current weather conditions. They described specific geographical facilities, the location of specific buildings and activities taking place years before the age of the internet. The locations and specifics of these observations were controlled, and confirmed as being otherwise unavailable to the viewer. Two particular viewers, Pat Price and Ingo Swann, were able to identify military installations around the world, including secret then-Soviet bases on the other side of the planet, including accurate weather conditions at the time of viewing. Other experiments included placing objects on a table in a room on the east coast. From a sealed room on the west coast, the psi observers were able to describe the objects in detail. Not only were most of the objects described in detail, but their positioning was specifically detailed (Puthoff and Targ 1981; Puthoff *et al.* 1981).

Other remote viewing experiments over the years since have confirmed that some of us the ability to "see" things not within our physical sensory range. Moreover, some have shown the skill can be developed. Targ and Katra (1999) describe being able to develop that skill by using a practice to "separate out the psychic signal from the mental noise of memory, analysis and imagination."

These controlled studies illustrate the existence of a seer existing outside of the realm of the physical senses and neurons of the brain. If seeing was merely a biochemical and physiological experience driven by a mixture of molecules and cells, then *who is it* that is able to *see* things that are beyond the physical range of the eyeballs? Who is it that can visualize and describe material objects half way around the world?

The limitations of our physical senses have been well established by science. As humankind has progressed technologically, we continue to gain new information about things we previously did not perceive through our gross sense organs. This growing technical observational facility increasingly makes us aware that our physical senses can only perceive a small portion of the vast spectra of wavelengths bouncing around us. Quite simply, the spectral range of our senses and technology are still only a tiny portion of the complete spectrum surrounding us.

Further outside the physical spectrum limitation is the *living spectrum.* Our physical eyes and physical instruments simply are not equipped to see into this spectrum. The spectrum of the living dimension is transcendental to our physical sense perception.

Perhaps I am the mind?

There has been a great movement over the last century proposing the mind is the all-powerful entity, and thoughts have the all-powerful capacity to manipulate the physical world. This was proposed a century ago by William Walker Atkinson in the book *Thought Vibration or the Law of Attraction in the Thought World* (1906). The positions put forth by Atkinson in this book, along with almost one hundred other books—some under a variety of pseudonyms—are similar. Atkinson's theory has formed the framework for a multitude of self-help books in the decades following and to the present day. Atkinson's theory attracted a number of followers, including influential writers such as Mary Baker Eddy of *Christian Science* fame and Wallace Wattles, author of *The Science of Getting Rich* (1910). The *governing mind* philosophy of the late Mr. Atkinson and Mr. Wattles has also influenced various other works, such as *Think and Grow Rich* (1937) by Napoleon Hill, *The Greatest Salesman in the World* (1968) by Og Mandino, and the wildly popular recent book and movie *The Secret* (2006), by Rhonda Byrne.

Of course, many of these works have attracted the masses because of their promise of material riches, success, and admiration. These appeals to our selfish natures appear to be grounded in the idea seemingly first proposed by Atkinson: The self is the mind, and the mind ultimately drives and controls the physical world. This has led to the unfortunate proposition that nothing real exists except for the mind, and hence the mind is the creator of the universe.

The interesting part of this very seductive proposal is that while the mind is proposed to be the all-pervading controller of existence, the intent of these numerous self-help writings appears to theoretically help people by *changing their minds*. The techniques proposed may vary slightly, but the intent is generally to help the reader gain greater wealth, fame, success, attention and influence by *changing* their thinking practices.

The problem of course with this proposal is that if the person is the mind, then *who* is it who will be deciding to *change the mind?* In order to change the mind there must be a driver and observer who can intend and initiate that change. Furthermore, as noted in these works, the process required in order to change the mind is quite difficult. *Who* is the constant force who makes the determination to change the mind despite all of its former habits of previous thinking? And lastly, *who* remains to reap the rewards once the mind has been changed? If the self is the mind, and the mind has changed, that former self would be gone. Therefore, no one would remain to realize any reward, since the last mind—the one who initially read the book—is gone, replaced by a new and improved mind.

The reality is that the mind is simply a tool of the constant living self. Like the body, the mind is an instrument the self uses through intention. The mind is a subtle sorting, translating and recording device. The mind reflects and categorizes the waveform interference patterns onto its mapping system, giving the self the ability to observe a holographic image of the information. With that holographic image, the self can concoct particular desires and intentions for the mind to execute through the neural network.

We can observe how the mind records this information when a particular vision or piece of music can be recalled minutes, days and even years after first being seen or heard. We can see it immediately by looking at an image, closing our eye immediately afterward, and seeing that image imprinted onto our mind. Our mind can also associate and compare stored waveform data with incoming sensory images of tastes, sounds, tactile sensations and other images our senses collect over the years. As the mind imprints these images, the self subtly directs the mind through intelligence to record these images, cataloging them according to priority. The mind is thus like a software program, designed to utilize the biochemical bonds within the neurons to resonate waveforms for storage and playback. This system might be compared to the recording capability of magnetic recording tape or diskettes, which store music, images, and data magnetically.

Like the hard disk recording operating system software of the computer, the mind transcends the body. Just as the operating system interfaces with the devices of the computer, the mind interacts closely with the limbic system and neural networks of the body to execute commands and feedback the condition of the body.

The mind is a changeable, subtle mechanism, yet distinct from the self. The separate existence of the mind can be easily shown in practical behavior: We can each observe the workings of our mind. We can watch images on the mind and see how sensory inputs become recorded and recalled. After watching a movie with special effects, we can close our eyes and watch the scenes' imprint onto the mind. We can also replay music recorded by the mind. We may hum or sing the words of a song we heard previously with the tune replaying on our mind long after the song was heard by the senses. Like a television or a radio, we can also turn and change the mind's images. We can decide to change our focus from one image to another. We can *change our mind.*

Changing genes reflect a living self within.

A newer version of the biochemical identity put forth by modern science is the notion that we are genetic information, or DNA. Admittedly, the mapping of the *genome* (the various sequences) and further mapping of the individual allele locations within *codons* (now referred to as *haplotypes* or collectively as *hapmaps*) reveals a complexity of design beyond human intelligence. Over the past three decades, tremendous research efforts have gone into creating statistical models to match the physical traits of humans and other organisms with particular gene sequences. As a result, thousands of genomes have been tabulated and various haplotypes have been connected with physical characteristics. In addition, different diseases have been connected to certain sequences. Although these efforts are laudable, science has unfortunately succumbed to a blurring of the relationship between these genetic traits and life itself. The erroneous assumption is that specific gene sequences; the particular arrangement of alleles or nucleotides at different positions of the DNA molecule; or the specific hapmaps created as a whole; are the *cause* of those physical or behavioral traits. While some might call this a chicken-and-egg problem, it is certainly clearer than this.

This assumption would be equivalent to saying a telephone is the source of the voice we hear through its speaker. It is elementary: The voice on the line is coming from a remotely located person. We may not be able to *see* the person while we are speaking with them, but we know the person is there because there is an exchange of personal communication. The voice on the other side responds to our statements with a clarity that can only come from a conscious speaker. In the same way, a specific sequencing of genetic haplotypes is a complex structure removing the possibility of chaos or accidental circumstance. This complex coding indicates a programming of sorts. As with any programming, there must be a source of the code. It is not logical to assume that a complex, well-designed code with specific rules (as genetic research connecting physical traits to specific codes indicates) comes from an accidental design. Just as we can connect the lucid voice on the phone to a personal consciousness, we can tie the sequencing of genes to a living component, ultimately driving the design.

If we extract a DNA molecule from our skin or body fluids, and place them onto the table or even in a test tube, we will find there is no display of life. Just as the body after the self leaves is lifeless, DNA or RNA molecules extracted from a living body become lifeless. We should also note that RNA transcription and genetic mutation is impossible without a living being present. While we can force a mutation upon an organism or its seed through the vehicle of a virus, the mutation will only become duplicated through the organism if there is a living force present in that organism.

The proposal that our behavior and traits are all determined by our genetic code is immediately refuted by common situation of children (who have inherited their genes from the parents) being born with distinct personalities, talents and character traits not portrayed in their parents or grandparents. While we quick to notice similar traits among our children, we nevertheless assume each child has their own character and personality. We can add to genetic inheritance that children also learn and mimic their parents to a great degree. Still, we can easily observe children behaving significantly different from their parents in similar situations. We can also witness the many conflicts that arise between children and parents. Certainly we know the extraordinary talents of child music geniuses or savants are not passed down genetically. In most of these cases, the parents have relatively little or no musical gift whatsoever.

Furthermore, if personality and behavior were based upon genetics then genetically identical twins would live parallel lives and have identical personalities. They would also make the same decisions in life, leading to identical lifestyles.

This is not supported by the research. Twins live very unique and individual lives from each other. Depending upon how much time they spend together, they will make distinctly different choices in life as well. In general, they display significantly unique and often diverse behavior. Hur and Rushton (2007) studied 514 pairs of two to nine year old South Korean monozygotic and dizygotic twins. Their results indicated 55% of the children's pro-social behavior related to genetic factors (i.e. where shared) and 45% was attributed to non-shared environmental behavior. (It should be noted that shared environmental factors could not be eliminated from the 55%.) In another recent study from Quebec, Canada (Forget-Dubois *et al.* 2007) an analysis of 292 mothers revealed that maternal behavior only accounted for about 29% genetic influence at 18 months and 25% at 30 months. In a study of 200 African-American twins, including 97 identical pairs, genetics accounted for about 60% of the variance in smoking (Whitfield *et al.* 2007). In a study done at the Virginia Commonwealth University's Institute for Psychiatric and Behavioral Genetics, (Maes *et al.* 2007) a large sampling revealed individual behavior was only about 38-40% attributable to genetics, while shared environment was 18-23% attributable and unshared "environmental" influences were 39-42% attributable. These studies are confirmed by others, illustrating a large enough variance from 100% to indicate the presence of an individual living being within each twin.

Distinct identity despite genetic sameness is further evidenced by the fact that such genetically identical twins will have distinctly different fingerprints, irises and other physical traits. Additionally, researchers have often discovered twins will make significantly different macro-lifestyle choices later in life such as sexual preference, drug abuse, and alcoholism.

We might compare this situation again to our car driver:

> *Say two people purchase the exact same model and year car. As they drive off the lot, their ongoing driving performance is examined. Comparing the two cars in the future will reveal the cars performed in much the same way: They had similar mechanical issues and had particular characteristics such as gas-mileage, top-speeds, and acceleration patterns. However, the researchers would also discover significant variances between the cars' usage in the future. While one was driven hard, the other was pampered. One was driven across the country several times while the other mostly stayed in the garage.*

As these differences stack up between the use of the cars, we will find a large variance between the two cars' comparative resulting performance. While the car type might have influenced a portion of the car's performance, the rest was due to a combination of environmental factors (where the car was driven and stored) and the discretionary choices of their drivers. In other words, their differences would stem from having two different drivers.

Because twins have the same genetics—just as the cars are the same make and model—the unique factors related to the eventual circumstances of their lives stem from the fact that each body contains a distinct inner self.

The individual self is the soul.

Empirical evidence reveals the existence of a transcendental living being operating the body. This is the "I" or the self of each of us. The self is the source of personality and life, which the body expresses through physical activity over its lifetime. Since there is energy, personality and movement in a living body prior to death, followed by a lack of movement, personality and energy afterward, the source of the energy and personality must leave the body at death. Since each personality is unique and different from all other personalities, each living being is an independent entity.

When considering the living being outside of the body or after the death of the body, many will imagine the living being looks like the physical body somehow—with the same eyes, face, sex and stature as their physical body. Many media depictions will illustrate this with someone who has died appearing as a ghostly version of that person's aged body before they died. Although a departed self might still be able to project a mental image comparable to a gross physical body shortly after death, the nature of the living being is thoroughly distinct from the temporary physical body. As Aristotle and Socrates described to their students, the physical body is completely abandoned by the self at death.

Many philosophers have proposed that after death, the living being either fades into "nothingness," or expands into "everything." This philosophy proposes that the living being does not have an individual identity after death: Instead, the individual person or living being simply vanishes and evaporates into space. This is often described as merging into "nothingness"—also called the void—or merging into "everything"—sometimes referred to as the white light. These two assumptions are basically the same proposition because either way there is no eventual individuality. There is no separate existence of the living being in these limited philosophies. To this, we can offer the simple observation of many ancient philosophers: Each individual is born with a unique and distinct personality. This individuality is expressed by the special talents unique to each of us. These special talents point to an individual existence prior to birth. If a person existed as an individual prior to birth, is it logical that a person would lose that individuality after death?

The living being is the underlying source of our personality; our feelings; emotions; desires; the ability to love; and the desire to be loved. This personality is distinct from the mental programming taking place through the brainwaves and neural network of the physical body. Beyond the programming, each of us is an independent, active living being with a central objective of receiving love. Does it appear logical that this active being—continually seeking love and relationships—would want to suddenly abandon these propensities to permanently lose our existence within a void or nothingness?

Still others contend that after death we merge into a vast ocean of consciousness. The question this brings is; what is the purpose of existing within a body as an individual, if we evaporate into a vague ocean of consciousness? What should the purpose of temporary separate existence be then? Could a collective vague consciousness have a purpose? Furthermore, the living self has maintained a steady active existence throughout many years of a changing physical body. Does it seem logical that the death of the body would affect a person's inherent will to survive and prosper? Should the death of our temporary body abruptly end our desire to love and exchange love? Should the active living being who is beyond the physical scope of our senses remand itself to the fate of the physical body?

Purpose and activity are the key distinctions between living and dead matter. Both of these elements (purpose and activity) indicate the existence of individuality. The very definition of *consciousness* requires individuality. Consciousness requires *awareness.* Awareness of something or someone requires a personality separate from that object or person being *aware* of. So an 'ocean of consciousness' would logically be an oxymoron.

Consistent with the ancient teachings of all major religions, the ancient philosophers and the vast majority of western scientists prior to the emergence of the concept of a chaotic accidental evolution of species, we propose the existence of a unique individual entity transcendental to the gross physical plane.

Plato, Socrates and most of the ancient Greek philosophers referred to the self as the *soul.* The translation is thought to originate with Aristotle (382-322 BCE), with the Latin *telos*. *Telos* most specifically translates not as a vague spirit, but as a personality with purpose, will, and character. In this context, we would emphasize that each of us does not possess a soul: we each are a soul. That being said, some might also refer to the soul as one's level of morality or even one's mission. As we seek not to confuse, we will refer to our identity as the *self* or the *living being* in this writing. We also may refer to the self as the transcendental living being to emphasize that the living being is not within the physical or material plane. Rather the living being accesses the physical plane via the vehicle of the physical body.

Of course, the word *spiritual* can also be misunderstood. Spirit can be confused with the subtle physical world of ghosts, which are living beings still embodied within the physical mind and subtle aethereal or plasma layer. They may be without the more gross physical body, but they still live within the confines of the physical dimension. For clarity, we will utilize the word *transcendental* as indicating the dimension beyond these gross and subtle physical layers. To this end we might also refer to the transcendental living being as the *inner self*, identifying the transcendental self occupying the physical body. Furthermore, we distinguish the term *living organism* as a physical body driven by and animated by the transcendental living being.

***

Conclusion: *Our basic identity is nonphysical in essence. The body is a vehicle temporarily housing the living being. Through these physical bodies we express our goals and desires. Though temporarily caged inside a physical body, each of us has an individual existence and personality, which existed prior to the body's birth. The living being continues to live after the death of the body. The physical body is a vehicle designed to allow us to forget our real identity and our real Maker.*

3

Science and Faith

The boy walked along a winding river in a place he'd never been. As he looked down the river, he watched the water winding around the rocks and wondered how long the river was. He was hot from the summer sun and though about going for a swim. He figured the river must drain into a lake at some point. He continued to walk, and saw the water moving somewhat faster. He became convinced that the end of the river was near, and the lake was getting closer. He imagined the size of the lake and guessed from the size of the river that the lake must be about a mile wide. He imagined the lake had docks to dive from and boats waterskiing people behind them. As these thoughts occurred to him, he became excited about getting to the lake. There he could swim and play with the other kids who must also be there.

As he walked, he came upon an older gentleman walking slowly in the opposite direction. The older man was barefoot. He walked slowly and carefully along the rocks on the other side of the stream. The man stopped the boy. He warned him that the stream quickly became a waterfall around the bend and unless the boy was careful, he might slip and find himself falling over a dangerously high water down into a small reservoir below. The man explained the reservoir drained out to a fast river which flowed to the ocean. "The reservoir will be difficult to get out of, and it's very dangerous," the man insisted.

The boy was not fazed. He had been studying the water over the past hour as he walked along side of it. He was convinced that it led to a large swimming lake. He didn't believe the old man. He thought that perhaps the old man was trying to trick him for some reason. Perhaps the old man hadn't even seen this waterfall, he thought. The boy said goodbye to the old man and kept walking, picking up the pace to reach the lake sooner.

Can faith in the Supreme Being be scientific?

The American Heritage Dictionary defines faith as a "confident belief" or "trust." Science, on the other hand, is defined as "the observation, identification, description, experimental investigation and theoretical explanation of natural phenomena."

Modern science—as promulgated by the scientific community today—is assumed to be based upon facts and factual evidence. Over the last century, using this assumption, modern science has attempted to distance itself from discussions relating to the Supreme Being. The seeming assumption is there can be no scientific approach to the topic of the Supreme Being. In many respects, since the evolution and big bang theories have gripped the scientific community, it has been assumed that science and the belief in a Supreme Power are diametrically opposed. In other words, modern science is leaving the lay community with the impression that the Supreme Being cannot be accepted as a scientific premise. Modern science seems to be suggesting the quest for truth is objective while transcendental knowledge is subjective. Modern science seems to suggest there can be no objective investigation regarding the existence of the Supreme Being. As a result, to even refer to the existence of the Supreme Being in scientific literature has seemingly become *unacceptable.*

The reason, some modern scientists seem to be saying, is that science supposedly uses a more stringent methodology for research, which supposedly excludes any evidence which cannot be directly observed. Therefore, conclusions or hypotheses regarding the existence of the transcendental world would supposedly lie outside of the scientific domain. Modern researchers claim to use a more rigorous set of principles and instruments in gathering evidence and making conclusions. They seem to suggest that the contemplation of the Supreme Being might damage the credibility of their research.

The scientific method is a platform for speculation.

Discussions regarding the Supreme Being supposedly cannot be applied to the scientific method. The *'scientific method'* is a collection of processes that result in a conclusion being drawn regarding the viability of a *'hypothesis.'* As such, the major component of the scientific method is the hypothesis. A hypothesis is basically a speculative guess about something currently not known by the scientist. Although *observation* can be utilized prior to the hypothesis, observation is the key element in the supposed *'proving'* of a hypothesis. Observation can be made visually, through other sensual experience or made through instrumental data. It can also be made through interview or controlled response. These observations will typically lead to an *analysis* of the data observed. Once an analysis of the data is made, a *'conclusion'* will be drawn. This conclusion is supposed to 'prove' the initial hypothesis, but in reality the conclusion is an interpretation of the data: Hence the use of the word *"theoretical"* in the definition of science.

Studies seek to prove theoretical hypotheses.

A modern scientific study is designed around a particular hypothesis, and is focused upon proving that hypothesis. Once a particular hypothesis is determined, a study protocol or this study *'design'* is developed. How observations are collected and accumulated are determined by the design of the study. The tools or instruments used for collecting data are also determined by the study design. The manner in which the data is assembled, whether charts, tables or other visuals are used, are also determined by the design of the study. The assembly of data usually allows for a particular type of data analysis: statistical, formula-derived, or trend-related. In some studies, there are a number of groups, allowing for a larger population and number of comparisons, theoretically providing more accuracy. Supposedly, the larger the study population and the more isolated groups a study has, the more accuracy the study will have.

Both hypotheses and conclusions are speculative.

Hypotheses and conclusions drawn using the scientific method are both speculative interpretations. The hypothesis is a working speculation prior to the study and the conclusion is a speculative interpretation of the results. Typically, the hypothesis will also require some consensus, either from previous studies, other observations or other references. The results of a study and the eventual data that arise from it do not typically create the conclusion, as the layperson might imagine. Someone, typically the head researcher of that study will *interpret* the data or the observation, making an official *conclusion* of the study. The conclusion thus draws a hypothetical meaning from the data. Data can usually be interpreted in various ways, depending upon the background and outlook of the scientist. Since the data requires interpretation, its presentation is not objective. If the conclusion did not require speculative interpretation there would be no need for an analysis of the data. If this were the case, there would be no need for a study to arrive at the conclusion. The conclusion would be obvious from the observation.

The variance of motives plagues modern science.

The hypothesis might be considered by some to be an altruistic formulation with an intent to understand the actual nature of things—a search for the truth. In reality, the hypothesis in modern science is often determined with the intent to advance a researcher's career or provide substantiation for a commercial purpose. The unfortunate state of affairs in modern science dictates hypotheses designed for publication and acceptance by peers, rather than for a real search for truth. Worse, many hypotheses are created to advance particular commercial purposes—in an attempt to accommodate a goal with a profit motive. A hypothesis may conveniently benefit the funding group of the study in one way or another. Most often, the institution providing funding will benefit either directly or indirectly from the eventual conclusion of the study. This may mean greater sales of a particular product or merely more credibility and rationale for the institution's specific purpose or mission. Even if the hypothesis is a personal vision of an individual researcher, it is usually only funded if its conclusion brings the university, publication, or funding group some kind of reward or benefit. This is simply because modern scientific study is an expensive undertaking. In today's economic environment, any money invested usually requires a return on investment.

Furthermore, the hypotheses and conclusions of a study are only accepted into the mainstream of science if its subjects and conclusions are acceptable by the editors, financiers, university provosts and/or other elements of the organizational hierarchy of modern science. As a result, research drawing conclusions considered radical or not interesting to the media are typically not funded, not published, and thus usually never undertaken. There is simply not enough financial or professional incentive for anyone involved to fund or undertake research outside of topics considered popular or valid by the members of mainstream science or commercial organizations.

Modern researchers are attached to controls.

Researchers try to capture and eliminate as many variables as they can during research. This is accomplished using *controls.*

Controls try to isolate variables that can potentially limit or skew results.

A well-known control in medical research is the blank test or "placebo." In placebo-controlled research, a portion of the study's subjects is given a sugar pill or other blank instead of the medicine or process being studied. This is to hopefully isolate the possibility that many patients will respond simply to being given any pill. Medical research has shown the placebo effect can taint up to about 33% of a group being studied. For this reason, most medical research considers results of less than 33% to be insignificant because a third of the group may be responding to merely taking any kind of pill.

Control is needed by those who do not have it.

Science's penchant for controls has become increasingly adamant. Modern science is perpetually dissatisfied with prior research. Previously unknown influences that skew results are constantly being uncovered, creating uncertainty among prior studies. As a result, newer studies are now subject to increasingly more rigorous controls. Older research is also increasingly being questioned and suspected.

This is illustrated by modern science's increasing demand for *double-blindedness* among its research. Blindedness is achieved when the subject does not know what is being tested or taken during the experiment. The subject is blinded to prevent the placebo effect. In today's modern scientific studies, not only do the subjects need to be blinded, but the operators involved in the study are often also blinded. This results in the well-known *double-blind study*.

The reason to keep both the subjects and the researchers blinded during the study is to prevent the bias of the personal expectations of either the researchers or the subjects from affecting the results. In other words, if a researcher expects a particular result, there is a greater likelihood of that result being achieved.

While this seems obvious and logical, it also indicates a deeper element among scientific study. If the researcher's leanings can affect the results of a study, barring any physical act pushing the results one way or another, science is assuming a nonphysical aspect of the study of humans. Perhaps this is an unintended admission of the element of consciousness among researchers.

Study controls do not include the researchers.

The designer or head researcher never seem to be blinded however. A study's operators and subjects are blinded because it has been shown their expectations can influence results. What about the head researchers and study designers? The person or persons who create the hypothesis, then design a study around proving this hypothesis have by far the greatest amount of influence over the study's results and conclusions. Yet these persons are not blinded. Not only are the study's designers not blinded, but they dictate the course of the study. Since the design of the study often influences the outcome of the study, it certainly is not logical that the person making the hypothesis should control or dictate the design of the study. Such a study would certainly be designed around arriving at a conclusion consistent with the study's hypothesis. Research designed by those who created the hypothesis should be immediately questioned for integrity and accuracy:

> *The researcher who designs a study around his or her own hypothesis is like a fox guarding the henhouse.*

A researcher whose hypothesis is proven wrong by his or her own study will lose professional credibility. He or she will lose respect amongst his or her peers and employers. There is thus an great incentive for the study to prove the researchers' hypothesis correct. As a result, studies are usually designed *specifically* to prove the hypothesis. While the researcher might attempt to provide an objective process for obtaining results, there is a strong disincentive to prove the researcher's hypothesis incorrect.

At the very least, alternative hypotheses may be ignored, and the data assembly process will reflect the researcher's view of how to best present the data. The presentation visualized and intended is certainly the hypothesis of the researcher. After all, we are speaking of the reputation and career of the scientist. How many professional researchers would be okay with their hypothesis being disproved by their own experiment?

Many studies are also designed by commercial parties interested in particular outcomes. In these cases, the initial hypothesis and the subsequent design of the study can either be determined or influenced by the profit motives of the commercial party.

Scientific organizations that have a commercial interest in the sale of particular pharmaceuticals or equipment often govern and document their own studies. Certainly these organizations also have a strong disinterest in research that portrays anything but a confirmation of success for the applications of their medicines or equipment. Nevertheless, research funded manufacturers is regularly allowed into and embraced by mainstream science. Quotes from manufacturer-funded studies are commonplace among popular media. Rarely do those quotes mention the study having been designed by scientists paid by the manufacturer. Rarely do announcements of research results mention that the research was funded by a particular manufacturer or perhaps a foundation funded by a particular industry.

We can quickly understand the enormity of the situation by considering the contrary possibility. Consider what might happen if a study funded by a manufacturer proved that the product of the manufacturer hurt people or otherwise did not work. Consider the significant investment of the manufacturer into the design and production of the product. Consider the enormous cost to perform one of these studies. A typical study with enough participants can easily cost many millions of dollars to complete. Consider the enormous loss to the company if the product did not succeed. Consider not only the monetary loss, but also the damage to the company's reputation.

For this reason, it is ludicrous that pharmaceutical companies fund and design their own studies, and these studies are accepted by the American FDA and other governmental agencies around the world as proof of the medicine's safety and effectiveness. We have seen the fallout of this corrupt system in some of the many dramatic recalls of widely prescribed medications over the years.

A researcher whose very survival depends upon the satisfaction of the group funding his or her studies is unlikely to design a study in a truly objective manner. Certainly this also goes for studies funded by educational institutions or media companies. Conclusions that include or point to certain philosophical viewpoints inconsistent with the institution's simply will not benefit the researcher's future earning potential. Publishing a study concluding or including a philosophical pretext outside the mainstream is not a common occurrence. Such a 'career move' would be a disaster for both the researcher and the institution supporting the researcher in today's scientific atmosphere. Such a study could result in embarrassment for the research institution, lost revenues for the commercial party or media outlet, and the loss of future employment potential for the researcher.

Design flaws in research are inevitable.

A researcher wanted to study the beneficial effects of ice tea compared to water. The study operators brew up some tea, ice it, pour into tall glasses, and put a slice of lemon on the top of each glass. The tea is given to some of the subjects, while others are given a normal-sized glass of room-temperature water.

This study immediately displays many flaws. First, both the operators and the subjects know which subjects were given tea and not water, and their preconceived notions of the tea's benefits or problems may affect the outcome. Second, the taller glass for the tea may imply that the tea is healthier. The lemon slice might also create an impression the tea is healthier as well. The lemon slice itself may add to the health benefits of the tea. The icing of the tea may give the tea a further advantage. Its coolness may add to the tea's perceived benefits. All of these issues may be just a few of the possible problems with this study. They are design flaws the researcher did not think were important.

> *The ice tea researcher decided to control these flaws by having both drinks look and taste the same and the operators didn't know which product they were serving up (i.e., double-blinded). Lemon and ice are put into both...*

The study may still be flawed if the design did not screen out subjects who were regular tea drinkers, for example. A subject who drinks tea or even coffee frequently would probably have a different response than a non-tea or non-coffee drinker. The coffee or tea drinker may be more tolerant to the caffeine levels in the tea. Someone who did not drink tea or coffee might have a response to the caffeine levels—becoming jittery or getting headaches, for example.

The researcher may overlook this flaw in the study possibly because of a preconceived notion that caffeine in iced tea did not have any negative side effects. Possibly the iced tea company funding the study simply did not want to consider that issue. Either way, the design and operation of a study may have so many potential errors, all caused by the views of those conducting the study.

A study designed by a human and upon humans will always have flaws. These flaws can come from a variety of sources. They can come from the designers; the researchers; the operators; the subjects; the environment; the product being tested; the tabulation of results; and the documenting process of the study. Beyond these, a scientific study can be flawed (intentionally or unintentionally) through the self-interests of the institutions who commit to the study or their sources of funds, as mentioned above.

With so many potentials for error, we can propose that a thoroughly flawless study conducted by humans upon humans is not possible. At some point, adding further controls can eliminate a study's ability to render meaningful results. If, for example, the head researcher were blinded, then there would be no one to oversee the study. That means the researcher would not be able to know what the study was about or what the possible results were. If another researcher performed the study they may not achieve a meaningful answer to the question. This is a contradiction in itself because by scientific method definition, a study is conducted to render results to prove or disprove a particular hypothesis. Indeed, the scientific method itself renders flaws.

The intrusion of a study affects its results.

The greatest problem in trying to conduct meaningful research is the intrusion of the study by the natural environment or the natural activities of its subject or subjects. In order to insert controls and capture data, subjects must to some degree be removed from their natural environments and brought to a lab, hospital, or study center. If they are left in their environment, control systems must be brought into their environment to alter their natural activities. This is necessary to remove bias.

Either way, the insertion of controls requires intruding into an environment something not typically there to measure results. This is accomplished by either inserting scientists or equipment to observe and document the results. Just as a camera will often affect events as subjects stop to have their pictures taken, instruments will invariably alter the normal environment and the normal activities of subjects in one way or another. We might see this as only effecting research on living creatures. In reality, any sensory perception with inserted controls will influence the results unnaturally. In the case of space observation, applying instruments to a visual star or solar system will funnel a narrow range of waveforms into the equipment, filtering the full spectrum of the object by the use of lenses and mirrors. An event or image displayed in wavelengths outside of those accessed by our observatory instruments will not be observed. Here the instrument's limitations prevent the observation. Instrument flaws can also alter the data collected, depending upon their inherent limitations and flaws.

Research involving the behavior of living organisms will be directly altered by the intervention of clinical research protocols. Often the most incidental occurrences can greatly affect the accuracy of the results. Influencing results through the intervention of instruments is well known. A camera inserted into a tribe of jungle apes by human researchers will certainly alter the activities of the apes, especially if the apes had never seen humans or the camera. The intrusion of the humans and their equipment will alter the ape's daily regimen in one way or another.

This same intrusion level is illustrated by the *white coat effect.* The white coat effect has been well studied over the years by researchers who noticed that many subjects responded differently to doctors giving medication than nurses or other hospital staff giving medication and treatment. Other studies have shown that patients will typically have higher blood pressure around doctors than at home or when blood pressure was taken by a non-doctor. This has led to the logical conclusion that if blood pressure is affected by the presence of a doctor, then results from research performed by hospitals and doctors may well be altered simply by the presence of physicians and researchers.

Many researchers have argued that the participation or even mention of participation in a study to subjects may affect the results. The clinical setting may affect the results. Any interference of a subject's ordinary course of existence may alter the results. Since the bulk of research by modern science is performed by clinicians intruding natural environments with clinical protocols and instruments, the trust we might have in the conclusions of these studies should be questioned.

Accuracy is limited by sense perception.

Outside of the limitations of modern science brought about by intrusion, design flaws, commercial motives and institutional bias, another key problem in modern research is the gross limitation of our senses and their instrument extensions. Human observation is drastically flawed by the gross limitations of the senses. Our eyes see a tiny fragment of the potential spectrum. Our ears hear another fragment. Our tactile senses feel another small fragment. Our taste buds and olfactory bulbs sense still another small fragment. Together all these senses still only pick up a small portion of the potential waveforms occurring around us.

We are not only limited by the range of observation among these senses, but also to our *scope* of perception. We are limited by our inability to fathom the breadth and size of the universe around us. While the expanse of the universe is inconceivable to us, the range of smallness is outside of our range of perception. Though we can see smaller objects with instrumentation than we have observed with our raw senses or prior instruments, we still cannot fathom the incredible depth and expansiveness of the world of the small.

The eyes are limited to receiving specific spectra.

Despite numerous technical advances in instrumentation, the eyes remain the main instruments of fact gathering in modern science. The eyes are cylindrical with a special lens and shuttering mechanism to focus and limit the entry of light to specific wavelengths. The cornea, the aqueous fluid, the iris, pupils, lens and ciliary muscles all operate in a coordinated fashion to focus on specific objects of particular wavelengths, distances and size. This takes place while the eyes blink to filter out other wavelengths, images, and debris, which may confuse or disrupt the image we expect to see.

Once the lens mechanics do their work to narrow in on particular wavelength ranges, inverted light is filtered into the eyeball, reflecting onto the retina. The retina is made up of cells (rods and cones) which translate the various wavelengths into bioelectric vibrational signals. These signals are then inverted and filtered again while they are transmitted through the optic nerve. The optic nerve carries these triple-filtered signals to specific neurons in the brain. The brain neurons convert the impulses to recognized images to be recorded onto the mind. The living being, under the illusion of false identification and expectations bound to desires, will then filter these images again in a manner that facilitates specific expectations and desires.

Beyond the tremendous amount of filtering, the visual senses yield various inaccuracies in observation. The eyes are trained to pick up specific wavelengths of light and not others. They do not pick up wavelengths outside of the 380nm to 760nm range. This means that any light outside these wavelengths will not be converted into impulses by the eyes and hence will not be transmitted to the brain at all.

The eyes are trained specifically on light and reflected light. This means we can only observe the objects or portions of objects that reflect or emit light within these narrow wavelengths. If light does not reflect off the object in this wavelength range, the eyes will not transmit an image of that object to the brain. If an object is made of a particular molecular structure that absorbs the range of wavelengths our eyes pick up, we will not observe that object. If the object emits an energy that does not allow light to reflect within our wavelength range, that object will not be transmitted to our brain. Should an object be moving at a speed faster than our eyes are trained to observe, we will not perceive that object. Should an object contain a molecular structure without enough density to reflect light, we will not see that object. Should an object lie in an atmosphere that bends light too deeply, we will note see that object.

We cannot see in pitch-blackness because there is not enough light available to reflect off objects bound in darkness. In a completely dark closet, our eyes are almost useless. There may be a small amount of light seeping in to provide reflection, which could allow shadowy outlines. In general, the less light available for reflection within our wavelength range, the less we can see.

There are a number of organisms stumbled upon over the years that do not reflect light in the normal sense. Certain jellyfish and bacteria varieties have been discovered only recently because they blend in to their backgrounds—they reflect little light. Our researchers are finding new species of life almost every day. Why? Because these species have been heretofore unavailable to our senses for one reason or another. Only through special instruments and staining techniques have we been able to see some of these and other organisms. It would certainly make sense for us to realize that we also do not have the ability to see an array of other life forms as well. With regard to the qualities of density, transparency, reflectivity, size, frequency and wavelength, our eyes can perceive only a tiny portion of the world around us.

Recognition is required for perception.

We must note that neither the eyes, the optic nerve, the brain nor the mind actually "see" anything. All of these anatomical instruments merely transmit or pass on oscillations of particular waveforms. *Seeing* is what takes place by a *seer*—the inner self. The self views a holographic imprint of the oscillations from the senses. Upon viewing the hologram, the self makes a value judgment as to what is accepted.

The self thus gives credibility to the information-gathering instruments. The assignment of credibility by the self is the only reliability factor for the holographic images transmitted by the senses onto the mapping system of the mind. We only place importance on what the eyes (or any other senses) capture and project upon the mind because we choose to. We choose to rely on images of our senses in order to observe the expected. As a result, our eyes tend to focus only on images we recognize and expect. The eyes will often completely miss patterns and shapes within our theoretical frequency range. It is our level of recognition and the expectation of an object's existence that precludes our viewing of it. As a result, we do not see many objects even within our visual range. If we do not expect or recognize them, they will either be filtered out along the way, or ignored by the self upon viewing the mind's screen. In order to perceive something, we must first have the inclination that the object may exist. Once we recognize and thus accept the object's possible existence, we then are capable of recognizing its image reflected onto our mind's screen.

Psychologists and psychiatrists sometimes use this propensity to test the mental state of a person. Opthamologists will also use this tendency to test for color blindness. Imbedded or interpretive pictures are often used in both instances.

> *We are shown an image of a butterfly imbedded into a drawing of a tree. While some will see the object, many will not. Unless we are told an image exists within the tree image, we may not see it. It is blended into the drawing, outside our realm of expectation. If we were told another image exists within the tree image, we are more likely to find it, although we still might have to find and recognize it. If we were told to find a butterfly inside the tree there would be a much greater chance of us seeing the butterfly image within the tree.*

In the same way, we can miss so much of existence simply because we are not aware of it and thus do not recognize or expect it.

> *Two people attend the same play. They get home and talk about it. They realize they each saw different things in the play. They realize they also interpreted the plot and its meaning quite differently.*

As we compare our observations with others we realize we each see different things in life; prioritize things a little differently; and even make different meanings of things.

Although we can objectively agree that particular events do happen with careful analysis, we also may easily allow our subjective interpretation of events to adjust what we perceive and conclude from observations.

Furthermore, peer-pressure often adjusts and distorts our perception of the information brought in by the senses. If our family members, friends, and researchers suggest our observations have particular interpretations, we are likely to assume those interpretations. This *suggestive* tendency of observation is well documented by hypnotherapy. Simply through suggestion, a person may be told to act differently, speak differently, or even believe something differently. In the same way, from the very beginning of our physical lives we are open to the suggestions of our parents, friends, teachers, and co-workers. As we hear these suggestions while interpreting our limited sense perception, we gradually align our recognition to the expectations of the rest of society.

Psychologist Solomon Asch established this tendency in our society in his research in 1951. Dr. Asch assembled test subjects into groups, asking each person in each group to answer a question about the length of a line everyone was observing. All but one in the group were instructed beforehand to answer the question wrong. The one true test subject in each group (not instructed on how to answer) predominantly answered the question consistent with the rest of the group even though it was clearly wrong. About 70% of tested subjects answered the question as the group did, knowing the answer was wrong.

Other experiments, such as the one done by Dr. Stanley Milgrim (1974) have confirmed that most people tend to follow the instructions of authority figures, even though they know those instructions are wrong and even harmful to others.

These studies illustrate how quickly most people will accommodate and even accept the conclusions of institutional thinking, abandoning their own observation and understandings.

We can also see how easily the *peer-review* process and the authoritarian institutionalization of science can lead to a mass acceptance of erroneous assumptions.

Perception is inseparable from ability.

Just as we cannot see bacteria or other tiny objects with the naked eye, we cannot see through mediums with densities or qualities outside of our atmosphere. For example, we cannot see through a different mix of gases. A room full of tear gas is difficult to see within. We also cannot see through dense matter such as mercury or gold. We can into some liquids but not others. While we can hazily see through water, we can only see clearly through water with special equipment such as masks or goggles. We also cannot see more subtle matter. While we can see water, we cannot see air. Outside of the molecular combinations that make up our atmospheres of air, earth and water, there are various other atmospheres made of other gases and molecular combinations around the universe. There are also other universes outside of our universe within even our Milky Way galaxy. Outside of our Milky Way galaxy, there are many other galaxies and many universes within each of those galaxies.

Since our eyes are made of specialized molecules set up for seeing objects reflecting at certain densities through *this* atmosphere, they are not equipped for seeing *other* densities through *other* atmospheres. While we may be able to retain a little of our own atmosphere in some spacesuits, we will not truly be able to *seeing* that planet because the molecular makeup and density of that atmosphere (including temperature and humidity and so on) are different. As a result, most objects existing within that atmosphere will reflect light differently than light is reflected within our atmosphere. This makes most everything existing outside of our atmosphere only partially visible if even visible at all to our eyes.

Most of us know that although water exists within our atmosphere, light will still reflect and bend differently in water than it does in air. Objects in water thus appear distorted to us. Light bends drastically different in other atmospheres as well. The objects in those atmospheres are outside of our sensory range.

> *Fish eyes are designed to see in water. Their lenses are more curved than those designed to see through air. As a result, most fish are blind outside of water and cannot see water itself.*

All our senses are limited.

Our ears work very much the same as the eyes do. The auditory canal is designed to bring in certain wavelengths of oscillation, which vibrate the eardrum, and move three bones—the malleus, incus and stapes—in such a way as to amplify and convert these frequencies into physical pulses. These pulses are pushed into the cochlear fluid where they vibrate tiny hairs. These hairs conduct and translate these pulses into bioelectrical signals, which travel through the cochlear nerve to specific brain cells. Recognized electrical impulses are then recorded onto the mind, where they are sorted and cataloged. During the entire process there is a filtering mechanism going on, removing information unexpected or unwanted. As a result, noises within range may or may not be perceived. They may still be recorded onto the mind if they haven't been filtered out. But since the mind's priorities are driven by the living being, the mind will focus upon the inputs most important to the living being's objectives. This is why hearing can be so selective. One person will hear one thing, while another hears something else—either a different sound altogether or a different part of a speech, for example.

The auditory sensory system also has a number of gross limitations outside of filtering. Like the eye, only specific wavelengths with specific parameters can be transmitted through. Dogs can hear frequencies we cannot, for example. This is because their ears were designed to pick up those different frequencies. Other species pick up from higher to lower frequency wavelengths. Dolphins and orcas use a sonar system with an entirely different frequency system to "hear" and "see" as well as "scope" objects at great distances. Beyond these functional differences, a person must also still be expecting and recognize certain sounds in order to identify them once they reach the holographic screen of the mind.

Thermal sensitivity, pain, and tactile senses are also specific to wavelength range. Sensing nerves located at different depths from the skin surface are designed to pick up specific vibrations from the skin surface and convert them into bioelectrical signals. These signals are converted by the peripheral nervous system into nerve impulses, and transmitted to brain neurons for imprinting onto the mind's screen. All of these sensory mechanisms are limited to a specific range of inputs. They are also subject to error. In medicine, an erroneous transmission of pain when there is no physical cause for the pain is called *psychogenic* or *noiceptic* pain, which is often considered either a neurological disorder or a psychological disorder. The human body's sensory system, as in all the other sensory systems in the body, is subject to a variety of limitations. Many animals and insects have tactile senses that pick up more sensitive vibrations than ours do. This is why animals can sense an earthquake much earlier than humans can. Furthermore, the slightest of vibrations can be felt by a spider or cockroach, sending them scrambling for safety.

Perception is limited by scope.

Beyond the sheer physical shortcomings of our senses is the gross limitation of scope. Scope is the relative relationship between our own physical senses—what our eyes are seeing or ears are hearing—and what interpretations we make. Our interpretations are relative to our conceptual training and background:

> *A flea lives on the body of a dog. The flea resides between the dog's hairs, munching on skin and blood. The flea is oblivious to the fact that the dog is running for a bone.*

We may be occasionally reminded of our limitations when we hear about or see unexplained events taking place around the universe. Instances of black holes, neutron stars, gamma ray bursts, unidentified flying objects, mysterious ancient relics, and other phenomena are reminders of our insufficient realm of scope and comprehension in understanding the universe around us.

Scientific instruments are limited by the senses.

Certainly, the many technological advances in instruments over the last century are credible. Instruments can magnify or amplify visual or sound radiation, allowing us to see smaller matter or matter farther away. Instruments can also extract and measure frequencies from a substance or bounce frequencies off a substance to indicate what elements might compose that substance. These instruments are nevertheless still limited by all the same types of physical limitations our senses have. They may allow for a *slightly* greater range of perception and a *slightly* greater range of scope. When one considers the entire physical spectrum range, we are still dealing with a very small range. We also are also missing entire dimensions and atmospheres. Furthermore, we are still stuck within what we recognize and expect from mental images when we observe instrumental data. When picking up wavelength spectra from compounds for example, we can only register what has been previously compiled from elements we were previously aware of. When we interpret bursts of wavelength data from space, we can only try to decode those with the languages we know and understand.

We must realize that instruments are built by humans. Human limitations are built-in. Even though instruments can pick up greater wavelength ranges, there is still a translation and recognition issue. Our processors are still programmed to translate the incoming data into something we can understand and perceive. The data will thus be narrowed down to the range we recognize and expect. Even if an instrument could, for example, pick up frequencies of communications between organisms from other dimensions: How could they be translated into the range we could understand if we did not build that translation capability into the device? We could not convert it unless we knew what we were converting. A language translator must know both languages. For many years, researchers thought animal sounds were simply random sounds without meaning, even though we had all the equipment to listen. Today we recognize that animals communicate through intonations, body signals and amplitude changes we were previously not aware of, even though we had been able to see and hear them for many years with our senses or instruments.

Communication vibrations are occurring all around us outside of our reception range. For example, plants have been tested for many decades for their communication and response capabilities with surprising results. As Peter Tompkins and Christopher Bird documented in their 1973 classic *The Secret Life of Plants,* controlled studies tested the electrical activity of plants, revealing that they communicate on a level we cannot perceive. For example, an indoor plant will respond with greater fear to someone who hurt remote plants outside. How did the plant know the outside plants were injured? Studies have also revealed that plants have an extraordinary sensory capability enabling them to respond to human activity, sound, and other occurrences.

Instruments compare observed data.

Much of the instrumentation researchers use today to view both the larger and smaller aspects of the universe are based upon the *crystal field theory* of the 1930s. When light travels through a substance, some of it will be absorbed by the molecules of the substance, and some of the spectrum will be reflected back. A ruby looks red because the chromium in the ruby absorbs some of the blue-green wavelengths (around 490 nanometers) while reflecting a greater amount of red wavelengths (around 650 nanometers). As these 650 nm wavelengths strike the retina of our eyes, we perceive the color red. Our physiological technology is analogous to the spectrometer process that chemists determine the atomic makeup of a particular molecule. Because atomic particles making up molecules interact distinctively with various radiation, the molecular configuration of a substance can simply be identified by the radiation they absorb and reflect.

Practically all imaging of atomic structures—whether by chemists wanting to identify a substance's composition or by physicists wanting to investigate particle activity—is performed through interaction with radiation. One such method is called *X-ray crystallography.* X-rays are shot into a crystallized version of a particular substance glued onto the glass of a diffractometer tube. The X-rays react with atoms of the molecular substance and these diffracted rays are recorded onto film or computer. These diffraction reflections are measured for amplitude and wave phase to yield the potential atomic structure and theoretical positioning of the electrons. Because X-rays are short-wavelength electromagnetic waves, they interact with the electromagnetic waves existing at the atomic level. As these interactions occur, they are absorbed or diffracted in a variety of different angles. These angles are plotted out onto photographic film, and graphed into position.

Each atom and molecule combination creates a distinct angle of diffraction. Using diffraction measurements and a formula created by William Bragg and his son in 1913, these plotted angles measure the level of wave interference these diffracted waves have, following their interaction with the substance. The distinct angles of diffraction were cataloged into a database as they are matched with specific substances. Gold has a diffraction angle different than copper for example. As the different atomic elements have been cataloged, researchers have been able to compare the cataloged data with current measurements to determine a substance's atomic structure.

X-ray diffractions have revealed numerous molecular structures over the years. X-ray crystallography revealed the fantastic double-helical structures of DNA and RNA, for example.

Another tool used to perceive atomic structure at the atomic level is called the *electron microscope.* The electron microscope fires magnetically manipulated cathode rays—thin electromagnetic beams—into a substance. The beam's interaction with the substance is reflected onto an electronically charged recording screen. With various magnifications, the researcher can observe somewhat of an *electromagnetic shadow* of the substance. It is the substance's relative response to the radiation—its absorbance or reflectance—that ultimately create the image.

A specialized form of spectrometry emerged after World War II called nuclear-magnetic resonance (NMR). Instead of firing continuous streams of radiation at a substance to elicit electromagnetic responses, NMR beams are magnetized and polarized during the firing process. This increases the likelihood of the beam *resonating* with the orbital patterns of the electrons. Once a resonance has been established, the scientist can make a number of assumptions regarding the qualities of that particular atomic structure.

Yet another development in this area of visualizing electrons using radiated reflection is *electron spin resonance* (or ESR) spectroscopy. By characterizing and cataloging the radiation response with known spin quanta, the spin characteristics of other substances can be comparatively determined.

These techniques are generally referred to as *spectrometry.* Spectrometry means literally the measurement ("metry") of the spectrum as it responds to molecular matter. While one substance will absorb a certain wavelength of some radiation, another substance may react to that wavelength by emitting other waves, referred to as *emissions.* Spectrometry may utilize various forms of radiation, including radiowaves, microwaves, and X-rays. Advanced telescopic spectrographic equipment may also use and interpret gamma rays, ultraviolet and sound waves in their analyses. As discussed above, newer instruments can polarize or otherwise modulate the probing radiation to elicit different responses from the substance. Those different responses again can be cataloged, creating a tool for the future identification of that substance's theoretical composition.

While modern science might want us to believe we are "seeing" those substances with these instruments, this technology renders a rather narrow understanding of the substance. The rest of our "seeing" is done through reference and inference. Instrumentation used in an attempt to understand atomic identity compares historical data rather than reveals direct information. This might be better called *referred* or even *inferred information.* Spectroscopy equipment will shoot radiation through a gas chamber or liquid medium, for example. This radiation will affect the particular molecules or ions, depending upon the waveform, the medium and the other characteristics of the radiation. The bottom line is that these instruments each yield a limited amount of information about the substance. The fact that every element responds uniquely is used as a foundation for cataloging each response. While we might be amazed at our ability to utilize different forms of radiation, we are still only deriving limited data, and this data only gives us a narrow bandwidth of real information about the substance itself. This might be compared to the three blind men each feeling a different part of the elephant. Unrelated portions of narrow information hardly reveal the makeup of a substance. Comparing that narrow information might tell us how the substance compares to others within those specific criteria, but not much else:

> *A young woman walks through a dark alley late at night. She looks to her left and sees a large shadow on the side of one of the buildings. The shadow appears menacing. It appears to be a large man with a large hat, holding a gun. The woman screams for safety. As she turns to run, she sees a child holding a broom, wearing a small hat. The child was apparently sweeping the alley next to a back porch light.*

Instruments with methods like nuclear magnetic resonance, X-ray crystallography, gas chromatography, mass spectrometry and other types of spectroscopy reflect a narrow set of characteristics of a substance, much as a light might cast a shadow of a figure on the wall. Understanding the object that created the shadow is another matter. Certainly the actual composition of the object may not be revealed by its shadow. If we have never seen that object before, seeing its shadow might conjure up a comparison with other shadows we have seen. If we have seen the actual object behind a similar shadow, our guess looking only at the shadow might be fairly accurate. Still we could make a critical mistake, as the woman in the alley did. Worse, if we can only compare a current shadow with other shadows—never having actually seen any of the objects creating any of the shadows, we can compare shadows but little else. The woman in the alley could well interpret the shadow as some kind of monster if she had never compared people with their shadows before. Comparing one shadow to the next might provide an interesting comparison of our shadow collection, but it would still not reveal the object creating the shadow.

We could certainly use our imagination to identify the object, but the accuracy of that imagination would depend upon the accuracy of our imagination. The expectation of the object's identity would certainly control our perception. This lands the accuracy of our instrument technologies squarely upon the limitations of the senses and our expectation of perception.

Cataloging data from instrumentation simply means correlating various instrumental data with our sensory data bank. We can measure elements we can see, touch or smell, then tabulate those, and try to extrapolate the data to obtain measurements for less tangible elements. Again, we are grounded by and limited by our sensory limitations. We can keep extending our speculations to fill the gaps, but with each extended speculation, we increase the uncertainty and decrease the odds of accuracy.

It is true that instruments may allow us to expand on a few of the characteristics of the world around us, but only to the extent we have the capability to physically perceive. At the end of the day, the capacity of our instruments is still limited to the scope, range, and perception of our basic senses. Elements outside of this capacity will be invisible not only to us but also to our instruments:

> *Our AM radio does not have the capacity to pick up FM transmissions. If we created a larger dial on the AM radio to zoom in on more distant radio stations, that radio still would not pick up any FM stations.*

In the same way, the processors and programs that convert and interpret information into charts, numbers, sounds, or visible representations will be as limited as the capacity of the humans who built the machines. The capability to measure existence outside of expected recognition simply will not be built in unless we possess those capabilities.

A history of instrumental observations certainly allows us to catalog and compare all sorts of observed characteristics among a population. It does not necessarily tell us anything outside of those compared observations. It is still therefore limited by our original knowledge of the observed object.

Instrumental data is limited by observation range.

Regardless of the capability of an instrument's output, the information obtained is still limited by the observation range and interpretation of its user. A typical instrument may receive a large range of wavelength and frequency emissions, for example. Only certain emissions will be considered significant by the observer, however. Those not recognizable will be discarded as unimportant. The person choosing what is significant is thus the *gatekeeper* of the information. It is the therefore the range of the gatekeeper's consideration which is critical. The gatekeeper determines which data is significant. The gatekeeper determines which data will determine what is used and understood. This gatekeeping process often takes place through a computer program built into the instrument. Such a translation system makes the programmer the ultimate gatekeeper of that instrument and information. As these instruments may display lots of charts, graphs, or raw numbers of various data, they still only gather what we instructed them to gather. They gather what we recognize and expect to be significant, and filter out the rest. As a result, even the most advanced instruments only display results that are within our range and scope of comprehension. The full data may well be *off the charts,* but we would never know it because we made the charts.

> *Not so long ago, researchers believed whales were big and dumb creatures. Researchers thought they cruised just below the surface, coming up for air occasionally, mating, and birthing. After more study, researchers now realize that whales are deeper and more complex than originally thought. Underwater researchers have seen whales swimming very deftly, performing miraculously graceful underwater ballets as they dive hundreds of feet beneath the surface. They have also discovered that their songs are quite complex, informing other whales over significant distances with precise communications. Researchers now believe these songs may also have sonar capabilities, allowing the whales to pick up information from the reflections of their songs. Researchers are only beginning to understand the complexity and intelligence of the whale. Despite modern computerized instruments and tens of thousands of hours of listening, researchers still do not know exactly what the whales are saying.*

Limited equipment yields limited understanding.

Our instruments are no more advanced than we are. Our development of instruments can only pace as fast as our understanding does. Hence, society's overconfidence in their technical capabilities is unjustified. Even if we accidentally stumbled onto a piece of equipment further evolved than we were, we would still be limited by what we could extract out of the instrument. Our range, scope, recognition, and expectations would all limit our ability to gain further information from that instrument.

Furthermore, just as we have errors in the transmission of sensual information, our instruments are also prone to error. An instrument may be calibrated wrong, yielding garbled information. The instrument may theoretically be thought up to observe one thing but actually picks up something else. An instrument could theoretically tell us blue is red and red is blue for example. Any successive instruments will be calibrated and built the same, continuing to yield the same error. An instrument can also filter and reduce information to yield distorted results. In order to convert the information into a range our senses can perceive, the instrument will have to translate and reduce the information into a different range. This process is prone to alter and reduce the information considerably.

> *Instruments are restricted to observe whatever type of information they are built and designed for. If we do not know something exists, we cannot design an instrument to observe it.*

For this reason, instruments are always undergoing revision and upgrades. Many instruments are simply replaced. Over the last century, thousands if not millions of machines have been junkpiled, never to be used again. They were either shown to be inaccurate, or replaced by better technology. Instruments are perpetually being improved because earlier versions are found to be inadequate in one way or another. Does this mean our current instrument is any more accurate?

The shortcomings of our technical instruments are all too obvious when reviewing the tremendous effort humankind has put into designing and building space observatory equipment. Billions and billions of dollars have gone into these efforts over the years. Today we find "advanced" observatories placed on the tops of mountains throughout the world. We also find lavish space observatories orbiting the planet. We find tremendously costly gigantic *arrays* of telescopes lining deserts for miles. All of these giant *ears* and *eyes* are tied in to our most advanced computers for analysis and imaging. With all this tremendous effort, money and time spent *listening* and *looking*, these scientists know very little about how the universe works and what is *out there*. In fact, all of this equipment has merely created more questions about the universe. Cosmologists are still struggling to understand the same basic questions asked five hundred years ago: What is a star? What is a galaxy? In addition to basic questions, the big ears and eyes have only opened up new questions like what are black holes and what are neutron stars. Black holes might well be called a prime example illustrating our instruments' inability to help us accurately understand the universe. Our observations have indicated the likelihood these holes may be swallowing matter, but where to or why is still at question. If we cannot see where things are disappearing *to*, we also will not be able to see where things are coming *from*.

Again, this is not to say that our instruments do not help us extend the range of the senses—they obviously do. We simply have to realize that the breadth of that extension relative to everything else. An instrument that lets our eyes see two more feet further is not much of an improvement if we are trying to view an object at several million miles. In the same way, an instrument that helps us view the same object with more magnification but within a limited wavelength range hardly provides a substantial improvement. It is important for us to not be overconfident, thinking we have perception abilities beyond what we actually have. To bring this into some perspective, we might mathematically consider roughly putting our senses on a realistic scale of maybe observing .000001% of physical existence. Meanwhile our instruments might be able to pick up an extra .00001 or .00002%, leaving 99%+ of *physical* existence—not to speak of transcendental existence—unseen and unobservable.

Incomplete information leads to speculation.

Our senses and their instrumental extensions are thus designed to pickup and translate limited information within a specific range, scope, dimension and atmosphere. These limitations result in grossly incomplete information. Furthermore, our recognition and scope potential does not allow us the ability to comprehend even the full range of what our limited senses can perceive. To fill in the gaps, modern science resorts to speculation. Speculation has even greater limitation: *speculation is limited by our previous faulty perceptions further distorted by our consciousness:*

> *A person wants to know what kind of insulation a house has between its walls without poking holes or taking apart any of the walls. He pounds on the walls with a hammer but this hardly tells him much. As he consults with others, he finds varying opinions. These various opinions only serve to further compound his uncertainty. He finally decides the best way to know is to ask the builder or someone who worked with the builder while the house was being built.*

Speculation reduces knowledge.

Relying on speculative information requires a faith in the speculator. Further speculations, rather than providing more clarity, only serve to create more uncertainty. Because we have no proof in the accuracy of a speculation, we are forced to look into the credibility of the speculators; their process of data gathering and conclusion; their motives; and the possibility of distorted, incomplete or incorrect data. The likelihood of error is compounded by the number of speculation variables applied to the situation. The question then becomes: *Can we trust that all of the variables are error-free all at once?* This is compounded by: *Which speculator can we trust?*

There are further questions these bear to mind: Is there one modern scientist whose speculations we trust over and above others? Are there types of studies or formulas we trust over others? Perhaps review studies—which combine results of other studies—will give us confidence in some of these theories. Perhaps we can trust theories accompanying gigantic equations we do not understand. How can we *trust* the varying multitude of information presented by and speculated upon by modern science? Perhaps the question should rather be: Should we trust modern science at all?

Groupthink increases uncertainty.

Considering the various flaws individual scientific studies can have, many researchers seem to rely upon *review studies* or *meta studies* to provide trustworthy conclusions. A meta study statistically combines a number of studies while a review comments on and reports comparatively on multiple studies. One might assume that the fact that more than one study *confirms* the same result gives that particular conclusion validity. In the same way, studies which are performed separately to test the same hypothesis often appear substantial enough to give someone trust in the results.

Confirmation studies do not necessarily provide more validity to an initial study's conclusions, however. Like the initial study, a second study is usually set up to confirm the same hypothesis. This leads to the likelihood that the second study will confirm the same hypothesis. Adding insult to injury, a second study done to confirm the first also most likely carries the same mindset and perception values used in the first study. The first study *paved the way for expectation.* Once the first study documents and concludes a particular hypothesis, and is published; debating that study's hypothesis becomes difficult. There is a greater likelihood the same hypothesis will be assumed in future research, as the institutional mindset moves in that direction. This tendency is often referred to as *groupthink.* Going against the grain in research is not an easy task. A new hypothesis may only come out of the second study if the first was blatantly faulty. Otherwise, if the first study is published, it will usually create the groupthink mindset. Other research will more likely emulate that study, simply because it was acceptable enough to become published. Once a mindset is established in modern research, *rocking the boat* with new theories becomes a risky proposition.

Meta and review studies are both groupthink speculations. In both types, the referred studies are *chosen by the author.* The author will use whatever criteria he or she feels is appropriate in choosing or commenting on research. Whatever biases the author of the meta or review study has, the study will reflect. Since the author will usually limit to using studies that confirm his or her own hypothesis—or those accepted by their peers—the review or meta analysis will merely facilitate the groupthink agenda.

Recently a meta analysis on vitamin E was published, concluding that vitamin E might cause risk of mortality with doses over 400IU per day. Although the meta study compiled 19 different clinical studies, it was criticized by many nutritionists and doctors because most of the subjects of the chosen studies were adults with greater mortality rates than most. Regardless of these obvious flaws, this meta study was accepted and published by mainstream medicine press and mass media.

Each individual study may contain unique variables and unknown influences: By compiling a number of studies in review or meta format, the total number of variables affecting the data only *increases.* With each variable comes a new potential for *inaccuracy.* The speculations in a certain direction are thus compounded, alternative views are further ignored, and the potential for inaccuracy is increased.

Formulation is limited to observation.

A mathematical formula is a relationship between two or more events or groups of data using variables for data input. The equal sign in the middle of the formula indicates an equal relationship between the two sides. This necessitates either a direct relationship, a proportional relationship or a variable relationship—where other events vary their equality. In the final analysis, an equation illustrates a pattern of events and a predictability or consistency between the events. When seemingly unrelated events are related, nature's design is partially revealed. We are usually amazed when previously-unrelated events are related through a formula. For instance gravity, force and momentum were all related through early scientific study, consisting of basic observation and the study of moving objects. Relationships such as *force equals mass times velocity* (F=ma) were developed by comparing relationships by early modern scientists, for example.

The problem with observational equations like these is that these equations are concluded *as if their relationships occur in a vacuum.* In the F=ma equation for example, the original observer related the speed and weight to the potential for increased speed, *assuming there were no additional influences.* In other words, even though events were repeatedly observed and their behaviors were confirmed, unobserved or unseen forces were not captured in the equation. They were simply out of observational range. In the example of gravity, only later was it found that atmospheric pressure played a part in this relationship, and thus new variables had to be added. This is why new formulae are arising from modern science. Is this because modern scientists cannot make up their minds? No, it is because we do not have the ability to see all the variables of influence:

> *Say an early scientist observed that whenever there is rain there are clouds. The scientist creates a hypothesis that clouds cause rain. After observing the relationship between cloud cover and rain, a formula is developed.*

We might say this postulate is correct because it is obvious—a relationship between clouds and rain is indisputable. However, such a narrow formula would ignore other important influences at play, including atmospheric pressure, water vapor levels, temperature, fronts and more. Our "clouds cause rain" theory would thus be overly simplistic and inaccurate, despite being easily observable. We can extend this same problem to the numerous other theories currently accepted by science. Theories concluded by combining speculation with limited sense perception are prone to dramatic limitations. The gross limitations of the human senses and their extended instruments restrict our ability to comprehend the entire landscape of influential events. Speculation derived from limited sense perception mixed with groupthink and/or fertile imagination can dramatically distance us from reality.

Scientific research is competitive and hierarchical.

In the real world, research is not the rational pursuit of knowledge many might imagine it to be. Rather, it is a system riddled with competitive forces; greed; profits; the pursuit of personal recognition; and quite simply survival issues for the individual researcher. The various private, university and public labs that produce most of the research are in a constant state of competition amongst themselves, each lab vying to be the first to the next *'hot discovery'* and each internally struggling to keep their funding sources going. The path to consistent funding and recognition is to beat the other labs to publishing the big particular discovery. Each researcher thus competes with every other researcher in their field: A real *dog-eat-dog* scenario, documented over the years by many a frustrated researcher.

There is a rigid hierarchy among researchers when it comes to getting recognition and credit for their work. Researchers with advanced degrees must gradually and diligently work their way to the top in order to lead or design research. Until that time, a researcher may assist other researchers or teams or confirm hypotheses established by others. Going against the grain is not conducive to professional growth in the *science biz*. This means that while complying with the groupthink speculations of other researchers, the individual researcher must focus energies towards one-upping fellow researchers in order to gain recognition.

Achieving credit for a discovery or any part of a discovery is the key to success in the *science biz.* Unfortunately, credit is only sparingly shared. Information and credit may be shared between researchers on the same team but researchers working from different funding sources will typically compete. As a result, research is usually kept quiet until findings are complete and published. There have been cases where research findings are stolen or otherwise gained from another lab. This adds to the need for secrecy, turning labs into high security zones. At the end of the day, the researchers who get published for a discovery will usually get the credit, even if other researchers reached the same conclusion prior to publishing. Sadly, this has resulted in many a researcher receiving recognition for another researcher's research work.

Credit for a discovery is the researcher's ticket to a successful career of funded research, job security, and name recognition. Achieving the respect of colleagues, university board regents, publishers and the public gives researchers clear incentives to *get there first.* Sometimes for the individual researcher, it is simply a matter of putting food on the table.

There are three glaring problems with this. First, the lack of collaboration between researchers slows the potential for further discovery. Second, the quality of the research and the potential for broader thinking are sacrificed as researchers race to try to discover and publish findings that follow the mainstream. Third, the system forces researchers wanting to be recognized to become *indoctrinated* into the mindset or groupthink of modern science. This pushes researchers to not only stay away from unconventional theories and conclusions, but also to stay within the confines of standardized equipment and accepted means of observation. This results in scientific thought continuing to be *inside the box.* Research with results or conclusions outside of mainstream hypotheses will typically not be done, as the path of least resistance is pursued. As a result, science publishers will not publish radical studies because no one wants to be ostracized. Thus, the body of documented science we see today is not *actual* science, but *acceptable* science, dictated by the masses of groupthink researchers wanting to protect and further their careers by through peer-acceptance:

> *Despite their individual speed, a pack of wild horses are easily driven into mass capture. This is because within a large pack, the animals are carefully watching each other. They do not want to stray from the pack because within the pack they feel protected.*

Modern researchers are assumed wise.

While many individual scientists certainly have been or are wise, much of the nonscientific media assumes that all modern scientists, either individually or collectively, are wise. Researchers may not have such a respectful opinion of each other, but they are particularly beholden to the club, and thus need to be protective. If a researcher scoffs another, he had better have a solid case, or face being embarrassed and even becoming ostracized. We might appropriately call this *peer-control.*

Meanwhile the public might assume that a researcher has undergone rigorous training, imparting profound wisdom from mentorship and study. It is true that higher degrees usually require a number of years of study and several mentorships with professors who may have an established history of research and writing. However, it must be understood that the *range* of study, and the ability of these professors to travel *outside the box,* is also severely limited by the educational institutions that employ them. Maintaining job security in these institutions usually requires the same sort of peer control process that research scientists undertake when determining hypotheses. Although speculation is obviously encouraged, the topics and range of speculation are thoroughly restricted.

In other words, a graduate student is discouraged to think *outside the box* in most institutions. Coursework is what other researchers theorized upon in the past, and it is assumed that the graduate student will further that same speculative mindset. A graduate student who wants to buck conventional theories of predecessors will quickly be under pressure to conform. On the other hand, a conforming graduate student will easily move through the system. The system is set up for conformity, and those who seek the path of least resistance conform. After all, conformity is what will be necessary to get and keep a job in the scientific community.

We can easily see this when we notice that many of the great scientists credited with landmark discoveries and speculations were ostracized and ridiculed by the scientific community of their day. The irony is that the graduate student of today is expected to conform to the speculations of these formerly ostracized scientists, or risk becoming ostracized. Modern scientists are thus being asked to *"do what I say, not what I do."*

As to whether this system creates wisdom, the question is whether we should consider the speculations of groupthink researchers as wise. Certainly we can accept that a person with a Ph.D. has worked hard and has undergone indoctrination into that area of study. Wisdom itself is another story. Spending twenty years in classrooms listening to people whose employers narrow the range of what they can say is not a recipe for wisdom. Classroom study may teach previous speculations, but this does not necessarily result in practical experience or appropriate application of knowledge. To this we add that laboratory testing—the study of isolated events—is not the type of practical experience known to necessarily cultivate wisdom.

Science does not happen without being published.

Research typically will not be accepted into mainstream science if it is not published. Being published means the research is written up and printed in a *respected* journal of science. There are not that many respected journals out there, however. Furthermore, there is a hierarchy among journals. The more esteemed the publication, the more acceptable the research will be.

In order to be published in a reputable science journal, a study will require a number of qualifications: It should be conducted by reputed researchers with advanced degrees. A doctorate degree is the standard. Studies can certainly be conducted by those with master's degrees or less, but their chances of being published by a reputable journal will be dramatically decreased.

Data and conclusions must be written up in a particular format and properly referenced. Although there is no guarantee a study will be published, a researcher with a good reputation, research from well-funded institutions, and conclusions that fit mainstream opinion on that subject will increase its chances. The conclusion can be new and interesting; just not too radical.

Some of the better journals use review boards to decide which research will become published. Or sometimes it may be the editor or editors of the publication who make the decision. The editor or review board members may or may not be researchers, or even specialists in that area of research. They sometimes simply have journalism backgrounds. Most of these journals will receive many papers from which to choose. Hence, many rigorous studies are never published. Often the decision is not driven by the appropriateness of the study, but by commercial considerations. The company funding the study may be a large advertiser of the journal, or a prestigious university lab. Perhaps the head researcher is *connected* somehow, or has enough recognition to raise immediate interest from the publication. Otherwise, the editor or review board may approve research for publication only if it appeals to the mainstream of researchers and/or their advertisers.

Publishing creates the illusion of accuracy.

Once a speculative conclusion or study is published, regardless of any lack of objectivity; ulterior motives by funding sources; lack of accuracy; or design flaws; the study will become part of the body of modern scientific *knowledge,* and from that day forward, will become *citable.*

When a study is published in a reputable scientific publication, other researchers and publications may then reference that study in their own writings. This is called *citing* the study. Being cited is also a competitive issue among researchers. The more a study is *cited,* the more successful the study has become. By being referenced in another article, the conclusions of the study become more acceptable to other researchers. If one were to say that their study was cited 250 times for example, other researchers would assume its speculative hypothesis must be accurate.

> *As higher bricks are laid onto lower bricks, the lower bricks become foundations. These foundation bricks cannot be removed without damaging the entire building.*

Theoretically at least, a fellow researcher can question cited research, claiming it to be flawed. This occurs rarely, though. It is usually reserved for those cases when an institution or well-known researcher has a stake in the results. In these cases, the protesting researcher or institution may write an editorial complaint about the study. The protesting researcher or institution must be reputable enough to get this criticism published, and be prepared to back up the protest with funded research, requiring a funding source prepared to be involved in the controversy. Should a second study be done, the research team or institution would also have to be connected and accepted enough to have the conflicting study published. The chance of this entire process becoming an eventuality to refute a study is fairly remote. In most cases, once a study is published, it simply becomes part of the body of scientific evidence. Writings may cite or not cite, but at the end of the day, and especially if it is cited, it is accepted as science.

This entire process of publishing a study and having other researchers read the study and possibly debate it is what modern researchers proudly call *'peer review.'* Although it is commendable that other researchers, if they have the gall and the backing, can criticize another study, this process also creates one of the worst aspects of modern science. Because their hypotheses and conclusions will be looked at by the whole of the scientific institution, in order to avoid criticism researchers will likely stay within the conservative norms of mainstream science. As a result, published research seems to stay within a narrow mindset while everyone in the process—including the publishers, the editors and the researchers—are careful not to *rock the boat.* This is one of the main reasons researchers will not reference the Supreme Being in their research. First, it would probably never be published, and secondly, if it did, it would probably hurt the careers of those researchers.

Commercial interests finance most research.

Because published research offers a high degree of visibility, commercial groups are often interested participants. As a result, funding is typically provided by a company or foundation which will benefit from the study being published. Some research is funded by non-profit foundations or government agencies that do not appear to have a financial incentive. Even this research may still be influenced by outsider commercial interests or the career interests of its executives. At the end of the day, most scientific research is funded or influenced by parties that benefit in some way from the published results. Whether it may be career-oriented or profit-oriented, the benefits are typically tangible, and sometimes even lucrative.

For example, a pharmaceutical company will fund a study on a drug that it manufacturers, possibly resulting in billions of dollars of sales. A salvage company may fund an archeological dig in order to be able to sell artifacts to a museum for millions of dollars. A government researcher may push to study a particular disease in order to increase his or her prestige amongst the industry, which may translate to a better job in the private sector. In many of these studies, millions of dollars are at stake and a financial disaster could be the result if the intended discovery or hypothesis and conclusion do not materialize. As a result, modern science seems to be increasingly wrought with deception and fraud.

Sometimes research is funded by a publication or media group which studies a particular area of science. Or it may be funded by a university steeped in a reputation for researching such topics. These parties are usually interested in hypotheses that confirm their reputation in the scientific community. The hypothesis and subject of the study are therefore carefully selected, according to the various agendas of the board members, or the institution in general. A publication, media group or university will usually still have an ultimate profit motive, negotiated through their reputation and the respectability of the research they fund. Research that does not further these agendas will simply not be funded.

Everything about the study—the initial hypothesis, the study's design, as well as its conclusion and write-up—may be arranged to satisfy institutions who fund research for economic reasons. Since the researcher's mortgage payment may depend upon the study being acceptable, the search for truth is compromised. This results in research and conclusions that adhere to conformity and respectability. While the educational institutions are ultimately driven by profit or the furtherance of their reputation, the publication may be motivated to attract a certain segment of paying subscribers or advertisers. Research drawing conclusions conflicting with the interests of educational organizations, publishers, or advertisers may simply evaporate due to lack of funding or publication.

Rather than retaining outside researchers, many studies are performed by the commercial concerns themselves. Manufacturers often employ scientists to conduct research on products the manufacturer produces. The agenda is simply to increase profits. The hypothesis and design are aimed at achieving this agenda. Even studies in natural sciences are often done by commercial companies who will sell the related products. In the business of science, research is typically not done without a financial incentive somewhere.

As a result of these incentives, much of modern science is not really that interested in a humble search for truth. Modern science is primarily a business concern. Objectivity is scarce in this business. The supposed peer-review control system modern science prides itself upon hardly provides objectivity, simply because the researcher who criticizes research may not have a job if he is wrong, and if the criticism is right, the researcher may not have a job for long. Either way, it is a straightjacket.

Modern science has not solved life's real problems.

Far from being an objective source of information, modern science is burdened with flaws, limitations, and bias. We have discussed many of these flaws. These include the limitations of the senses and sense perception. They include the limitations of instruments that only extend these limitations. They include the limited experience and knowledge of the researchers who decide what and how to apply science. They include design flaws created by imposing research onto natural subjects and environments. They include the problems created by designing research to confirm the hypothesis of the researcher. They include the profit agendas of researchers and the institutions that fund and publish research. They include the competition and secrecy among researchers in order to earn credit and climb the ranks of respectability. They include the limitations created by scientific journal publishers who determine what becomes published and what does not. They include the peer control and groupthink to stay within a conservative mainstream of presentation and conclusions. Finally, above all these points is one over-riding flaw of modern science: *it is speculative.*

With this massive collection of flaws, it is doubtful that modern science is qualified to help an individual gain an actual understanding of existence. Modern research simply does not provide the proper platform for the discovery of Truth. Although each individual researcher may be earnestly try to contribute some good, the institution itself is riddled with bias, over-confidence and speculation. Due to this behemoth of a system we refer as modern science, research meant to supposedly provide a clearer understanding of the world around us has merely provided further complexity and uncertainty for those seriously looking for Truth.

Society has faith in modern science.

Why does the institution of modern science seem to be so confident of its conclusions? With an institution so laden with flaws and bias, there must be a reason why our society renders so much respect for modern science's conclusions regarding the universe around us. The only logical answer for this is *faith*: Members of our society have developed a *faith* in the speculations, institutions, publications, and conclusions of modern science.

Faith is required to *'buy-in'* to speculative theories not supported by solid objective evidence. For example, there simply is not enough objective evidence for modern science's fundamental theories describing an accidental, purposeless basis for life. To fill in the many blanks provided by this lack of solid evidence, modern science has inserted many speculations. Because the senses and sense instruments are limited, modern researchers are given the opportunity to insert their theories, as outrageous as they may seem. Thus the complex ruminations of *'quarks'* and *'membranes'* abound. A purposeless view of existence is propounded and accepted, as modern science conveys to the public that there is no life *'out there.'*

In order to buy-in to these current theories, we have to trust in the speculations of these possibly good-intentioned researchers and their institutions, overlooking (or most likely just being unaware of) the various pressures upon both the individual researcher and the institution. We have to overlook the *system.* We have to overlook how the system pressures scientists to sacrifice the search for truth in order to retain their jobs and reputations. We have to overlook how the system pushes editors and review boards to publish articles that please the stockholders and advertisers. We have to overlook how the media will only quote from *respected* journals as they try to pass on new discoveries to the masses. All of these individuals, possibly well meaning but forced to comply with a system built upon motivates of profit and respect, have to be trusted to tell us the truth.

As a necessity to reinforce the various speculations of modern researchers, we often find dramatic media displays put on to try to convince us of modern science's expertise. This requires extensive photography, colorful graphics, elaborate artwork and deftness in communication. Proudly displaying complex instrumentation together with arrays of technical photos and drawings, modern science is able to woo the public with its graphic displays of apparent technical wizardry. The scientific community seems to have also become expert in the politics and techniques of *spin* to maintain the trust of the public.

Remember that *faith* is defined as *confidence* or *trust*. Western society currently *trusts* these researchers and their institutions, regardless of whether their conclusions are adequately proven or objectively assembled. (Remember that leeching and bloodletting was also trusted at one time.) Our modern society has developed an overriding yet unjustified confidence in the institutions of science. Since much of the information we have discussed here is not often discussed, it might be more accurate to call the mass confidence and faith in modern science *blind.* Since modern science has amassed speculation upon speculation like thousands of bricks in a high-rise building, questioning science might be compared to pulling the foundation out from under such a top-heavy building. Disturbing any lower brick could render disastrous results for the entire building.

Now consider someone who did not believe anything unless they were able to observe it directly or it was physically proven to them. Most of us have heard the phrase:

"I won't believe it until I see it."

Consider the massive effort required to enable such a person to re-enact all the research now accepted as basic science, let alone the hundreds of thousands of scientific speculations that followed, many of which had no physical evidence. Would this person, if they were able to see or hear all the actual *evidence,* end up with the same conclusions modern science has concluded?

Even famous scientists of the twentieth century, some near the end of illuminated careers in modern science, have written stark criticisms of the institution of modern science. If even our respected scientists have a hard time with the institution, where does that leave the layperson who is just trying to figure out the truth regarding our existence?

Real science requires reliable authority.

Blind people use the sense of touch and hearing to make their way around. A blind person will walk through a building touching the walls and corners with a cane to find the way around, listening carefully for pertinent sounds. In using only the sense of touch and sound, the blind person may develop vastly inaccurate perceptions, however. They might think a new twenty-storey high-rise is an older two-storey duplex, for example. Nonetheless, it is likely that a blind person will also be aware of and accept the limitations of their blindness. Because they are aware of their blindness, they are more likely to rely upon and trust someone who does have the sense of sight. They are more likely to ask and trust a more reliable source.

We must also consider a better alternative: Consider a Source of information without flawed perception, ulterior motive, hierarchy, or struggle for recognition: No publishing roadblocks or stubborn groupthink positioning. Consider a source of information from someone who not only knows the relationships and the causes, but is the cause of all physical occurrences. Assuming we could be connected with and hear from this reliable source; wouldn't this be a more scientific method of obtaining the truth regarding our existence?

Accepting information from a reliable source is the oldest and most reliable method of information gathering. This is why every classroom has a teacher. Throughout history, learning from reliable sources has been the standard method for gaining an understanding of any topic. If a person wants to know something, who better to ask than the person who truly knows?

The difficulty here is in connecting to a true authority. Finding a true authority may require a serious effort. However, is this process that much different from the effort assumed to be undertaken to gain any kind of scientific information? Can a person be expected to understand the theory of relativity without first enduring rigorous training in basic math and sciences?

Science is founded upon faith.

Despite science textbook versions, there is a long tradition among our greatest scientists of a fundamental acceptance of the Creator. Much of modern science's foundation was built upon the research and conclusions of those who at the very least, assumed the existence of the Almighty. Nicholas Copernicius, a well-known Polish astronomer, was the first to calculate the rationale for planets encircling the sun during the sixteenth century. Copernicius was also a Canon in the Catholic Church and his published reports were supported by the Pope of that era. A hundred years later, it was Galileo Galilei who sparked controversy with the proof of the tidal elliptical, implying that the earth circled the sun—though his determination to support scripture was well known. It was Sir Francis Bacon of the sixteenth-seventeenth centuries, who devised the scientific method of deductive reasoning and research, and wrote among others, *De Interpretatione Naturea Prooemium.* Bacon once wrote that one must "fly to Providence and Diety." During this period another important scientist, Rene Descartes, was also well known for scientific reasonings and his contribution to the scientific method. Descartes' purpose was intent on establishing a scientific basis for the existence of the Supreme Being.

To these we add that it was Johannes Kepler, an astronomer and mathematician, having developed the basis for the understanding of light and gravitation, who was a devout Lutheran and professor at the Catholic University at Graz. Meanwhile Isaac Newton, the brilliant and multi-talented physics and mathematical genius of the Renaissance, who became convinced in his later years that the arrangement of nature was due to the existence of "an intelligent and powerful Being."

Sir Robert Boyle and Michael Faraday were two highly esteemed nineteenth century chemists and physicists and authors of peer-accepted scientific theories (ergo, *Boyle's Law* and *Faraday's Principle*) and many other treatises on electricity and magnetism, respectfully. They both carried strong religious beliefs into their scientific work. The mathematically gifted Gregor Mendel of the nineteenth century provided the calculation proofs for the existence of genetics. Mendel was a monk who later became the Abbot of his monastery.

Twentieth century science was not devoid of researchers grounded in faith. William Kelvin, known for his discoveries in modern physics, was known to be deeply religious. Max Planck and Albert Einstein, who were instrumental in their mathematical derivations which brought us understandings of light, relativity, sub-atomic matter, quantum theory and more. Both of these men were believers. Planck said in his 1937 lecture *Religion and Naturwissenschaft*, that *"the holiness of the unintelligible Godhead is conveyed by the holiness of symbols."* Albert Einstein commented often about the role of the Creator. Einstein once quipped, *"I want to know how God created this world. I am not interested in this or that phenomenon, in the spectrum of this or that element. I want to know His thoughts. The rest are details."* Einstein also coined *"God does not play dice,"* and famously, *"Science without religion is lame; religion without science is blind."*

Each method requires faith and devotion.

Both modern science and Truth from the Supreme Authority require faith. Ascribing to science requires faith in the many speculations of scientists and their institutions; while ignoring ulterior motives or faulty perceptions. To understand modern science, one must become devoted. Even after many years of education the modern scientist must diligently study the various scientific papers to keep up with science's changing theories. In connecting with the Real Authority, devotion is required as well. Just as one must study and mentor under respected scientists to become a scientist, one must mentor with the Almighty and His devoted messengers. Just as any science mentorship would require, we must build a mentoring relationship with the Creator to allow a reception of knowledge.

Trust is the necessary doorway to obtaining information in either case. To read and accept a science journal's version of reality, one must have a trust in the particular scientists proclaiming those theories. One must not only trust the researcher. The entire institution must be trusted. In the case of information from the Supreme Person, trust must also precede learning. While some trust institutions, this is certainly not required. Trusting directly in the Supreme Person and His representatives is the only key to obtaining this knowledge.

We may doubt that the Supreme Being can directly impart pure knowledge to us. This doubt is the reason we are not connected with Him now. Doubting can be a necessary tool while we are discerning various philosophies. Doubting the very existence of the Supreme Being is another matter, however. This type of doubt blocks *access* to the Supreme Being. A general trust in His existence, combined with a general humility regarding our ability to know through speculation is required to open the potential for a real connection with the Source of knowledge.

Today modern science seems to have convinced the public that there are only two choices. We should either trust "factual science" or trust the ecclesiastic positions of religious institutions. Focusing the debate between science (as if faith cannot be scientific) and a particular institution distracts the debate from the real issues. Can we trust modern science to be truly scientific? Instead of clarity, we find arguments that appear to communicate *that we can trust science more than we can trust a particular religious teaching*. This of course unfairly narrows the debate down to only one option outside of modern science. It also slants the issue with an assumption that the existence of the Supreme Being cannot be scientific. It also eliminates the possibility that knowledge can come directly from the Source.

Consider the depth of knowledge available from the all-knowing Original Person. Unbridled by time, and unflawed with limitations, the Source of the universe can impart knowledge to each of us in a *descending fashion*. The descending process is quite simply more reliable than our attempts to *ascend* with limited senses and mental speculation. Noting that modern science has primarily increased confusion and complexity through this speculative process, the descending process is prudent and clear. The descending method is also sustainable and empowering to the individual: Confidence is being placed in the hands of Someone reliable, and access to that knowledge is available to everyone.

It should be known that this method may not satisfy an immature demand to know it all. Science does not offer this either, however. The descending process works on another format. The information we receive through the descending process is more applicable to us. It is more practical. It is more personal. It is also timed perfectly with our ability to understand

and our progress towards utilizing it. This type of knowledge is not simply information: It is wisdom.

Wisdom comes from within and without simultaneously. Through the Supreme Being's ability to expansion next to the inner self, He can teach us from within. Externally the Supreme Being may utilize various events or lessons to teach each of us. These are confirmed by authorized external sources such as His messengers and scriptures. Through these three sources—the Supreme Being within, the Supreme Being as His messenger, and the Supreme Being as scripture—He can teach us each directly, raising our wisdom according to our faith and ability to understand and apply it.

This does not mean we need to abandon scientific endeavor. We can certainly apply science to our everyday lives, finding ways to live harmoniously within nature while serving and honoring the Supreme Person. There are many applications of science to be used in His service. There are applications of science that can be used to raise our consciousness rather than simply increase our doubts. As mentioned earlier, many of the great scientists and mathematicians who contributed much of the foundations for the sciences of physics, chemistry, math, and natural sciences had a deep faith in the Supreme Being. The wisdom of their science reflected an understanding that the universe was part of a larger, personal design. It has been only the last few decades that modern science has abandoned this scientific grounding in the Supreme Authority, seeking instead to pursue speculations that contradict His existence.

Modern science has not led to real advancement.

One might argue that modern science has given man many technological tools, which have led to the advancement of our society. This assumption is subject to debate:

- *Is the poisoning of the earth's air, water, and land a sign of the advancement of human civilization?*

- *Is the killing off or threatening of many specifies of life around the planet a sign of human advancement?*
- *Is the mass murder of millions of people using atomic energy a sign of human advancement?*
- *Is the production and assembly of poisonous gasses and viruses as weapons a sign of human advancement?*
- *Is the development and mass-production of toxic chemicals that cause numerous forms of cancer a sign of human advancement?*
- *Is the development and mass-production of machines that cannot be recycled without toxic waste and dangerous forms of radiation a sign of human advancement?*
- *Is the stressful daily modern lifestyle—full of traffic jams, overwhelming noise, tiny apartment/cages, toxic pollutants, sexually-transmitted diseases, and terrorists with home-made bombs—a sign of human advancement?*
- *Is the genetic manipulation and overuse of antibiotics, resulting in dangerous and potentially destructive mutations of species a sign of human advancement?*
- *Is the extinction of many species and the threat of more extinction, including our own, a sign of human advancement?*

This bears the question: Why are technologies that work *with nature*—achieving survival while sustaining natural resources—not considered viable scientific endeavor? Why must modern science continually push our race towards artificial circumstances conflicting with nature? Is there any wisdom to cutting off humanity from the very natural resources for which our bodies were designed? Since the human body was designed to live among fresh air, around nature's resources, and on natural foods: Is the removal of our physical bodies from this natural environment a scientific approach to life, knowing that doing so causes disease and toxicity?

It is modern science that is responsible for paving our path towards the very destruction of life on our planet. Through our greed, modern science has created technologies in an attempt to create artificial comforts and enjoyments for us. In reality, these technologies only further complicate our lives and poison our bodies. Where does wisdom and intelligence fit into such an endeavor of folly?

As archeologists dig up civilizations in search for our origin, the gauge for the advancement of that tribe or culture is typically how many complex tools are found around the dig site. Archeologists assume that stone and clay tools are a sign of a primitive society. The real sign of advancement should be how *few* complex tools the culture needed to survive however. The fewer tools needed—and the more those tools were able to naturally decompose without threatening the future environment—the more *advanced* the culture. What archeologists have missed about ancient cultures is that these cultures were often extremely devoted to the advancement of wisdom. Many chose to develop spiritual qualities over technologies. Many chose to focus upon the aspects of internal wisdom, rather than the search for *what is out there.* Within the perspective of wisdom, many of these former societies were quite a bit more advanced than our modern one.

Science and profit are diametrically opposed.

From a societal point of view, when one examines some of the institutions of the modern scientific machine—the manufacturers, the publishing houses, the universities and the various institutions that advance modern scientific endeavor—there is a *disincentive* for science to accept the science of the Supreme Being's existence. This is because profit and the Supreme Being are diametrically opposed. Because these institutions put profitability and reputation above the principles of Truth, the Supreme Being is left out of the equation. The assumption of a separation between church and state is often claimed to be the reason modern science does not explore the existence of the Supreme Being. Freedom of choice and separation does not require that one *deny* or *contradict* His existence, however. On the contrary, modern science has created its own *new faith:* one which denies and ignores the Supreme Being's existence—proposing an accidental creation. By ignoring His existence and scoffing at those who explore it, modern science has put believers—many of whom are credentialed scientists by trade—in the closet, afraid to admit their faith in their research or teaching.

Knowledge from a superior source is scientific.

Accepting the fact that the Supreme Being is in control, a deeper understanding for these developments is available. This understanding lies within the character and personality of the Supreme Being and His purpose for this universe. Certainly if the Supreme Being wanted to force His existence upon us, He could easily appear and prove it without a doubt. However, the Supreme Being has enabled us the freedom to ignore His existence. He has created for us a world where we could pretend He does not exist should we choose to. This is ultimately based upon the fact that He gives us each the choice to love Him or not. This is because, after all, real love requires freedom.

We live in these temporary physical bodies away from Him because at some point, we *chose* to be away from Him.

Not only does He allow us to live in the illusion that He does not exist if we want, but He gives those of us who want to ignore Him the "scientific" rationale to do so. This gives those who want to ignore Him an acceptable process to justify their intent to ignore Him. To give us this choice, He also provides enough mystery to allow us to equally *weigh* His existence against scientific scrutiny. This forces us to make a choice completely based on our freedom to trust Him or not. This is what *doubt* is: Doubt is a reflection of our complete freedom of choice.

Despite the fact that we can logically and scientifically deduce and understand His existence, we are faced with not being able to physically see or hear the Supreme Being. We cannot prove His existence with our physical senses or our physical instruments. This is no accident. This is by design. It forces us to trust. If we trust someone, we have *faith* in them. If we have faith in someone, we trust they would not lie to us:

> *If a friend tells us something we haven't seen for ourselves, this tests our trust in that friend.*

Since we have to choose to trust *someone*, should we not choose the Being who owns, controls, and creates everything? Like the boy walking down the river, we have the choice to either trust someone who knows or trust our own theories based on limited information. A choice to trust the Supreme Being certainly indicates a more scientific approach, because the Supreme Being is a more reliable and trustworthy Source of scientific wisdom.

***

Conclusion: *Modern science has led us towards the cliff of transcendental ignorance, into a ravine of doubt and confusion. The institution of modern science has become a platform for those living beings who choose to ignore the Supreme Being's existence. As modern scientific discoveries choke us off from nature, surrounding us with stress and toxicity, modern science makes us doubt that our very existence has any meaning. The Supreme Being—in complete control—is allowing those of us who want to play independently the rationale to do so. For those who may choose a higher scientific existence—one of fulfillment, love and joy—there is a process of trust available to guide us with wisdom toward the scientific Truth*

4

The Intentional Creation

The woman had lost her memory. She found herself alone in a empty white room. She lay on a clean mattress in the corner of the room, surrounded by nothing but white walls and a closed door. She fell asleep. After a deep slumber, she awoke to find a table in front of her bed. On this table was a sumptuous meal with a glass of cold milk. A set of silverware and a napkin were neatly arranged around the food and glass of milk. Again, there was nothing else in the room, only her bed and this table. Looking around, she wondered where the food, the table, the fork, knife, and napkin all came from. Pondering all this, she concluded there is no one outside the room—the food and the table must have accidentally appeared.

Was it all a big accident?

Interestingly enough, this is what some scientists unfortunately seem to be proposing. They seem to be proposing that all of the multilayered, synchronized, and sequenced activities and elements of nature are all random accidental occurrences. They seem to propose that all of our intellectual abilities—all of our tendencies to think, communicate, love, learn, etc.—are accidental occurrences. They seem to propose all this somehow developed without reason or purpose. We are being asked to believe that in this white room of a universe, everything living came into existence spontaneously from non-life. All of the varied species of life, bringing forth unique personality, emotion and a striving for survival, all originated from an accidental freak accident.

Obviously, the sane person would assume that the food was prepared outside the room. People outside the room obviously came in while she was sleeping and brought the food, the table, and the silverware. A sane person would conclude that these people must be caring for her in some way. She might also assume that she was put in this room for a reason. She might guess that she was being rehabilitated for something. Maybe she did something crazy or hurt someone.

Unfortunately, modern science has seemingly concluded on this accidental origin hypothesis. It appears that modern science is not even offering possible alternatives for consideration. The conclusion has been drawn, the papers have been published, and the textbooks have been distributed.

Two imaginative speculations are assumed.

Modern science has seemingly concluded two hypothetical assumptions: The first being that the universe began with an accidental large explosion called the *'big bang.'* The second assumption is being that life descended from an accidental combination of chemicals arising from a *'primordial soup' of some sort.* These two theories are assumed in scientific literature across the disciplines. They are generally assumed as factual. From textbooks to news media, these once radical and rejected theories are now being accepted as fundamental foundations upon which other theories are laid. Not even a century ago, these theories were considered bold and controversial—even crazy by most of the science institution. Yet now these theories have become integral in the development of newer theories on everything from archeology to genetics.

Neither of these theories has any solid evidence, however. To the contrary, these theories deal with issues so gigantic; with time factors so expansive, that humans have little ability to collect definite evidence, let alone supply controlled data. The tiny mind of a human with its tiny scope of sense perception is simply no match for this task. Even the relatively sophisticated radio telescopes and other relatively advanced machinery we may launch into outer space does not establish clear evidence of life's origin. None of the information provided from all this research conclusively proves either theory. Yet amazingly, these a*ccidental-event scientists* (as we will call those who postulate these theories) speak of these hypotheses with no hint they are speculative and thus could easily be wrong. This is the real crime in the promulgation of science and the advancement of knowledge.

A rather flimsy piece of information accidental-event scientists seem to rest their 'big bang' thesis on is the direction matter appears to be traveling through space. Apparently, rocks and meteors appear to be traveling in one direction. Accidental-event scientists propose that this direction is outward from a theoretical center. Supposedly this indicates everything is traveling away from one point of origin. It is speculated that this origin point is the big bang.

Again, it is assumed that everything is flying away from the center only because these rocks are all seemingly moving in one direction. This observation has been made without a clarity of which point in the universe is truly the center however. The trajectories are not quite so simple because there are so many other potential gravitational and magnetic effects. Our galaxy appears to be a gigantic spiral with several arms, and we see among the distance stars many other apparent galaxies. Where is this theoretical center? Accidental-event scientists cannot pinpoint the center because they do not know where the center is. Maybe it is towards direction of the stream of matter, or maybe it is away from it. Our range of perception is simply too small to know this for certain.

Most accidental-event scientists will admit we have little understanding of the width and breadth of the universe. While we can see distant galaxies, and it appears that our particular solar system is part of a galaxy (the Milky Way), we do not know how many galaxies there are. Some of the galaxies we see through our telescopes are so tiny that it is perfectly conceivable that there are numerous galaxies beyond the range of our senses. The bottom line is these scientists are merely making bold guesses based on incomplete information. Accidental-event scientists have no idea how big the physical universe actually is and what is actually *out there.*

Over recent years, physicists have continued to add new speculative postulations onto these in an attempt to explain the details behind these accidental creation theories. We note a number of theories such as the *'string theories'* and the *'membrane theory'* (or *'M theory'*) have recently been postulated. These ruminations propose that the universe was once composed of membranes or strings, and their collisions might be the basis for the big bang. These theories again assume a random, meaningless, and accidental creation. They assume no design, no purpose, and no intention.

In general, modern science's theories on the origins of the universe and life appear to be founded upon three basic assumptions: 1) events of the universe are accidental; 2) the human senses have the capacity to perceive the true nature of the universe; and 3) there is no design, controlling, or organizing source of existence.

The origin of life must address life itself.

To properly analyze these assumptions of the origin of universe, we must reflect upon the nature of life. This is because the universe now supports life. As we have illustrated previously, when the physical body or body part is separated from the transcendental living being, that body or part becomes *life*less. When this lifeless condition—death—has arrived, these organic parts begin to decompose. The life force that once drove and maintained the physical body is gone.

As we look around us on this planet, we see the entire planet is teaming with life. There is life in every nook and cranny of this world. We see life among nearly every element. We see life in water, in rocks, in soil, in the air, and of course walking the surface of the earth. While life around the rest of the universe may be beyond much of our senses and information-gathering equipment, many scientists are beginning to assume life exists on other planets, and are even starting to observe a few signs of life among other planets. To separate the living nature of existence from the process of creation would simply not be logical.

Realizing within each living organism is a transcendental inner self opens the discussion regarding the origin of life to more than the physical evidence presented to our senses. The consideration must also include the source, purpose, and activities of the living forces. Rocks and other debris flying through space may be interesting, but alone they can hardly explain the complexities and design of the living forces around us.

With these points in mind, let us discuss the big bang and primordial soup theories with a little more depth:

The big bang theory assumes no life.

The big bang theory states that billions of years ago there was nothing: no life, no planets, just a mixture of hot gasses and particles. Suddenly from a combination of supposedly unstable, volatile gases, very hot temperatures arose. For no particular reason, at some point in time there was a gigantic accidental nuclear explosion, sending various rocks flying in all directions. From this supposed fireball, some rocks that flew out began to slowly cool, and others stayed lit. Cooler rocks began circling some of the still-burning rocks. Out of this magical accident and subsequent re-gathering of spherically- and elliptically-shaped rocks, our particular universe supposedly and randomly assembled into the unique and beautiful sun and planet arrangements we have today. All these various rocks somehow randomly settled into separate solar systems, accidentally forming precise elliptical patterns. Bunches of these solar systems somehow connected together to form galaxies of accidentally formed spirals with spiral arms. Somehow, the multitude of galaxies and solar systems aligned accidentally into precise elliptical or spiral formations throughout space. All the various stars aligning our beautiful nighttime skies are accidentally providing us with navigational aids and interesting ephemeris positions. Somehow one big accidental explosion did all of this.

The proposed chemistry within the supposed initial gas cloud (or 'membranes') and the resulting amazingly gigantic nuclear explosion is quite complex. It is also beside the point. The critical questions relate to the source of the initial nuclear explosion:

1. Where did these initial chemical elements necessary for that first explosion—whether atoms, strings or membranes—come from?

2. Where did the initial energy necessary for the fusion or fission reactions among these initial elements creating the potential for such a gigantic theoretical explosion come from?

Although modern science has observed many chemical reactions, never have we seen a new element or subatomic particle *spontaneously* come into existence. We have seen elements combine to form what we think are new molecular structures. We have observed supposedly new molecules forming when we combine different elements. We have also observed elements become isotopes after bombarding them with subatomic particles. Nevertheless, we have never seen a new element suddenly come into existence, nor do we know how and when the original elements were created. We also have no idea how the theoretical building blocks—the electrons, neutrons and so on—came into existence.

Where did the 'big bang' particles come from?

Since the supposed gigantic big bang explosion required a precise volatility among then-existing nuclear units, these nuclear units would have had to be in existence before such a bang. Moreover, if the nuclear elements we observe today are arranged with precise molecular properties now, what would be the rationale in supposing they arose from chaos in the past? What accidental force suddenly created the beautiful orbital molecular structures we can observe today?

If these original subatomic units contained enough nuclear energy to create such an incredible explosion, these original elements must have somehow contained and stored such incredible energy. To retain and release energy, any molecule, atom or particle must first *acquire* it. Where did these original elements obtain their capability to *acquire* and *store* so much energy?

The big bang theory was founded upon the observations of chemical and nuclear explosions observed in laboratories and in space. As scientists have traced these explosions, it appears that they proceed along a systematic cascading reaction. The reaction requires an assembly of atomic elements that react in a chain-like process. This process is hardly a chaotic process. Rather, it is systematic and step-like. Where did these original nuclear elements come from and how did they come to be arranged in such a way as to allow for such a dramatically gigantic explosion?

Theoretical physicists appropriately call this the *'Singularity Problem.'* In a nutshell, this is the problem of not knowing what existed prior to the supposed big bang.

Nuclear energy had to exist before any 'big bang.'

If atoms and subatomic units retain a common energy eventually be released, there must be an initial *source* of the energy. The common energy driving subatomic particle motion also appears to hold them into precise orbital patterns. These nuclear forces—which have been broken down into various components by quantum physics—appear to be necessary for both holding atoms and molecules together as well as providing the energy for such an explosion. Where did these energies originate prior to the supposed big bang? This means not only would a *source* of the energy have been required; but also such a *source* would have had to exist prior to this supposed creation.

Heat and energy are released in an explosive fire. Like any fire, an explosion must have available combustible elements for consumption and an energy source for ignition. In other words, the big bang must have had an ignition source, enough energy to push forward such an explosion, and something combustible to burn. Where did this ignition come from, where did the energy come from and where did the combustible elements come from for such a monumental bang?

Modern theoretical physicists and cosmologists twirl technical jargon around like skilled jugglers. They try to substantiate their speculations, avoiding the basic problem of something coming from nothing. Note that there have been hundreds of different theories documented to explain the nuclear and chemical process. Among those are the *'string'* and *'membrane'* theories mentioned above. This latest theory has the big bang elements created initially by a random crashing of *'membranes'* into each other. This theoretical *membrane* crash somehow produced all the elements for the explosion. Assuming these chaotic *strings* or *membranes* could somehow create the precise dynamics of nuclear physics, the *singularity* question remains: Where did the membranes or strings come from and where did they get their energy from?

The bottom line is, regardless of which terminology is used, the nuclear gas big bang theory, the membrane big bang theory cannot explain the existence of the initial energy, nor can it explain the creation of the initial elements required for such an explosion to occur. As the classical *Law of Conservation of Energy* states; energy is never lost or created in an explosion or process. Energy can be transformed to another state, but an original energy must be present to convert to explosive energy. This would mean any potential energy available to cause such a huge bang event would have had to have originally existed prior to such an event.

Over the past few years, some cosmologists have proposed that recently discovered *'gamma ray bursts'* emulate the big bang scenario. The hypothesis is that a neutron star is formed through a grand explosion, followed by a short-lived existence and an eventual implosion into a black hole. Although these gamma ray bursts are far from understood, cosmologists insist their substantial energy emissions supposedly created by these *'star births'* come from nothing. Then of course, when these dark stars implode into theoretical black holes, all that energy, along with surrounding matter, supposedly also disappears into nothing.

Energy with enough potential to create these sorts of tremendous explosions and implosions would certainly require a powerful source. The energy must come from somewhere, and in the case of black holes, must go somewhere. If the source of the energy existed prior to the explosion then we could hardly claim the universe was created by a bang. Where did this energy come from? We would have to concede that a source of energy existed prior to any such explosion if indeed it took place. Such an explosion, if it did take place, would have had to have been an event further down the line from creation. If such a theoretical explosion took place after the elements and energy was created, then the big bang could not have been the event of creation.

Energy is organized.

The proposition contending that the current systematic arrangement and rhythmic movement of energy, matter, and life around us today had its origin in an accidental cloud of random gases or floating membranes simply does not make sense.

> *The harmonious energies which give way to the songs of birds; the rhythmic lapping of the ocean onto the shore; the soft light of the moon; the warmth of the sun; the magnificence of the stars; the flight of the butterfly; the beauty of a conch shell; and the leaping of a dolphin could not logically arise from a chaotic grouping of gases or membranes.*

The precision required for any molecular reaction should in itself refute any notion of randomness or chaos.

Harmony refutes randomness. The pulse of nature, complete with harmonious rhythms, simply does not correlate with a chaotic origin. Our universe is pulsing with rhythm. Throughout nature we see repeating rhythmic occurrences. Each day we observe the sunrise and sunset, establishing a cycle that is repetitious, adjusting slightly in each cycle by another cycle. Seasonal changes with the rotation of the earth with respect to its orbit and tilt are apparent. With this seasonal oscillation, we see a rhythmic rise and fall of plant-life—waxing in the spring and waning in the fall. We see birds and other migratory animals in precise movements, traveling with the seasons under magnetic influence to different parts of our planet.

For any rhythm or pulse to exist, there must be a source of that pulse. When we see larger rhythmic waves pounding onto the beach, we know a storm out to see created these pulses. As we can see in everyday life, every vibration must have a source of motion causing the vibration. In the same way, the movements of the planets, the tides, our heartbeats, and the migrations of animals are all consistent with precise rhythmic cycles. The various pulses and cycles of nature we see around us are thus *harmonic.* Their cycles work with a synchronicity. They are also precise, measurable, and predictable. The harmonic pulse moving through nature is *organized.*

Chaos results without organization.

Observational science indicates that particles must have an outside organizing force or face virtual chaos. Without an organizational force aligning and organizing particles, there would be no cohesive force allowing particles to constructively bind to atoms. The behavior of atoms would be unpredictable and unreliable, making for unstable and unpredictable molecular structures. Molecules simply could not align with other molecules in stable structures without organizational energies being exerted upon them. Not knowing what forces really hold and align the components of matter, scientists have created theoretical but empty descriptions of these energies: Names such as *'gravity'* and *'electromagnetic forces.'* Gravity and electromagnetism are just words. But what *is* gravity?

The basic force of gravity has perplexed humankind for thousands of years. While easily observed, gravity still evades comprehension. After centuries of ancient scientific endeavor, Galileo Galilei's sixteenth century hypotheses developed through observation and measurement still ground much of the science. Sir Isaac Newton later proposed the *universal gravitation theory,* composed of the inverse-square law and planetary gravitational orbit hypotheses. This proposal became the foundation for Albert Einstein's *field equations* of general relativity, which described a realm of gigantic orbits and predicted the existence of black holes. Dr. Einstein spent nearly thirty years of his life in this effort, trying to connect gravity to other natural elements such as electromagnetism. Today Einstein's field equations and Newton's gravitation theory are loosely tied together and packaged within a theoretical quantum mechanics particle model called the *graviton.* Einstein had departed from Newton's model substantially, however. Einstein's theory of *general relativity* states that gravity is not due to forces pulling two masses together as hypothesized by Newton and Galileo. Einstein's general relativity postulation says gravity is caused by the four-dimensional space-time system curvature responding to motion through time. The field equations and the theory were considered so complex at the time Sir Arthur Eddington joked that no more than three people in the world understood the theory. This is probably still true today.

Recently the assumptions of general relativity are being challenged. Dr. Subhash Kak, a Professor at Louisiana State University, has published findings that introduce a new element to the relativity model: *Time relative to a distant star.* In Dr.

Einstein's equations, the relative ages of two people were compared: One relative to a spaceship and the other relative to the earth. By introducing relativity to a distant star, the theories of relativity begin to approach a broader foundation for time and motion. This reveals the context of the situation: Our observations are limited to our relative position and smallness in relation to the size and breadth of the universe.

With all of the considerable time and focus on this subject of gravity, are we any closer to knowing where gravity comes from? Do we know how and why is it so precise that we could predict almost the exact time something dropped from the sky will hit the surface of the earth? Why does gravity always pull objects down to earth at the same speeds? Can this level of precision be the result of chaos? Could such an organized force of precision come from nothing?

At the very least, we can recognize gravity as one of the *forces outside our perception.*

Atoms have precise structure.

An atom is a precise and balanced unit made of various subatomic particles, seemingly held together by another *force outside our perception.* As physicists are still debating over whether subatomic particles are indeed particles or waves, we will call them wave-particles. These wave-particles are termed subatomic because they are parts of the atom, just as planets are part of a particular solar system. At the atomic level, physicists like Neil Bohr theorized in the early twentieth century that atoms have systematic *valences,* or orbital regions that accommodate these electromagnetic wave-particles propelling around an atomic nucleus. A covalent region is an area of space where observations indicate it is statistically likely that region will contain a subatomic particle. (Note that no one has ever really *seen* an electron.) This nucleus supposedly has a positive charge while the subatomic electrons theoretically have negative charges. Early nuclear physicists told us that these opposite charges somehow have repulsion and attraction forces keeping the atom together. Meanwhile each type of atom—each element in nature such as hydrogen, oxygen, nitrogen—somehow developed a unique yet precise arrangement of subatomic particles, giving each element unique properties such as molecular mass, boiling points and so on. Each atomic element also was found to display a unique electromagnetic frequency.

In the decades following the development of the atomic theory, various studies have been performed to watch how atoms and particles respond as they are collide or are bombarded. Through these experiments, physicists have observed a tremendous stability and balance exist between the subatomic particles within an atom. As a whole, the *quanta*—or particle characteristics—are extremely cohesive and intricate. What makes them so intricate and precise? While nuclear physicists speak of chaotic beginnings, the result is a series of rigid and quantifiable rules of engagement between these wave-particles. Could such a precise arrangement, which keeps these smaller parts organized with their larger parts, be accidental? These quantifiable units are theoretically the building blocks of matter. What actually makes these units so precise and organized are again, *forces outside our perception:* Forces precise enough to allow these units to become perfectly aligned in countless numbers, elegantly arranging the geometric structures we see around us: Precise enough to render consistent, predictable and measurable properties.

Molecules illustrate precise functionality.

Atoms combine in a synchronized manner to form the various moving and functioning structures around us. Modern physicists tell us that atoms are uniquely designed to sometimes become ionic, allowing them to then join one another by sharing subatomic particles within mutual orbital regions. In other words, via *forces outside our perception,* atoms are brought together into an assembly of precise sequences we refer to as molecules. The atoms of a molecule are bound together in such a way that they lose their independent characteristics. Together they display completely different features. Just as modern scientists do not understand what is holding the subatomic wave-particles together within and around an atom, they do not understand what brings ions into molecules. Though complex terms have been ascribed to these forces—such as *'small and weak nuclear forces'*—modern science does not actually understand these forces or their source. Modern science also does not understand why atoms come together to form molecules with such precision and beauty:

> *Bonds between atoms can form various shapes, resulting in distinct and measurable designs and structures. Molecular bonding can take on linear, trigonal planar, trigonal bipyramidal, octahedral and many other uniformly balanced and symmetrical structures. These various bonding patterns form molecules, which will stack together into crystalline or lattice structures to form still greater complexes of three dimensional shapes such as snowflakes, glaciers, diamonds and every other object we perceive around us.*

As we observe the various structures molecules combine to form, again we see tremendous precision and quantification. Each type of molecule in nature displays distinct, precise, measurable, and consistent characteristics. For this reason, a chemistry professor can confidently draw an outline of the shape of a particular molecule occurring in nature. For this reason, each and every molecule in nature has unique quantifiable characteristics. Although every molecule is distinct, groups of the same molecules also show precise and exact properties. Each has a unique melting point. Each has a unique boiling point. Each has a unique specific gravity, density, viscosity, surface resistance, osmotic pressure, equilibrium, solubility, and neutrality. Furthermore, molecules within different states form have different characteristics. Solid molecular forms display precisely distinct melting points, tension, height, width, mass, and shape. Gas molecular forms will display precisely distinct vaporization points, pressure, volume, molar mass, and even precise kinetic particle speeds. Each type of molecular arrangement, whether it is liquid, solid or gas, has precisely distinct and consistently quantifiable measurements for each of these characteristics. This means that every glass of pure water under the same conditions will have the same surface tension, and every block of pure ice will have a particular lattice structure with a particular strength and cohesion. As these molecular substances are arranged in nature, each has a distinctly precise, predictable, and measurable structure and characteristics, which change predictably with environmental changes.

This quantifiable precision among atomic elements appears with any molecular combination, allowing scientists to catalog and identify each type of element and molecular substance by its distinct characteristics. Countless molecules combine to form structures or solutions, yet they are all so organized that each type can be measured, catalogued and identified. These specifications are consistent from the smallest groupings to the largest volumes of the substance.

> *A methane molecule is arranged in a perfect ring structure. Its tetrahedral carbon-hydrogen arrangement provides strength and powerful reactivity, giving it a precise explosive specification when it is exposed to specific temperatures: Not one degree more or less will suffice for either one drop or an entire tank-full. Methane is among a family of hydrocarbons such as ethane, propane, butane, pentane and hexane. Each of these has a unique hydrocarbon polygon form. From propane's triangle molecule to pentane's pentagon and hexane's hexagon, each has a unique shape and is combustible at a precisely unique temperature.*

All molecular bonds provide beautifully unique structures like these. Some form fantastically shaped rings or other patterns with precise and symmetrical arrangements outside of our comprehension. The precision is so accurate that complex mathematical formulae and bonding angles can be applied to each type of molecular structure. These *quanta* will occur both for large and small volumes of that substance, distinguishing it from any other substance.

Elements are sequentially arranged.

The 19th century Russian chemist Dimitri Mendeleev—given the distinction as the formulator of the chemical periodic table of elements—is said to have realized the periodic table one day as he awoke from a dream. Today the basic structure of this table is still used. The precise arrangement of the table of elements within the table follows each element's unique atomic number, weight and position relative to other elements. The natural groupings of the table display a commonality among elements in the same region of the table, despite have significantly greater atomic mass and number.

Mendeleev's table, formulated before many of the quantifications on the elements were made, accurately predicted elements that were in that day unknown. The existence of such a precisely structured table of elements arranged by atomic number and weight illustrates how nature, even to the tiniest subatomic particle, is sequentially arranged. Despite our inability to physically observe or comprehend the subatomic particles and their various forces, we can indirectly see the absolute precision of the design and repetitive nature of the periodic table.

Scientists have observed events indicating that each orbit of an atom must hold tremendous energy. Furthermore, it has been observed that each atom has a specific electromagnetic frequency within the bonds holding its subatomic particles together. Along with this energy specification, observations have suggested that atoms and molecules also *release* precise amounts of energy when these bonds are broken and particles or atoms are released.

Scientists have shown that this released subatomic and molecular energy can create the potential for explosive forces.

When energy is released sequentially from a large number of atoms or molecules at once, tremendous explosive forces have been observed. The example of the atomic bomb comes to mind. Again, scientists do not understand the underlying causes for these powerful *forces outside our perception*, and thus struggle to describe their origin.

Subatomic particles have memory.

A Japanese university mass accelerator study resulted in a stunning observation in the late 1970s: tiny subatomic particles would—once they were torn away from an atom through bombardment—apparently return to the same atom they departed from. While there were millions if not billions of seemingly identical and closer particle-hungry ionic-atoms available to assume the particle in the medium, each particle would somehow remember their origin. In 1982, a physics research team led by Dr. Alain Aspect at the University of Paris determined that subatomic particles could instantaneously communicate with one another somehow. Though some were separated by relatively long distances, they were able to signal each other. Although these studies were soon forgotten, the results illustrate a deeper mechanism and design within the smallest elements of nature.

The theoretical memory of a substance repeatedly diluted in water has been illustrated through over 200 years of clinical homeopathic medicine. Given in doses considered so small that the substance's original molecules, the innumerable clinical results for homeopathic treatments speak for themselves. Homeopathy is now one of the largest of the alternative medicines, and practiced around the world.

The implications of homeopathic dilution memory have been expounded from research by a number of scientists over the past two decades. Some of this research stemmed from the work of a medical doctor named Jacques Benveniste, M.D. Former research director at the French National Institute for Health and Medical

Research (INSERM), Dr. Benveniste's career was very distinguished, having been credited with the discovery of the platelet-activating factor. During experiments on the immune system, Dr. Benveniste and his research technician Elisabeth Davenas inadvertently observed the activity of the basophils despite dilution levels so low it was doubtful any molecules of the biochemical remained in the solution. Over a four-year period of continual trials, showing repeated confirmation while instituting further controls, Dr. Benveniste and his research team concluded some sort of molecular memory of the substance was retained after dilution.

In further research, as Dr. Benveniste and his team continued to dilute substances through the ninth dilution, the activity of the substance began to increase with successive dilutions. This was almost precisely what Dr. Samuel Hahneman—the founder of homeopathy—discovered over two hundred years ago.

Dr. Benveniste's research became controversial. Particle and substance memory had vast implications in the study of medicine and our knowledge of physics. Still, Dr. Benveniste, until his death in 2004, along with other researchers, confirmed these findings conclusively (Bastide *et al.* 1987; Youbicier-Simo *et al.* 1993; Endler *et al.* 1994; Smith 1994; Pongratz *et al.* 1995; Benveniste *et al.* 1992).

The obvious conclusion is that all substances have a form of design, which can translate to a memory system through the proper carrier. We already know each element remembers a particular type of wave-particle bonding pattern, a specific boiling point, freezing point, melting point, and so on. A substance retains these characteristics despite rigorous environmental and time challenges. This memory system indicates a larger governing factor within the electromagnetic bonds of atoms and molecules. This memory basis is at the very root of the Bohr atom, with its valence orbitals filling out to a distinct number. As we investigate orbital bonding angles and orbital shell counts among molecules, we find that these quanta and bonding angles are distinct unless the atom comes into contact with a greater force of change, or interference. Moreover, particular forces, such as radiation, create predictable responses as they impact with the bonds of atoms. What makes the atoms respond in precise and measurable ways?

Consider the ability of an iron-oxide tape to memorize the electronic pulses made by sounds. Our ability to tape-record a song or speech onto a magnetizing substance like iron-oxide indicates nature's memory systems not only exist, but they can be manipulated to work for us.

When we press a bar magnet upon another magnetic metal we change the polarity of the molecules making up the metal. The polarity has been said to be changed through a restructuring of the electron orbital orientation, rendering an electron-heavy side and a proton-heavy side. This polarization causes an effective memorization of the positioning of the magnet. After removing the magnet, some molecules revert to their original polarity. Others will remain in the same direction. Among the molecules remaining in the changed polarity, there is a residual memory of the positioning of the field from the magnet or magnet head.

At the very least, these observations illustrate a deeper mechanism within the smallest of particles, allowing for a memory system. Despite this, accidental-event scientists have persisted. Their assumptions that matter is dumb, and its origin is chaotic are clearly refuted by these studies along with common everyday observations. They tell us something we intuitively know already:

Within every atom is a deeper force that connects all matter together.

Considering memory at the most minute levels, we can know also that the largest, most complex structures around us are not moving randomly. Organized energies on a micro basis will reflect the same behavior on a macro basis. *Unseen* organizational forces link structures and functions together in a constructive, meaningful manner, from the subatomic particle on up to the largest and most complex of structures.

Memory requires designation.

If memory is resident even among the smallest of particles and atoms, then each atom is uniquely identifiable. Differentiation requires identification: In order to be distinguishable from another, an object must be identifiable. In order to be identifiable there must be uniqueness inherent within each particle and atom, and there must be an energy giving the particles and atoms the ability to identify each other. In other words, there must be a *coding* resident within each atom:

> *Each human has a distinct fingerprint. Every creature has distinct DNA. Every snowflake is unique. No two rocks are identically shaped. Every butterfly has a unique wing print.*

These coding systems allow each distinct part and living organism to be uniquely identifiable. Amongst this uniqueness, we also see precise structure and repetition of design. There is replicated order, yet this is harmonized within distinction and uniqueness. The uniqueness among precisely repeating structures illustrates that everything has been designated and coded for a particular reason. Designation illustrates a larger design and intelligent force moving among every part and parcel of the universe.

Designation indicates assembly.

The coding of particles and atoms would also indicate that every atom is *assembled* by subatomic particles, and thus each subatomic particle *belongs* to that atom. Since each atom is distinguishable, we must also realize that every molecule is *assembled* by the distinguishable atoms. Therefore, each atom *belongs* to a particular molecule.

If a smaller part specifically belongs to larger part, then the smaller part is *specified* to the larger part. If something is specified to be part of another part then this creates an overall *specification* as to the combination of all the parts. Furthermore, if there is a specification designating each smaller part to a particular larger part, then the larger part must be specifically *assembled* with the smaller parts, *according to its specification.* Consider how a part—say a starter motor—to an automobile has a specification:

> *The specification of a starter motor will show a number of smaller parts fit precisely together to make up the starter motor. Each smaller part belongs in a certain position and arrangement on the starter motor. Furthermore, each of the smaller parts will fit in a particular way, requiring that one small part is assembled before another small part can be attached. A cotter pin, for example, might be put on last, after the various nuts and bolts have been assembled and tightened. Since the cotter pin prevents the other parts from falling off, it must be assembled last.*

In the same way, if we assume that subatomic parts make up atoms, and atoms make up molecules, then there is a particular *assembly* required. If we further realize that the different atoms are identifiable and distinguishable from each other, they have designation. This means that physical matter is *specifically assembled.* Furthermore, we must realize that any *specification* requires *design.* The question then becomes: Where did this assembly and design come from?

Life organizes matter.

A living organism will assemble molecules into complex and precise structures. *Forces outside our perception* within living organisms determine how to convert and combine molecules from one form to another, utilizing them for cellular parts. An example of this is how a living organism will ingest and process purines and pyrimidines together with other nutrients, and with them, assemble specific complex DNA structures through a complex process called replication. This is a form of specification coding: The living organism duplicates tracks of instructional information onto DNA strands, laying nucleotides together in a helixed ladder of hydrogen and sugar-phosphate bonds. These coded DNA molecules provide a chemical specification *blueprint* for each living cell's designed functions.

There are trillions of cells in the body and each has a specific function. Lung cells process oxygen. Muscle cells produce energy and force. Intestinal cells assimilate nutrients. Each cell is organized precisely to operate within specific tissue systems in a highly complex yet coordinated fashion. Each cell is like a little factory. A cell has a DNA replication and transcription center, little organelles which produce energy and other substances like enzymes. Each cell also has a precisely-structured cell membrane, which allows certain molecules and ions in, and certain molecules and ions out. Tiny gates called *ion channels* provide the pathway. Ion channels also have gates that scan and permit particular molecules in and out, precisely restricting access to unauthorized molecules. In much the same way each atom contains precision in specified assembly, each cell is also designed with an intelligent coding system, enabling it to function in a precisely specified and coordinated fashion.

Groupings of these precisely arranged and organized cells move to a rhythm of guided macro-organization. *Forces outside our perception* organize these groupings into tissue systems, and each cell does its part to contribute to the tissue system function in a display of utter coordination. These tissue systems bring together specific functions into larger, coordinated functions as they intelligently perform operations necessary to keep the entire body healthy and alive. Without *forces outside our perception* organizing the assembly of particles into atoms, atoms into molecules, molecules into cells, cells into tissue systems, tissue systems into organs and organs into physical bodies, chaos would be the result. Yet rather than chaos, we have a beautiful functioning orchestration of design and assembly.

The universe is designed with precision.

Within all natural structures and functions, precise assembly is apparent. While the growth patterns of leaves and flowers might appear random at first glance, in reality every leaf of every plant grows within a precise pattern of assembly, sequence and angle:

> *Flower petals and leaves have precise geometrical relationships as they grow around branches. Flowers have precise petal ratios when counting around the stalk: From 13/34 to 34/89, and always in Fibonacci sequence.*

The *Fibonacci sequence* is a series of numbers, 0,1,2,3,5,8,13,21,34,55.... observed throughout nature. A Fibonacci number is found by adding the two preceding Fibonacci numbers together, i.e. 1+2=3, 2+3=5, 3+5=8 and so on.

> *The angles of outward projection of branches and leaves from trees and plant stalks are always assembled in precise Fibonacci ratios: ½ in grasses, lime and elm; 1/3 in sedges, beech, hazel and blackberry; 2/5 in roses, oak, cherry, apple and holly; 3/8 in bananas, poplar, willow and pear; 5/13 in leeks, almond and pussy willow; and 8/21 in pine cones and cactus.*

Attributed to Leonardo Fibonacci around 1200 A.D., who traced a family tree of rabbits, the Fibonacci sequence can be seen all around us and throughout nature. It can be seen in plants, fish, insects, animals, and humans, both from a perspective of dimension and appendage. Plants are not sprouting leaves and branches randomly. They are producing these precisely specified arrangements due to *forces outside our perception.*

Symmetries in nature's design surround us. When sequential Fibonacci measurements are arranged into polygons, they form rectangles which, when laid against a square of the next Fibonacci number, becomes the famous *'golden rectangle:'*

> *The golden rectangle is made from two adjacent 1x1 squares, which become a 1x2 rectangle. This can be laid against a 2x2 square, becoming a 2x3 rectangle, which if laid against a 3x3*

> *square, becomes a 3x5 rectangle, and so on. The Fibonacci rectangle is observed throughout nature, including the outside dimensions and inner segments of the bodies of plants, animals and humans.*

This proportion is sometimes referred to as *'Phi'*. Another natural pattern observed throughout nature is revealed when golden rectangles are assembled around each other into a spiral:

> *The 'golden spiral' is formed concentrically outward by the golden section dimensions of 1:1.618. The golden spiral is seen repeatedly throughout our natural world. It is seen in the nautilus shell. It is seen in storm systems such as hurricanes and tornados observed from above. It is seen in the cross-section of an ocean wave hitting the beach. It is seen in the swirl of water down a drain. It is seen among the tops of plant florets like cauliflower and broccoli. It is seen in the cross-graphing of the sine waves within radiation frequencies.*

The golden spiral and golden rectangle are thus connected together throughout nature in three-dimensional precision. They can be seen linked in sequence, seen from above, appearing through movement and structure amongst living organisms and natural phenomena. To an untrained or uneducated eye, nature may appear wild; in reality nature is precisely designed and arranged with sequence and precision. The whole of nature and all of its parts are working under a grand scheme, driven by *forces outside our perception.*

Herbal medicine illustrates nature's programming.

Over many thousands of years, humankind has been using herbal medicines to cure and prevent all types of illness. Modern science has for decades, scoffed at herbal medicine. Yet approximately 60% of pharmaceuticals are based upon plant constituents. Furthermore, rigorous medical research over recent years has confirmed that a wide range of herbs have properties that have significant healing effects against various diseases: each plant specific to particular diseases and particular actions. What is it about these various plants that happen to heal or prevent particular diseases?

As research on herbal medicine has advanced, we have discovered that each plant species produces a unique combination of constituents. These constituents and/or their combinations have been linked to specific healing actions within the human body. Many of these constituents have been isolated and synthesized over the years by pharmaceutical companies. Once the synthetic version is patented, it can be mass-produced as a pharmaceutical. The major problem modern medicine has encountered during this process is that when particular constituents are isolated and produced synthetically, along with a healing effect they can produce various side effects within the patient.

This problem of side effects is not a problem with the natural herbs, however. This is because along with the specific healing constituents, plants also contain various buffer constituents that balance all constituents perfectly, rendering the herb effective without the dangerous side effects the synthetic isolated versions have. While providing precise healing constituents, nature's herbs also provide buffering for safety.

As researchers have investigated herbal constituents of various plant medicines, they have found *specific designation* among the plants and the diseases they heal. While some plants provide healing for chest congestion, others fight infection by stimulating a greater immune system response. Meanwhile others increase circulation and still others help the stroke volume and strength of the heart. These healing designations among specific plants also coincide with their growing season and growing locations. In hotter climates where water is more apt to stand and become contaminated, there is an abundance of hotter plants such as peppers, which have been shown to be antibacterial in their action upon the body.

The ability of particular plants to have particular physiological effects upon metabolism would be analogous to having a label on each medicine bottle, linking each medicine to a particular symptom or disease. Such a system of linking a particular herb to a particular disease would entail not only specification but also a sort of *programming*. Such a designation of plants linked to particular diseases occurring in other species indicates a type of *programmed design.*

Function design requires programmed placement.

A functional design would be something that is not only *arranged,* but something that continues to function within that *arrangement.* For example we could arrange our furniture, putting each furnishing in place. That would be an arrangement or a design. However, should we arrange things so that the furniture re-adjusts itself, or moves to accommodate guests when they come in: That type of arrangement goes beyond a one-up (or single-operation) design. This type of arrangement has been *functionally programmed.* Such an assembled functional arrangement would require not only precise design, but programmed systems of cause and effect to allow for a variety of decisions and actions, each linked to eventual results. In other words, to allow someone the choice of more than one course of action, the potential results of every possible choice must be established and coded into the system. This is what we would call a *program.* For example, a computer functions using programs that allow an array of possible outcomes, with each action linked to a particular result:

> *If A happens, then X results; if B happens, then Y is the result. If C happens, then Z is the result.*

Now if these were random events, then A would not be linked specifically with the Y result. In a random event, sometimes A might result in Z, and sometimes A might result in Y or even X.

> *There would be no designation between actions and results whatsoever if life were chaotic.*

In our everyday lives we can personally observe this designated cause and effect in action. We can see that our activities each have particular consequences. If we take a certain action, we will have a particular result or type of result. If we choose another path, we will have another result altogether. Although we may not always understand why, we usually learn from this cause and effect relationship. Since we can observe particular results for particular actions, we can realize that some actions are preferable to others. This also allows for social order and lessons of morality. If life were chaotic, it would not matter what actions we took. Any action might result in any type of result.

Chance and programming are opposed.

Chance has been the object of increasing study by modern scientists over the past few centuries. Early modern scientists studied the possibilities and the mathematics of chance using coin-tosses, dice throws, and card games. Because the larger tosses did not consistently close the variance between 50%, most researchers assumed the dice or coins themselves had some sort of inborn bias towards landing on one side or another. Perhaps a slight weight differential on one side or one edge of that coin existed. Perhaps other gravitational effects or wind resistance were preventing an unbiased coin toss.

Over the last few decades, these tools have been replaced by computer-controlled devices to more closely study theoretically random events. Some very interesting observations have resulted from these experiments.

In 1969, a machine called the Random number generator was invented by Dr. Helmut Schmidt, a physicist at Boeing. This device utilized a mechanical basis to produce a theoretically random flashing of one of four lights. An observer could predict the result by pressing a button under one of the lights, signaling the light the observer though would light up next, using the decay emissions from the strontium-90 isotope to confirm theoretical, natural randomness. With a choice of four selections, the statistical average over a large number of guesses should be no more than 25%. However, large trial numbers resulted in levels closer to 27%, indicating some sort of ability to predict the result (Schmidt 1969, Palmer 1997).

Following these studies, questions arose (Wagenaar 1972) as to whether the effect was kinetic or precognition. In other words, were the observers predicting the results or affecting the results? In an attempt to isolate this, Dr. Schmidt refined the methodology and instrumentation of the RNG (or REG for *random event generator)*, which performed randomized calculations resulting in either an even or an odd result. This machine was set up to duplicate the theoretically random result of a coin-toss: heads or tails. With this sort of programming, large volumes of results could be compiled quickly and accurately.

Over its history of research, coin-tosses traditionally resulted in a decreasing variance between a 50/50 result when the number of tosses increased—up to a point. As the tosses get higher, the variances do not decrease as expected. This notion perplexed researchers, because a seemingly accidental series of results should continue to trend towards the unbiased 50% level as the number of tosses increased.

Dr. Schmidt's series of studies with the RNG confirmed this problem. As the number of results increased, significant variances remained, staying above 1-4% higher than the unbiased 50/50 level. What could be preventing the expected and gradual descent to 50/50?

In the early 1970s Princeton Professor Dr. Robert Jahn refined random number generator research. Dr. Jahn improved upon the machine, increased the number of controls in the protocol, and expanded the range of its study. Like Dr. Schmidt's, Dr. Jahn's machines would randomly produce either a one or a zero in a random sequence, but with any possible source of bias removed.

As hundreds of these RNG studies were compiled by Dr. Jahn and others, the same results emerged. RNG variances from 50/50 continued with larger runs, with substantial differences. After investigating all the potentially related causes, Dr. Jahn began investigating various unrelated outside events in an attempt to correlate the variances. The first of Dr. Jahn's discovered variances related to the attendants monitoring the RNG run. Amazingly, variances trended differently for females than for male observers. Investigating the human even further, his trials began asking observers to wish for one result or another. These resulted in larger variances. While some observers tended to 'wish" the result towards the wish, results for other observers resulted trends away from their wishes. In other words, some observers could affect the RNG results more than other observers could, while still others might produce still opposite results. Note that these observers were not physically able to affect the results, and most were not considered gifted in psi. They were merely observing the results (Jahn and Dunne 1987; Jahn *et al.* 1985; Jahn *et al.* 1987).

Dr. Roger Nelson, an emeritus researcher and professor at Princeton, took over the research from Professor Jahn. Dr. Nelson began taking the RNG machines to group events and discovered that group intentions could influence the RNG results in an even greater way. Everything changed on September 6, 1997. On this day, billions of people throughout the world watched the funeral of the once Princess of Wales Diana. On this day, the RNG machine also made a massive spike, illustrating some kind of relationship to population consciousness (Radin 1997; Jahn *et al.* 1997).

Shortly after, Dr. Nelson brought together a team of seventy-five researchers from around the world and connected forty RNGs through the internet—naming these linked RNG satellites "EGGs." The EGGs essentially brought RNG data from all over the world into a central computer for analysis. At first, the data did not seem to reveal anything of great significance (Radin 1997; Jahn and Dunne 1997).

The first events to stimulate the EGGs around the world were the bombing of American embassies in Nairobi and Tanzania in August of 1998. After these extraordinary results, the *Global Consciousness Project* was in full swing. Dr. Nelson and his associates began watching other mass events. Events like the Super Bowl, the Olympics, O.J. Simpson verdict, and the Academy Awards produced spikes in the RNG graphs. Major catastrophes such as earthquakes or even major sporting events would move the RNG results significantly one way or another. In other words, events involving greater levels of consciousness among large populations affect RNG results significantly. It became clear that globally relevant events are followed by leanings of mass consciousness, which somehow affect random events (Radin 1997).

A stirring RNG result took place on September 11, 2001. Of course, the RNG charts were spiking significantly after the bombing, associated with the world's reaction to the bombing and the death toll count. However, something even more mysterious happened: *The shift in RNG results began four hours before the first plane hit.*

While the RNG research initially focused on the ability of humans to influence events, another relationship began to emerge. A theoretically random event—supposedly isolated and thus unattached to any other event—appears to be connected to various unrelated events after isolating all known forms of bias. Since the RNG machine is the ultimate test of isolated, seemingly random and control events, it is the perfect vehicle to test modern science's notion of a chaotic universe of randomness. These test results, performed by researchers with integrity and impeccable credentials, reveals a universe of design and programming: *An intentional universe.*

Nature's events are connected.

The mass movements of migratory animals illustrate large-scale organization in nature. The movements and actions of large populations of animals have long been observed by biologists, yet not been well understood. It is mysterious that somehow a migratory bird will return to within meters of where they were originally born, flying from many thousands of miles away at the same time each year to that very spot.

From the symmetrical flight of birds in formation, to the migration of caribou, whales and butterflies, these mass movements show design and assembly with a precision beyond the scope of these creatures. Yet we can observe other events connected to these migrations and mass movements. We can see that migrations are connected to movements of the sun; magnetic influences; and environmental conditions existing at the origin and destination of the migrations. In the same way, *our* movements are also connected and organized. Just as the migrations of animals are outside of their scope of understanding, our movements and events are outside of our scope.

We often marvel at how organized and beautiful beehives or ant farms are. We can easily see that each individual bee or ant is not aware of this incredible level of organization. Similarly, when we fly over our cities we can see the same sort of master organization. Like the bees or ants, we did not have a conscious awareness of how the city might look from above as it sprawled over the centuries. Curiously, cities look a lot like our computer chips: our highways look very much like a computer data bus, and our factories and warehouses look amazingly similar to our computer capacitors and memory chips. These illustrations of organization beyond an organisms' conscious planning also reveal *forces outside our perception* working within a grand scheme.

All events are interconnected.

All events are interwoven in a grand scheme outside of our comprehension. Events we observe on a daily basis may *appear* to be random, but each event has a way of affecting something else, creating a new possible event or circumstance. When we apply this to events taking place in our lives, we can easily connect action events to resulting events. This connectedness allows us to choose actions that create positive results, and avoid actions that create negative ones. When these lessons of action/results are added up, they become *morals.*

Science fiction writers and movie producers like the theme of connected events, as they reflect the reality of our personal existence. Movies and books typically connect events in fictional lives to particular outcome themes. These create what we call *"the moral of the story."* Producers and writers will also sometimes play with the slipstream of time in their stories, creating *"time capsules."* These time capsules move the characters back or forward in time, exploring connected events and their relationship with time. Such a time capsule story might put the actors back a few hundred years, enabling them to change an event that took place in the past. These story scripts portray even an insignificant change in a past event as creating numerous dramatic changes in present and future conditions. These time capsule stories may be fictional, but they are based upon widely accepted observations portraying a grand scheme of connectedness among seemingly unrelated events. Some have termed this scenario the *'butterfly effect.'*

Connected events contradict randomness.

If two events are related, it means they are connected in some way. If connected events are related, there is no isolation between them. *Related* means there is a *relationship* between the events. A relationship means that there is a *bond* between the events. We can often see these bonds simply because the two events are bound by the participants or the subjects of the events. For example, we know that if we chopped down a tree, the tree could fall on something and possibly damage it. The bond between the tree being chopped and the tree damaging something was the tree itself and the tree chopper. The two events would be connected by at least two common participants.

There is not always an obvious common participant seen between related events. This does not mean a bond doesn't exist, however. In the RNG research, there is no obvious bond between the event and the RNG results, yet there is a definite relationship, illustrated by their mutual occurrence outside of coincidence. They may seem outwardly disconnected yet they are invisibly bound by *forces outside our perception.*

Often in our own lives, we will see seemingly disconnected events unfolding to reveal a *moral:*

> *A man walks down the street and stops to help up an elderly woman who has fallen. He carefully props her up, making sure she is steadied onto her cane. Later that day the man trips going down some stairs and just as he was about to tumble down the stairs to his injury, someone catches him, preventing his fall. In thinking how lucky he was, the man remembers how he helped the elderly person earlier in the day.*

We might immediately relate to such a relationship between our own actions and events. For doubtful, regardless of whether we can physically relate these two occurrences, they are absolutely related by the fact that the man remembered his good deed after someone did one for him. That remembrance in itself connects the events, and hence creates the *moral.* We experience so many of these occurrences throughout our lives. While some of us may dismiss them as mere coincidence, others will connect them. Yet even the thought that they were coincidental connects them and makes us entertain life's connectedness.

We can also see how every event is *linked* somehow to at least one other event. We can see that every event has *at least* one prior event, which caused or influenced its result. Since we can say that every event is connected to other events somehow, this would create a *lattice* of interconnected events. This lattice of events makes up an entire array of events, of which every event is connected to a few others. This means that all events are interconnected by a master design of connectivity:

> *Every piece of wood in a house is connected to at least one or two other pieces. No wood is floating around without being connected. Even though one piece of wood is only connected to only a few other pieces, because all pieces of wood together make up the entire house, each piece is connected to every other piece by the master design and purpose of the house as a structure.*

All events are connected because there are *forces outside our perception* running through every event, just as there are *forces outside our perception* running through each atom and through each cell of the body.

Random events do not exist.

These facts together with the RNG research illustrates that while events may *trend* toward a natural result; any particular event is driven by unseen influences and connected to other events. Event outcomes may be affected by observers, other events, or both. Even seemingly unrelated events taking place thousands of miles away may be affecting events unfolding before us. This means that seemingly random events are not random after all. Seemingly unconnected events are actually connected. No matter how hard we try to produce random events, all occurrences are, at the end of the day, connected to other occurrences somehow. Therefore, no occurrence can be absolutely random.

Events are programmed with precision.

Modern science has determined that nature can be measured and quantified through so many mathematical relationships. Most of these quantifications relate one event to another somehow, predicting their measured relationship with precision down to the decimal place. Various formulae have been developed over the past 400 years, connecting physical characteristics like mass to velocity and speed to gravity. There are hundreds of formulae in each and every one of our science books, each illustrating precise relationships between two or more natural elements or events. These formulae connect events in mathematically predictable ways. Only non-random events can be connected in predictable, precise and measured ways.

If each event influences others, and events can be related to other events with predictable and precise formulae, a coding system has been set up among events. Coding calls for particular rules that create specific relationships between events. As we discussed earlier, this is called a *program.* A program is a coded process that specifies how particular events create specific resulting events. Such a coding system in nature indicates that nature has been *programmed by forces outside our perception.*

Conversely, if an event could take place in a vacuum, without any other events affecting it or being affected by it, we could say that this event was an *isolated* or *random* event. In this case, it could not be the result of programming. Have we ever observed, in this life, an isolated event though? Have we ever been able to even create an event isolated from other events? Certainly once we even try to *set up* an isolated event it is no longer isolated because the event is automatically related to our set up of it. An attempt to design an isolated event would fail simply due to the design itself.

Connected events require assembly.

A set of dominos is lined up into a formation. When the first domino is tipped, it hits the domino standing next to it, which then tips the one next to it, until the entire stack—which had been precisely arranged—has now tipped over into a neat design, falling with a whirring sound as each domino goes down. Each domino tipped over because it was affected by the domino next to it tipping onto it. In order for this to happen, dominos had to be stacked in formation prior to the first one being tipped.

Events are connected to the events that influence them and the events they in turn influence. Like dominos, in order for an event to be particularly affected by another, there must be a *design* connecting events in particular and predictable ways. Like the domino formation, connected events require precisely programmed assembly. Like the domino formation, events are connected by a system put in place before the connected activities commence.

Assembly requires outside influence.

A designed system reveals outside influence. If we accept that today's universe has the complexity of cause and effect, then we would have to accept that this complexity was programmed prior to the actual connection of events. If the programming preceded the connection of events, the source of the design—the designer—would also have to precede the events. If programmed events were preceded by a designer-programmer, the designer-programmer must exist outside of the field of events.

According to the *Law of Energy Conservation*, the only way to change the total energy of any system is through an intervention from an outside force. Since assembly requires energy and programming, an outside designer-programmer exerting force from the outside is necessary. Such a designer-programmer must exist prior to design and assembly of the program. Furthermore, it is logical that in order to adjust such a programmed system, the designer-programmer must be able to intervene with enough energy to make necessary adjustments.

Outside influence indicates purpose.

Events are connected because they were arranged and designed for a particular purpose. Programmed assembly requires planning. The initial impetus for such planning requires purpose and intention. Planning, design, and programmed assembly would not logically be initiated without a purpose. Coding events to affect and connect to other events indicates a grand scheme created for a particular purpose. If not, what would be the use of such a tremendous coding effort? What would be the logic of programmed events without a reason? Any movie with a plot and moral comes with a purpose—why expend any effort otherwise?

The 'primordial soup' assumes random events.

The modern primordial soup theory goes something like this: At some point in time, billions of years ago, there existed a random pool of lifeless chemicals. The pool was accidentally struck by lightning or some other form of tremendous heat. Out of this accidental impact, various proteins were created, and DNA somehow evolved, which supposedly led to the first living single-celled creature. The environment needed for such an event has been debated over the years by modern scientists. Some propose that an environment like the current one existed, while others claim the earth was frozen back then. Still others have argued that a hot, molten environment had to exist to allow for such a fantastic accident.

In the late nineteenth and early twentieth centuries *accidental soupists* postulated that not only could life have evolved from a chemical soup, but that spontaneous life could form at any time from any number of possible soups. At the time, microscopes were undergoing vast improvement and bacteria were just starting to be noticed. Eventually Louis Pasteur, known for developing pasteurizing techniques to inoculate bacteria, proved to the scientific community that life could not spontaneously arise from even the richest of initially sterile soups. He showed that sterile soups would only lose their sterility if bacteria or fungi came in from the outside.

The *soupists* did not give up easily, however. The soup theory was updated with each passing observation and theory through the twentieth century. Today the modern version is based on a supposition that a random combination of molecules such as methane, ammonia, water and hydrogen sulfide supposedly *accidentally* came together to form simple peptides and nucleotides. These supposedly formed complex DNA structures and proteins that would eventually (and spontaneously) come alive. This spontaneous-DNA theory has come to be the linchpin in this soupy theory.

DNA and protein cannot be spontaneously created.

Scientists believe that protein is the building block of life and DNA is the instructional facility determining the function of a living system. Proteins are made up of a mixture of 20 different amino acids, into complex molecules consisting of hundreds of combined amino acids. The protein molecule is often a twisted, semi-helix molecule with extremely complex properties and activities. Some proteins act as enzymes; some act as hormones; and others perform various other activities inside the body. The chemical make up of just one protein molecule is extremely complex. It has been noted by a Dr. Francis Crick that just a small protein of some 200 amino acids has a one in 10^{260} chance of being produced by accident. And this is just one simple protein molecule. The typical organism makes billions of *different* protein molecules each and every day.

Meanwhile, double-helix deoxyribonucleic acid, or DNA, is also a very complex molecule. It is elegantly designed, yet complexly coded. A DNA molecule is made up of long sugar-phosphate chains linked to combinations of four possible purine or pyrimidine nucleotides. As a result, DNA molecules have tremendous helix-spiral shapes. The specific ordering and combination of the nucleotides on the DNA chain makes up a particular code, often called the *'genetic code'* by scientists. It has been estimated that one human DNA molecule will have over 3 billion base (purine or pyrimidine) combination pairs: Not an easy molecule to come together by accident.

Researchers have observed that living organisms will assemble special RNA molecules, which will make copies of the DNA's coding and relay (or *replicate*) that coding to make new DNA. To accomplish this, an RNA strand will wrap against the DNA strand and extract the code to form a copy. Once it has a copy, it can either help make another DNA, or transfer the coding on to structures that manufacture proteins. Scientists believe that there are three basic types of RNA: messenger-RNA, transfer-RNA, and ribosomal-RNA. Although they have found several other types of RNA, these three types are basic to passing along the instructional messages of DNA coding. At least that is what has been theorized by modern scientists. But we ask: How would an arrangement of *"chaotic"* chemicals somehow have the ability to *instruct* an entire organism's chemicals and tissues how to function?

Regardless of this lack of logic, scientists assume that this chemical arrangement of DNA provide the instructions for the arrangement and function of a living physical body and all its tissue systems. Somehow, accidental-event scientists postulate, simple chemicals accidentally came together to form these utterly complex coded helix structures of instructional DNA and RNA. Then somehow these lifeless magical chemical combinations spontaneously became living single-cell creatures, complete with the need to survive.

Because DNA cannot replicate (or reproduce) its coding without RNA, some accidental-event scientists have proposed that RNA somehow accidentally formed first, and from the RNA, DNA was created. The problem with this theory is that RNA cannot replicate anything without any DNA to replicate. If RNA was first, what could it have replicated, and what would it have replicated from? Of course, DNA cannot be formed without RNA, because RNA assembles the nucleotides to make the DNA. So we have the classic *catch-22:* DNA requires RNA to be produced, and RNA cannot replicate anything without any DNA coding to replicate. This means that neither could have come first.

Is it even logical to assume that accidental events resulted in the incredible complexities of DNA and RNA? From a purely chemical and biological standpoint, it has not been possible to duplicate DNA creation from basic chemicals in any lab. A few real basic polypeptides have been formed in labs, but these were hardly accidental events. No complex DNA and RNA structures complete with protein-mapping, replication and translation abilities have been synthesized from dormant chemicals, even intentionally. Dr. Crick's analysis of this potential is parlayed analogously:

> *An accidental formation of DNA from a batch of chemicals might be compared to dropping 1000 typewriters and 1000 illiterate monkeys out of an airplane and expecting the books of the Library of Congress to be typed up and ready for printing when they all hit the ground.*

DNA has not been synthesized because DNA is manufactured only by living organisms, and its coding has been engineered through *forces outside our perception.* Chemical combinations can certainly be arranged by putting certain elements together with heat and mixing. When combined with heat, most elements will become volatile and can form bonds with other elemental ions. Without an organizing principle, these bonds will typically be very basic. Replicating double-helix DNA is another animal altogether.

DNA does not create life—life creates DNA.

Neither DNA nor RNA is functional outside of a living organism. As soon as either is disconnected from a living organism, they become lifeless chemicals, subject to immediate decomposition. When an organism eats, the DNA in its meal will first be digested and broken down into basic components before the organism can assemble its own signature DNA molecules with it. If DNA were alive, it would be able to *function* outside of the living organism, and *act* independently inside of any organism that ate it. Instead, when DNA is eaten, the organism will simply break it down into basic components just as fats and sugars get broken down during digestion. Furthermore, the living organism is not dependent upon any particular DNA or

RNA molecule. If a chunk of DNA is extracted from a person's body for a DNA test for example, this is no loss to the body. The living organism will simply manufacture more of it.

If a living organism manufactures DNA by assembling nucleic acids from raw nutrients, how could a living organism be created by DNA? If only living systems manufacture DNA, then life would have to precede DNA manufacture. While DNA may be resident inside a living cell, it is hardly the cause of the life of that cell. This is illustrated when the cell dies: The DNA will still be resident in the dead cell. If an organism dies (i.e., the living being leaves), all the DNA will be retained by the dead body of the organism. Before decomposition breaks apart the dead body's DNA and various proteins, intact DNA will lie lifeless with the rest of the body parts. Pumping in new DNA will not bring the dead body back to life. If DNA were the cause of life in a living organism, why would it still be there after death? And why couldn't fresh DNA bring a dead body back to life?

Quite simply, the living organism produces DNA because DNA is a *product* of life. DNA is assembled by living systems to reflect a larger blueprint for future growth and activities throughout molecular change. Life is not a product of DNA. Yes, DNA coding is passed down to new physical generations by parent organisms that blend their DNA coding when mating. The living being is drawn into the sperm prior to fertilization, and from there the genes adjust to perfectly reflect the ongoing consciousness of the inner self. The initial gene combination is thus a reflection of the consciousness of the self, who *existed* before the egg was fertilized.

We can easily become confused by gene transplanting in laboratories. Should DNA be extracted from a living cell and inserted into a donor cell, the donor cell's genetics may become altered. Inserting genes into a living body will typically require a virus in order to create any significant mutation however. A virus has the ability of infecting multiple cells, forcing its genetic makeup onto these cells, potentially causing mutation (note that while bacteria are alive, viruses are not). Without such a genetic carrier, a hapless gene or two will rarely have any affect upon a living organism.

Genetics illustrates a deeper mechanism.

In a multi-cellular organism, scientists have observed that each cell has a copy of the genetic code of the entire organism. The ramifications of this are beyond our speculative mental abilities. Through assembly and design, each cell contains the body's entire coding, yet each cell has only a small part of that coding to accomplish.

What mechanism gives each cell the DNA master code yet instructs each cell to use a specific part of that DNA? Modern science cannot fathom such an amazing feat of symmetrical *holography*. Holography occurs when each part of a structure reflects the whole structure while the whole structure supports each part. Each cell of the trillions of cells within the body reflects the entire organism; yet each cell functions in its own independent way to contribute to the functions of the whole organism. Each cell has a different yet aligned purpose. This level of sophistication, coordination, and reflection could only take place through forces beyond our comprehension: they could only take place through *forces outside our perception.*

Chemicals are organized from the outside.

Classical physics proposes the *'First Law of Motion,'* which states that every body will continue in a state of rest or uniform velocity unless compelled to change by an external force. Translated into chemistry, progressive formations of chemical bonds must be organized by an outside force. Otherwise their bonds could not be continue to progress. Protein molecules and coded DNA structures are highly progressive formations, illustrating an external organizational force. Noting that DNA and protein are manufactured and assembled only in living organisms, the only logical view of their existence is that they were ultimately designed and coded by an external living Source.

When we consider the complexity of these various chemical structures and their formation only in living organisms, the only logical conclusion is that life is their basis for assembly and function. Furthermore, since the chemicals themselves are not alive, we should understand the *Source* for the assembly is *alive*. We have seen that living organisms will draw lifeless nutrients into its system to reassemble them into complex structures that support a continuance of life. What gives the living organism this capability? Since we know these processes only take place when the organism is living, and cease only when the life is gone from the organism, we should understand that the *life* of the organism is the source of those capabilities. Since that *life* can leave the chemistry of the body at death, we should also understand that *life* has its source *outside of the physical dimension*.

Time problems lead to a seeded life theory.

As accidental-event scientists have worked hard to support the math of the primordial soup theory, many have run into a major time dilemma: The planet simply does seem to be old enough to support the length of time required for all these accidents to have taken place. This has presented a real *'fly in the soup'* because where then, could accidental chemically derived organisms arise from? For this reason, previous primordial soup advocates have embraced the *'directed panspermia theory.'* This theory postulates that tiny microorganisms or DNA supposedly "seeded" earth from another planet which supported life, and it is these seeds that supposedly evolved into life as we know it today.

Understanding that life is contained within the physical forms of living organisms, the question remains: How did life arise on that "mother" planet? To this, *panspermia soupists* have suggested that older planets may have had more time for accidental soup creation. How long did they need, and which planet are we talking about? These accidental-event scientists cannot tell us. After all, *they are guessing.*

Every seed must have a progenitor.

Within each living organism, we find a unique living being. The physical body is a structure of complexity and amazing design, driven by this living being. The living being is *injected* into the sperm prior to fertilization. Without this injection the seed does not grow. Likewise, if the living being leaves the fertilized seed, the seed will die. No scientist has been able to physically perceive this living being. This is because the living being is transcendental to the physical body and the senses of the physical body. It is of another nature. Since it is of another nature, *our origin must be from another nature: life.*

Life is not produced by matter. Rather than life being a product of chemistry, life moves from *outside* chemistry *through* chemistry. Life is pulsing through matter, yet is distinct from matter. The physical world is *injected* with life in the same way that a sperm is injected with the living being.

Living forces outside our perception move through the universe. These forces assemble and structure matter with precise design and programming; measurable and predictable functionality; sequential and symmetrical arrangement; memory and coded designation; specification; interconnected events and activities; mathematical precision; and event morality indicating intent and purpose. All of these characteristics are synchronized and meaningful because they are *living, conscious forces.* These intelligent forces running through matter are conscious because they extend from a Conscious Supreme Being—*the Ultimate Progenitor.*

The two basic components of creation—matter and life—both originate not by accident, but through intentional design by a Transcendental Intelligent Being. We say "transcendental" because He—like all of us—is from a realm outside of the physical dimension. This transcendental realm could also be considered the *permanent dimension because it is the dimension of life.* This Intelligent Being from the permanent dimension of life has assembled nature as a temporary realm, and pulsed through every atom and organism His own conscious living energies. Furthermore, He impregnated it with permanent living beings. He thus has intentionally *charged* the physical world with design and living beings.

The universe is a holographic structure.

Within a hologram, every part reflects the whole. The energy and functionality of the universe is reflected within each living organism. The energy and functionality within each organism are reflected within each cell. Cellular DNA reflects the organism's total DNA. The energy and functionality of each cell are reflected within each molecule and the energy and functionality within each molecule are reflected within each atom.

Like the physical body, the universe is made of progressively smaller subunits, which also combine with synchronicity to form a greater whole. At both the atomic level and the universal level, the living energies—forces outside our perception—of the Intelligent Being have been inserted, charging the universe with programmed functionality and purpose. Interconnected events illustrate these pervading intelligent energies. Because they originate from a single Source, they are harmonically resonating throughout the universe—reflecting that single Source just as a heartbeat reflects the presence of a living being in the body.

The Supreme Being manifested the universe and the living beings with intention: From Him originated every chemical, and from Him come the energies that keep every subatomic particle together within every atom and every atom within every molecule. His living forces thus surge through every physical structure, from the smallest to the greatest.

Producing and driving the machinery of a physical vehicle the size of a universe is no ordinary task. It is also no accident.

The precision we see around us reflects intelligent planning and organization. The mass of intelligence required to create this interplay of interconnected functionality is outside of our realm of comprehension. His energies emanate its holographic structure in a display of incomprehensible reflective perfection:

> *When we look at a mirror facing another mirror, we see an unlimited duplication of reflections, smaller and smaller until the smallest of reflections are too small to see.*

The combination of two mirrors creates a two-dimensional duplication, while the Supreme Being's reflection is duplicated in a multi-dimensional manner. The Supreme Being reflects His energies through the universe to drive every atom, every planet, and every organism within a functional array. This is simply beyond the scope of language and mental cognition. What we can understand is that the functioning machinery of the universe illustrates a *conscious* and *intentional* purpose for the various events taking place within it. Without a conscious and intentional effort, the precision of the geometrical and mathematical interplay of galaxies, solar systems, planets, atoms, cells, organisms and the machinery of nature simply could not exist.

The various systems of life are precisely interconnected yet interwoven with flexibility and choice. This illustrates a conscious purpose and intent, requiring an Intelligent Living Force with the capability to design and assemble such a grand scheme. Only such an Intelligent Living Source could impregnate the universe with subordinate living beings and maintain it at such a tremendous level of conscious involvement. This complicated structure naturally requires skills beyond our comprehension. Why should subordinate living beings be able to comprehend their Creator? Is it a given that we should be able to understand? Any ability to comprehend the entirety of existence would certainly require a gift from on high, far greater than the speculations with tiny minds and tiny telescopes.

Living beings reflect a Supreme Being.

The fact that the entire universe is holographic indicates a Supreme Being who has produced, and thus contains the potential of all the parts of the universe and more. These parts include the living beings. The living beings are separated fragments of the Supreme Being. We are fragments in that we originated from the Supreme Being, but we are still independent beings. We are of the same *quality* of the Supreme Being, but we are *not* Him. We *reflect* Him on a fractional basis, yet we are *not* Him. We are connected, yet we have some independence. He is also an Independent Person. It only makes sense that we are separated yet connected. Consider not only our ability to each make independent decisions, but also our inability to control nature.

This aspect of reflection goes both ways. While the created reflects its creator, a creator is also reflected by what is created. In other words, a creator must have, at the very minimum, the qualities of what was created. How could a creator not have the capabilities of what was created? If each living being is complete with individuality, personality, decision-making ability and the quest for love, then the Supreme Being also has at least these minimum characteristics. By the reflection of the created, we can understand that the Creator has an independent personality, wishes, desires and distinct consciousness, just as we—each of His living creations—have.

Personality comes from a Person.

Some like to speculate that the Supreme Being is somehow impersonally spread throughout the universe like a cloud or gas. Some vaguely describe Him as the *Force,* implying only impersonal characteristics. This would not be logical because function, design, and assembly can arise only from purpose and intention. Purpose and intention require individual personality, because individual personality renders specific wishes and desires. A gas, cloud, or vague force is diametrically opposed to individuality, purpose, and intention. Furthermore, unique personality is evident among each of us. The creation of unique personalities must logically arise from a personality. From a void comes a void and from a purposeful individual personality comes unique individual personalities with intention and purpose.

The Supreme Being is a distinct, Intelligent Personality. His energies may be all-pervading and expansive, but He is ultimately a Unique Individual.

Regardless of how deep humans probe into the nature of the universe, we always find deeper levels of organization and purpose. Logically as well as intuitively, these levels of organization illustrate how far beyond our mind's ability this creation goes:

> *The geometrical structures of the molecular bond; the individual hexagon shapes of the snowflake; the logarithmic spiral of the nautilus shell; the concentric pattern of biorhythms; the undulating motion of waves; the elliptical movement of planets around suns and electrons around nuclei; and the holographic nature of the subunits within the whole, illustrate complexity beyond our scope of imagination or speculation.*

The mysterious assembly of the universe and all the *forces outside our perception* arising from a Transcendental Supreme Being run deep, forging upon physical existence particular events and experiences that leave each of us touched individually as we each make our journey through physical life. For this incredible assembly to be called *random;* for this incredible design to be called *accidental;* for this incomprehensible symmetrical structure of holographic symmetry to have come from *nothing;* is simply folly.

Time is a physical element.

Thinking through creation one might ask: "*Who created the Supreme Being, and when was He created?*" However, this question presupposes time is a constant outside of the physical dimension. It assumes that the transcendental dimension is subject to the physical laws of time, and since time is a factor of creation, there was a beginning to the Supreme Being.

As Dr. Albert Einstein once proposed, time is relative to other physical movements within this dimension. This relativity exists because time is a physical element. Thus time is relative to how fast physical bodies are moving and where physical bodies are positioned within the universe. This is also why a fly's lifetime is very short compared to a human's, yet is still a full lifetime to a fly. Time's existence is part of the programming of the physical universe. It measures the functionality of physical elements relative to the living beings who access them. Time is thus the *intentional pacing* of the physical universe.

The concept that the transcendental or actual world is outside the realm of time may be difficult for the physical mind to grasp because the mind's input is *from* the dimension of time and space—the physical dimension. Suffice to understand that because time has been created by the Supreme Being, the Supreme Being is not subject to it. Because the Supreme Being is not subject to time and space, there no beginning or end to the Supreme Being, nor is there a physical restriction on His presence: His existence is—also beyond the grasp of the mind—eternal and unlimited.

The mechanics of creation stem from intention.

The various elements of each universe are *reflections* of His energies: part of the effulgence of the Supreme Being. The chemically reflected energies are his *inferior* energies, as opposed to His *superior,* living energies. There are two types of *superior* energies of the Supreme Being: His Original Self and Personal Expansions, and the separated living beings. We are the separated living beings.

As a result of the creative potency of the Supreme Being, there are innumerable universes, each having slightly different characteristics, and each harmonizing with His Personality and design. Once existing, each universe is charged by His conscious energies—*forces outside our perception.* These energies drive the production, maintenance, and destruction of each universe in a unique by synchronized manner.

Within each organism the Supreme Being creates a reflective connection, broadcasting His personal energy into every life form. Thus, along side of each and every living being, within each physical body, dwells an reflective expansion of the Supreme Being, guiding and observing the living being's activities within that body, traveling with each of us as a Friend and Companion. Thus some refer to this as the "Lord in the heart," or the "Holy Ghost."

His personal *forces outside our perception* are thus transmitted into each atom and particle, into the universe as a whole, and into each living organism. These impregnations of His personal energy into the physical matter of the universe make the universe *operational* and *connected.*

This world is intended as a training facility.

As each of us travels through this lifetime of this physical body, we are engaged in a multitude of learning experiences. When we look around us, we see that all of us are undergoing unique learning experiences. We are all dealing with the reactions to our various independent decisions. The universe is designed in such a way that our decisions and actions cause specific reactions. Those reactions tell us that certain decisions are good and other decisions are not so good. It is thus no accident that decisions with positive results are also good for us and good for other living beings. This is all occurring by His design.

This programmed process of individual learning can eventually lead us to a state of wisdom. Should we learn the lessons His programming teaches us, we become better, wiser living beings. As we become wiser, we evolve, and become elevated.

The intention is to resume a relationship.

Why is it important we become elevated? What is the purpose of becoming a better person? If we consider that our most important goals are connected with loving relationships or obtaining love, it is only logical that the Supreme Being is the source of love and loving relationships. A loving relationship between the self and the Supreme Being is actually the most elevated form of existence. Such a relationship is actually our reason for existence: to exchange a loving relationship with the Supreme Being. Consider this logically: if we were the Supreme Being would we want to hang out alone, producing universes for everyone else?

The living beings were manifested by the Supreme Being expressly for the purpose of exchanging loving relationships with Him. This is our ultimate reason for existence. In order to exchange loving relationships, He manifested unique separated parts and parcels of Himself. Thus, our intended purpose for existence is to love and serve the Supreme Being.

Loving relationships require freedom, however. How could real love exist without freedom? Freedom is also key factor explaining why we are living in a separate world, each going through separate learning experiences. This is also why some of these experiences are not very fun: These are all meant to teach us, and encourage us to come home. The Supreme Being has designed and structured a universe where we can learn to rise above our current desires to enjoy separately. Through His programming, we are faced with various learning experiences relating to our decisions and actions. He has designed a process to encourage us (but not force us) to choose to resume our loving relationship with Him.

Modern science's various speculations regarding creation align perfectly with this purpose: By creating theories of accidental creation, modern science has given us the rationale to continue to pretend that life is random and meaningless. This allows us to pretend there is no Supreme Being. The various accidental creation theories enable us lock ourselves up into our neat, white rooms while we pretend there is no one outside: We can pretend that no one outside this world cares for us. We can pretend that no one outside this world loves us. Although this is not rational, we still have the freedom to believe it.

***

Conclusion: *The universe was created by an Intelligent Being for a specific purpose. This purpose is related to the living beings who occupy the various physical bodies within it. At the root of this purpose is love. The Supreme Being originally manifested separated living beings to exchange loving relationships with. Since love requires freedom, He allows us complete freedom to love Him or not. For those of us who chose not to love Him, He has produced a dimension designed to allow us a facility to pretend to be away from Him. Along with this facility, He has programmed in an educational system enabling us the ability to regain our relationship with Him should we choose to do so.*

5

Evolution of the Living

One day long ago, a young man and his new wife bought a small broken down house in need of repair. They moved in and began a new family. The man immediately began to repair the house and make various improvements. Over the years, he worked very hard to upgrade the house to fit his family's needs and desires. He rebuilt the kitchen to suit his family's cooking needs. He rebuilt the living room to allow for greater comfort. He added on a master bedroom with big windows to increase his scenery. He added on two new bedrooms for the children. He built a recreation room for family recreation. He landscaped the yard to be able to sit on the lawn relaxing, while his kids played in the yard. Over many years, the once small broken down house became a beautiful, larger home with wonderful landscaping and many amenities. All the wood of the old house had been replaced by new wood. The house had practically been rebuilt. It had been added on to, painted, re-roofed, re-floored, and re-furnished. It was not the same house the man had moved into so many years before.

After many years, their children had grown. The man and his wife decided the house was too big for them. They wanted to buy a smaller house more suited to their elderly needs. They sadly put their home of many years up for sale. A young couple became interested to buy the house. As the couple toured the house, they were pleased with all of the man's many improvements. They purchased the house.

The man and wife moved out of the house shortly thereafter. They found a smaller house across town. They found a house with many of the same features they enjoyed in their older house. Still this new house was smaller, and better met their current needs. After a few years, the man and wife felt comfortable in their new, smaller house. They practically forgot about their older home.

Evolutionists say we evolved from lower species.

Did the small house accidentally improve itself? As unreal as that sounds, this is seemingly how modern science has approached the design of the human body and the rest of the other species of living organisms. Modern science has assumed the human machine simply evolved accidentally. Some scientists have assumed that all of the gifts, talents, and skills that are unique about the human organism are all accidental genetic mutations. The human body supposedly accidentally evolved from monkeys, which accidentally evolved from lower creatures, accidentally accumulating increased complexity and intelligence. The theory claims that every creature supposedly evolved from the simplest of single-celled creatures through processes of *'genetic mutation,' 'survival of the fittest'* and *'natural selection.'*

This is the *'theory of evolution.'* We might also call it the *accidental evolution theory* here. It explains that single-celled creatures, over billions of years, randomly developed multi-cellular functions, organs, appendages and other more advanced tools for survival. Although there is no definite scientific proof for this theory, it has become broadly accepted throughout modern science, and assumed throughout much of modern western society.

The theory stems primarily from observations of physical specimens, breeding observations and to a lesser degree, fossil findings. Its central rationale is the visual similarities between the various species and their body parts. In addition, observations of slight mutations through generations of breeding have illustrated mechanisms that allow organisms to adapt to environments. More recently, modern science has observed various genetic mechanisms that appear to relate to this adaptive tendency. This genetic refinement of the evolution theory has become known as *"Neo-Darwinism."*

This accidental evolution theory has been the subject of hot debates over the last 100 years. Its most outspoken critics have been *fundamental creationists,* who teach that all the species appeared approximately 5000 years ago when creation occurred. The creationist history has been scoffed at by many scientists who consider the many fossils found and dated by radiocarbon dating systems. This dating system ages some living organism fossil remains at thousands and even millions of years old. Modern science therefore asks: *How could life on earth have been created 5000 years ago if the fossil dating systems show living creatures living millions of years ago?*

These two diametrically opposed theories have held the spotlight in the debate regarding our origin over the past century. In the last few decades, *'intelligent design,'* has been offered in an attempt to reconcile the some of the concepts of accidental evolution with the existence of a Supreme Being. *'Intelligent design'* accepts the plausibility of accidental evolution together with the notion that it all took place somehow with the Supreme Being's involvement.

In order to accurately understand our past and how we came to exist today, we must be able to view it within the context of a scientific understanding of our identity and reason for existence. This must be logically considered together with the evidence. If we accept the existence of the inner self within the physical body, the context of the theory of evolution changes. The debate must incorporate this reality. To assume otherwise would be to claim that living organisms are merely walking chemical accidents.

A lifeless body does not evolve.

While science debates the accidental evolution of the physical body, we know a body is lifeless without the living being present. While the evolution debate has focused on whether and to what extent our physical bodies have evolved, a complete understanding of our existence must consider the nature of the inner self:

> *We might study the development of racing cars over the last 100 years and how they evolved into faster cars, but it would be ignorant not to consider the people who raced in these cars, those that designed and built them, and the development of the racing industry which developed around them. The cars surely did not build themselves; nor did they circle the track on their own.*

Since each living being has an individual personality, complete with feelings, emotions, desires and the need to love and be loved, it is essential that this reality is not ignored or factored out of the equation. Sadly, the debates and theories of evolution have focused specifically upon the physical body as though it was a walking bag of senseless biochemicals. Unfortunately, the unproven theory of accidental evolution has become firmly fixed upon the mistaken notion that life is simply a purposeless mixture of chemicals and chaos.

Life cannot be created by chemicals.

Over the last few decades, since the discovery of DNA, there has been conjecture that DNA is the key to life and the driving force of accidental evolution. Yet the DNA molecule itself, being comprised of merely chemicals (nucleotides attached to a sugar-phosphate substrate) is not living, nor can it create life. Many attempts have been made to conjure living organisms in isolated chambers by combining various chemicals. The spontaneous assembly of life from chemistry has never been accomplished.

The theory of *spontaneous generation* or *abiogenesis*, was embraced to some degree in Europe during the middle ages and Renaissance periods. The theory held that lower species of life were spontaneously generated through exposure to certain elements. Examples included insects, maggots, and microorganisms. The later two were thought to spontaneously generate from exposed rotten meat. Around 1660, the Italian physician Francesco Redi demonstrated that maggots were not generated from meat. In 1768, Italian scientist Lazzaro Spallanzani illustrated further that microorganism-containing solutions could be sterilized and freed from microorganisms. German Theodor Schwann further demonstrated this with experiments in the 1830s. In 1862, Louis Pasteur published findings illustrating how unsterile mixtures led to microorganisms while sterilizing and enclosing would prevent such contamination. Uncertainty remained regarding the generation of microorganisms, however. British physicist John Tyndall cleared this up by testing sterile and unsterile containers with light beams, illustrating the relationship between dust particles and microorganisms. Tyndall's demonstrations put to bed for good the notion that living organisms could spontaneously generate.

How could chemicals have a desire to survive?

As the accidental evolutionist theory has been expanded over the last 100 years, it has been merged with the *'big bang'* and *'primordial soup'* theories. Combined with these ancillary theories, the accidental evolution theory now states that following the big bang, life spontaneously arose from chemicals. What is curious is that these chemicals somehow developed the desire to survive. Have we ever observed any lifeless chemicals develop a desire to survive? Have we ever seen chemicals doing anything but predictably reacting to each other?

In other words, the accidental evolution theory says that out of lifeless chemicals single-celled living creatures have arisen, miraculously displaying a desire to survive. A desire to survive means having a need to improve survival factors and eliminate threats to survival. The need to improve survival means there is an intention to survive, and a value is put onto survival. Eliminating the threats to survival means survival is valued enough to put an effort into changing, adapting to, or destroying potential encroachments and dangers that could shorten life. These factors compound the problem presented: how could lifeless chemicals develop the ability to even *recognize* life, let alone value life enough to take persistent action to sustain it?

The quest for survival requires awareness.

Accidental evolutionists have yet to explain how a batch of chemicals can suddenly obtain a desire to survive. In order to desire to survive, an organism must be aware, consciously or subconsciously, that it *is* alive. A living organism must be able to differentiate itself from a pool of dead chemicals somehow. If there is no distinction of life then why avoid death? Why would a living organism desire to avoid becoming nonliving chemistry without distinction between itself and dead chemicals? Certainly, it would be easier to become dead chemicals than to struggle for survival in the midst of the tremendous environmental challenges. A small organism who could be killed by direct sun exposure, for example, would have gladly accepted death by the sun if death and non-survival meant no further struggles to avoid the sun. If there was no distinction between the living and dead chemicals, then the path of least resistance for the living would be dead chemicals. As a result, no living creature would bother to avoid death.

The struggle to survive requires self-distinction.

If a living being could not distinguish itself from a nonliving entity there would be no urge to survive. Without the urge for survival, there would be no motivation to adapt. There would be no reason to survive or evolve. It is like wondering why no boulders were rolling up hills. Without an incentive to survive, there is no urge or underlying rationale for doing the work to stay alive. Furthermore, without an underlying motivation to remain alive, the concepts of the theory of evolution such as *'survival of the fittest'* are meaningless. The urge to survive requires the living to distinguish themselves from the nonliving. Without such distinction, life would have ceased already. All of us would have preferred the easier path of dead chemicals.

Chemicals do not make decisions.

Accidental evolution would require not only living chemicals somehow distinguishing themselves from dead chemicals, but also chemicals desiring to lengthen the lives of their descendent chemical combinations. What mechanism gave living chemicals the impetus to increase the chances of their descendents' survival? The implication of this is that not only will a batch of chemicals struggle to survive and avoid death, but they will also adapt in ways that won't necessarily help *them* survive any better, but will help their descendents. What gave these chemicals the ability to calculate structural changes to improve the chances of survival for future species?

Accidental evolutionists seem to insist that through a desire to survive and adapt to environmental challenges, an organism began altering its anatomy for better survival. These alterations or mutations were theoretically passed on to offspring. While it may seem speculatively reasonable to consider as we see alteration in nature, there is still a gaping hole: How did such a mechanism (of adapting and passing genetic improvements to future generations) arise? What incentive would lifeless chemicals have to create this unselfish mechanism for their future generations? How and why could they have coded this ability into their genetic mechanisms?

These questions bear the larger issue of why would a lifeless or previously lifeless bag of chemicals decide it was important that future generations even exist, let alone improve their chances of survival. While we might quickly assume that living organisms would want to produce offspring with greater changes of survival, there is no rational reason for this desire. Why would a selfishly motivated newly living organism care about a future generation?

First accidental evolutionists make a huge leap assuming that life somehow spontaneously generated from chemicals. Then they make a huge leap that these newly living chemicals somehow preferred survival and pain as opposed to a painless existence of nonlife. Then they make another huge leap by assuming that these newly living chemicals could and would want to dilute their strength to produce offspring that require only trouble and work to maintain. Then against all odds, evolution theory proponents take the leap in assuming that these newly living chemicals somehow created an "unselfish gene" that somehow passed on improvements for the future survival of future generations who do nothing for that newly living chemical itself. All of this was done by newly living chemicals that not much different in substance from their dead chemical cousins?

The only answer accidental evolutionists seem to give us to these questions is that this all must have been a series of random accidents. It should not have happened, but accidentally did, they claim. This is seemingly accidental evolutionists' only answer to all the real puzzles of existence:

It was an accident that should never have happened.

The assumption that accidental evolutionists seem to make is that each required event, from the initial conversion of dead chemicals to live chemicals to each genetic mechanism and every improbable variation, took millions if not billions of years to occur. With this much time at their disposal, all sorts of accidental variations could possibly happen, they maintain. They claim that from all the variations that *did* take place, the ones that extended or improved life were retained because those variations made for better survival. The other accidental variations did not work so well, so those species must have died off. All the one-legged accidental variations did not survive. These types of variations fell to the wayside as these weaker creatures were killed off. This part of the theory is called *'survival of the fittest.'* Improved variations were supposedly selected through *'natural selection.'*

While these theories might resonate as we consider already developed species continuing to develop and adapt, the formations of the original mechanisms as mentioned above are completely ungrounded and illogical.

Fossil records do not support gradual variation.

Logically, if variations occur randomly, and only the better ones survived, this implies that many thousands of variations *other than the one that survived* should have occurred. If this took place then we should see many fossil records of thousands if not millions of other variations. Why are there so few fossil species of each type if they all were accidentally forming all sorts of variations, from which only a few eventually progressed?

Another problem that seems to plague the accidental evolution theory is *transitional species.* If we consider that each major change from one species to the next required—according to accidental evolution theory—millions of years and many small variations to accomplish, then we should see many fossils half-way or partially-through the change from one species to the next. The step from invertebrate fish to vertebral fish is an example. This step supposedly took 100 million years to accomplish. Where are all the partial-vertebrate fossils? Why didn't any of these transitional species survive? We should also be seeing transitional species between every other species—not major leaps from one to another. Furthermore, many of these transitional species would not be so inferior as to eliminate their survival. We should see half-long necked giraffes. We should see zebras with only a couple of stripes, then some with a few more, then some with many stripes. Where are the occurrences of the myriad of transitional creatures that varied but were not inferior in any survival context?

Instead of transitional species, the fossil record has shown a consistent pattern: fully developed species appearing for a period of time before becoming extinct. Analysis has shown that some 99% of all species found in fossil records have become extinct altogether. Yet in these records we find little evidence of these extinct species transitioning into the species we see around us today.

There are so many extraordinary features that different species have that sets them drastically apart from other species. Animals with complex brains provide a good example. While it is presumed that the complex human brain was an evolutionary accident, it appears that many species outside of the human evolutionary chain of apes on down also have complex brains. While it is supposed that this hereditary "abnormality" might have accidentally occurred once in an accidental evolutionary cycle, to propose it occurred by accident multiple times is illogical.

In the case of fossil finds, the assumption seemingly has been simpler organism fossil finds have outdated more complex organism fossil finds. Yet researchers continue to find complexity among even the oldest of fossil finds. In recent digs from the Australian outback and reported by University of California researchers Droser and Gehling in 2008, fossils of *Funisia dorothea,* a type of tube worm dated at some 565 million years ago showed a complexity among organisms far older than previously thought. It was assumed that at this point, organisms were quite simple and asexual, contrasting to the sexual reproduction of *F. dorothea.*

Dinosaurs are thought to have lived well over 200 million years ago according to carbon dating, and their mass extinction is said to have occurred about 65 million years ago. Outside of the water-borne organisms more easily preserved and located, there is not much of a fossil record either prior to the dinosaurs or after their mass extinction. During this rather short period of 65 million years after the cataclysmic event that likely destroyed just about every significant species of life, a new series of evolutionary steps would have had to begin. This post-cataclysm evolutionary phase was necessary to graduate microorganisms and possibly the few fish and horseshoe crabs remaining. This leaves the evolutionary process little more than 60 million years to land on the human.

In the final analysis, most biologists and archeologists are disappointed at the lack of fossil evidence proving a clear timeline of evolution from simple to complex organisms. The physical evidence simply does not indicate clear evidence for accidental evolution.

'The Fittest' have not always survived.

One of the major assumptions of the *'survival of the fittest'* concept is that the strong variations with better chances of survival make it. Why then, are there so many weak species around today? Why have these not been stomped out by the stronger variations? Why was the tender butterfly not taken out by the dragonfly? Why was the black ant not eliminated by the fire ant? Why was the field mouse not taken out by the cane rat? While accidental evolutionists may maintain that each surviving species has special characteristics that somehow allowed it to survive, there is no explanation given for obvious weaknesses appearing within surviving species. If *'survival of the fittest'* was indeed the case, through all this evolution we should be left with primarily a few super-species: the less fit species should have been wiped out by now.

The laughable part of these concepts is the current human condition. While the *'survival of the fittest'* and *natural selection* elements of the theory are supposed to improve successive species' chances for survival, the human form of life has "evolved" to the advanced stage of not only endangering its own survival through the poisoning of the earth and atmosphere; but endangering the survival of nearly every species on the planet. Could this be a new twist in the evolutionary process, perhaps?

The fact is, we have a very stable number of species and varieties, and they each have their arranged roles to play. There is a balance between these various species. The balance is easily seen when humankind intrudes into the environment with clear-cutting of forests and the like. While individual species are certainly adapting to changes in their environment, these adaptations maintain the balanced distinctions between species. Outside of the drastic imbalances humans have introduced, the subtle environmental changes and variations in nature are—like the rest of the universe—precise, measurable and designed.

Assumption limits archeological evidence.

Because of a lack of substantial and certain findings, geologists and archeologists have had to make far-reaching conclusions about our origin. Fragile assumptions have been made using limited archeological evidence. This has resulted in a few new findings immediately and dramatically contracting previous assumptions. As a result, debates rage over the interpretations of these few findings. The major mistaken assumption has been that the fossils and bones found to date in archeological digs truly represent the reality of our past.

Finding a place to dig where there may be a preserved fossil or bone fragment of any consequence is tremendous guesswork. As a result, a dig will rarely unearth anything really significant in terms of humankind's origins. Frankly, this is because most of that history has neatly decomposed into the earth. The rate of organic decomposition is extremely fast, and relies greatly upon where an organism died and how. With regard to humankind, it also depends upon how that culture buried their dead. It is the rare occasion that an ancient skull or bone fragment will be preserved enough for reliable identification. The earth has had a volatile geological past. There are now oceans where dry land was. There are now deserts where large bodies of water were. There is evidence of massive and widespread volcanic eruptions and floods that covered huge regions around the world at one time or another. Finding a few spots here and there to dig might give us brief glimpses of a single individual's or family's situation. How reliable are such findings? Are they reliable enough for scientists to make bold statements regarding our origin? Many of the skulls and bones that have been used to make bold statements are mere fragments or pieces of skulls or other body parts. Large assumptions fill in the gaps in determining what the whole body may have looked like. Further assumptions create additional risk of flaws as the bone fragments are pieced into the grand scheme of our origin.

How many gaps have archeologists had to fill with liberal assumptions and speculations about man's ancestry? Perhaps the question should focus on the inverse: How much real evidence do we actually have? How many old clearly identifiable bones have been found? Of the few bones we have found, how reliable is the information they provide?

In reality, we have found only a few significant bones and pieces of skulls over many decades of digging. The scant number of significant findings is obvious from the impact each finding has made: Each time a really old bone fragment or two has been found, drastic changes in perspective regarding human history seem to have resulted. In total, we have only found a total of five or six groupings of older distinguishable human bones dating over a period of some 200,000 years. Each finding has dramatically changed the theoretical timeline of human origin and evolution.

Out of a potential population of billions of people living over hundreds of thousands of years and we've found only a few bones? Note also that most of these finds are bone *fragments* or skull *fragments.* From these fragments, models are simulated to approximate what the body or shape of the head must have been like. For this reason, some archeologists debate the reliability of many of the findings. Do accidental evolutionists base their theories on our origin on these few controversial bone fragments? No. Accidental evolutionists first established speculative assumptions to comply with the accidental evolution theory. The bones have been *pieced into these assumptions.* Archeologists stubbornly fit their findings into the accidental evolution theory because this is today's *accepted theory.* Dates and locations may be juggled based on findings of remains, but the assumption of accidental evolution has been steadfastly abided by over the past century. To do otherwise would risk that archeologist's credibility amongst peers and research funding organizations. An archeologist without the funding to dig is not much of an archeologist.

For example, recently an Indonesian dig found a few bones reputed to be from a species of pigmy humans. This shocked historians and archeologists, creating controversy because of the possibility that much of man's history would have to be rewritten. Africa has been thought of as the location of the *'the dawning of man,'* and all species of humanoids have been apparently traced to Africa--outside of this pigmy humanoid dated at around 100,000 years ago.

To illustrate this further, the bones archeologists have called *'Lucy'*—the supposed missing link between monkeys and humans—were apparently found scattered over an area about a mile wide. Is it reasonable that the bones of a dying or dead animal would become spread out over this distance? Also note that archeologists appeared to conclude that Lucy was neither a male nor female, and didn't have the ability to reproduce. What kind of missing link cannot reproduce?

Note that for a long time only a few decades ago—after the finding of two sets of bone fragments—archeologists assumed that humankind was about 25,000 years old. They believed that only apes or Neanderthals existed prior to that. Then a few decades ago, a few skull pieces were dug up in Africa dated at about 130,000 years. This dramatically changed the various theories of man's origin. Then archeologists dug up some bones in Africa estimated at 160,000 years old surrounded by a host of stone tools. From this, they made a number of new assumptions about human origin. Then the 130,000 year-old bones were re-dated at about 200,000 years old using the surrounding seabed for dating purposes. Again, assumptions on human origin were significantly adjusted.

From these few finds, archeologists have assumed that humankind is a substantially older than previously guessed and must have evolved from apes in Africa about 200,000 years ago: All this from a discovery of a few bones? It is quite a leap from 25,000 years old to 200,000 years old based upon a few bone fragments. Does this sound like a methodology creating certainty? Should this we now conclude that man originated from apes 200,000 years ago? We may be able to agree that humans might have *lived* 200,000 years ago. Any other conclusive understandings would be impossible from the finding of these few bones:

> *A blind man walked into a theatre full of people. As he approached the stairs to the balcony, a young child approached him and politely took the man's hand, and guided the man up the stairs towards his seat. The blind man thanked the child, wondering why theatre was filled with children that evening.*

Surely making such a grand conclusion about our origins using a limited amount of evidence could not be considered reliable. When we consider the tremendous land-mass, water and ice changes that have taken place over the age of this planet, and we consider the various civilizations that may have lived in different places—on mountains and other places now covered with water or volcanic rock—the likelihood that we've missed entire civilizations of humans becomes a definite possibility. We also have not considered the many cultures that may have cremated their dead. Certainly many traditional cultures practice cremation. Yet modern geologists seem to be present their data *as* if these few bones are conclusive evidence of man's history. Why do accidental evolutionists seem so confident of their theories with such a shortage of evidence? To this we bear witness to the pressures of research funding, publication and groupthink.

Is radioactive-dating accurate?

Another assumption accidental evolutionists appear to rest their theories upon is that radioactive dating systems are conclusive. Radioactive dating of carbon-14 and other isotopes assume several factors unknown to modern scientists. In the case of carbon-14; when a cosmic ray enters our atmosphere, it will bombard atoms, creating neutrons that will bombard nitrogen molecules. These nitrogen atoms then initiate carbon-14 production. Theoretically, carbon-14 is consumed by trees and other living matter at a linear rate. Once that tree or other living organism dies, the carbon-14 will decompose without new carbon-14s being added (because the organism died). This means that a researcher can measure the amount of carbon-14 left in the dead matter, compare it to the amount of carbon-14 in a living form of a similar species today, and determine the age by extrapolating the theoretical half-life (how long it takes for half of the molecules to degrade) of carbon-14.

We are not debating this method's ability to determine that something is *very old.* However, there are a number of problems relating to the method's accuracy. First, we are assuming the same rate of cosmic radiation is entering the atmosphere over the expanse of time between that date and the date of measurement. Variances in the sun's emissions, the universe's movements, and other atmospheric changes we may not be aware of can all affect the levels of cosmic rays bombarding organisms in our atmosphere. Some records show that the earth's magnetic fields have dramatically decreased through the years, which would directly affect carbon-14 levels. Second, we are assuming the atmosphere has remained constant, allowing the same amount of isotope creation. For example, today's living creatures will not be able to be dated accurately in the future because fossil fuel burning and industrial pollution has dramatically changed our atmosphere. As a result, the amount of carbon-14s in today's atmosphere will not match the atmosphere even a hundred years ago. This should also mean that volcanic activity, floods, and other general atmospheric changes, which we have seen evidence of, could also significantly impact the rate of carbon-14 decay. These types of events can dramatically affect the atmospheric balance, which can significantly change the rate of bombardment. Third, many researchers are assuming that living creatures of the past consumed carbon at the same levels they do today. Consumption rates vary greatly from species to species. Nutritional requirements adjust to size, age, environment, sun exposure, and food availability. Breathing rates change with atmospheric conditions. Certainly, the assumption that over hundreds of thousands of years, consumption rates will not vary with environmental conditions change is a stretch. Yet another assumption being made about carbon dating accuracy is that carbon-14 decomposition rates are predictable in every occurrence. Physicists propose that carbon-14 deterioration is not subject to the effects of the outside environment. Despite this confidence, the rate of decomposition of many substances—their half-life—is still a theoretical model based upon extending a small sampling of decomposition for a short period into much larger time periods. Quite simply, no one has been able to accurately test the accuracy of the half-life period because radiocarbon testing was only developed in 1949—by Willard Libby.

Because of the precision that nature was designed with, such a *clockworks* system of isotope decomposition can be a useful measuring device, as long as it is used with humility and practicality. Currently these methods are highly theoretical, as we do not fully understand all of the variables. Therefore, their reliability has limitations. Modern scientists have done tests by ring-dating trees to confirm that carbon dating has, at least in the short range (1000-5000 years) the ability to get in the ballpark. Comparison tests with Bristlecone pine trees about 4000 years old (dated through ring dating, which is also not conclusive because during some periods trees do not leave rings) have shown carbon-14 dates could be from 600-700 years short. Though modern scientists call this a confirmation of accuracy, it does show a 17.5% discrepancy. What will the discrepancy be as older objects are dated?

Assuming accuracy levels within 80% at under 5000 years, how can we reliably count on dating extending to 50,000-100,000 years or more, as carbon-14 is often being used for? Assuming this variance would remain constant as the age increased would also be foolhardy. The number of variants as mentioned above—cosmic ray levels, atmospheric levels, consumption rates and decomposition rates—all increase the possibility for error as the age increases. Assuming the 20% variance at 5000 years, would 50% at 50,000 be out of the question? This would make something dated at 50,000 years be 100,000 years old, or even 25,000 years old if the variance went the other way. Consider the effect of this sort of variance on a timeline of 200,000 years. The bottom line is that science is making vast timeline and origin assumptions based on this dating system.

When radioactive dating is extended into other isotopes like argon-40, lead-206/-207, and strontium-87, many of carbon-14's uncertainties are compounded by new ones. As a result, different dating systems often conflict when they are compared to each other in dating the same objects. Typically, geologists analyzing digs are confounded with radically different dates using the different dating systems. We illustrate this with the 70,000 year adjustment in bone remain aging mentioned earlier.

As archeologists date something, they often do not use the isotope dating alone to determine the date. They will typically have other considerations. They might consider the surrounding environment. They might consider the tools and pottery also found on the site. At the end of the day, these researchers will generally blend in the isotope dating with the accepted timeline acceptable to their peers. After all, the find must not be too radical. If it is too radical—such as what happened with the Indonesian find—controversy will reign. What researcher wants to be caught up in a media controversy, where their reputations and methods are questioned? It is far easier to come in line with the expected result, as we have discussed.

Again, we agree that these bone fragments may be *very old.* We are not proposing creation took place 5,000 years ago. The point is; unreliable aging methods and the sporadic finding of a few mysterious bones over theoretically hundreds and thousands of years—even millions of years in the case of dinosaurs—hardly gives accidental evolutionists the ability to reliably make claims of *conclusive evidence* for determining the history and origin of the human race and life on this planet. In reality, archeologists are speculating using limited information, limited experience, and limited perception. These limitations are compounded by the stubborn groupthink version of the theory of evolution—an accidental, random and chaotic version of our past.

Complex organs require multiple mutation.

A question that seems to be posed by and to accidental evolutionists is how gradual mutations could have resulted in incredibly complex anatomical parts such as the eye:

> *The eye is an incredible instrument resembling an advanced camera. It has a shutter; a lens; delicate cells that convert light into data; and the ability to constantly keep the lens clear from blockages.*

Accidental evolutionists will respond that it would be easy to imagine primitive creatures having light-sensitive cells, which gradually over billions of years, developed into the complex eyes we have today. *Yes,* they proclaim, there is *just* enough time for all these developments. Just enough time for *accidental* developments? Is there evidence of partial improvements? Are we seeing various types of *transitional eyes?* Simply the mention of a timetable for random, accidental developments is contradictory to say the least.

We must remember that we are not just talking about gradually improving just one eye. We are talking about *every complexity existing within the human body.* We are talking about the liver, the heart, the lungs, the genitals, the nervous system, the brain, and the intestines. Every physiological mechanism of our bodies are made up of tremendous complexity and synchronicity of composition. These specialized organs and tissue systems consist of many layers of networks traveling through each of them, including neural, circulatory, lymphatic, biochemical, and more. All of these layers work simultaneously and within biorhythms tuned not only to each other, but tuned into the larger rhythms of the universe. Human beings with advanced technologies have worked for many years trying to *purposely* recreate only a few of the functioning parts of the body. And we are saying that all of these complexities *accidentally* developed? More importantly, are we saying that all these complexities accidentally developed among all the biomolecular structures on an *interactive* basis to simultaneously develop into complex systems? In other words, the complex eye could not have developed independently of a complex nervous system to transmit its reception, or a complex brain to receive those impulses.

Biological functionality is collaborative.

Accidental evolutionists suggest that it took the supposedly first single-celled creature possibly trillions of generations to accidentally develop into multicellular creatures: This is just this *one* simple mutation. How about the rest of the mutations necessary to get the single cell to the human? Apparently, the assumption is that each progressive improvement took place in a stepped fashion. Can cellular systems proceed with stepped progress? In other words, will complex organ systems make individual partial changes in tiny steps, accumulating these improvements at some point into the grandest of complex behavior? Since cellular systems work on an integrated basis, we must assume any change would have to have occurred collaboratively, as mentioned above. Did all these changes collaboratively happen accidentally? Which mutations took place first?

> *Did the complex nervous system develop before the complex eye did? Or perhaps the complex eye developed before the complex*

> *nervous system. This would make that complex eye a lazy eye for a few million years, while the nervous system caught up.*

A basic contradiction exists between collaborative cellular behavior and eventually-drastic changes in organ and tissue behavior. If we consider the various functional complexities of advanced organisms, while stepped mutation from one behavior to another could not be functional during transition phases, individual components could not change separately because they are each interacting with other components for overall functionality:

> *This might be compared to one man building the Empire State Building by forming each brick out of clay, then putting* one *brick up at a time. If it took the man five minutes to make each brick one at a time, mix the mortar and then put it in place, it would take this bricklayer 400 years to lay all the bricks in the building, assuming a forty-hour work-week.*
>
> *Now consider how long it would take if we could only have one man form and put up each brick, make the mortar, but a new, untrained man had to come in to make the mortar and put up each next brick. Each man would not know what a brick was, how to form one, how to make the mortar, nor where or how to lay the brick even if they figured out how to make one. Each new bricklayer would have to learn from scratch, with no teaching from the previous bricklayer. How long would this building take to build?*

Most would conclude that if each man did not know how to lay each brick, the building simply would never get built. If it did, it would certainly collapse through a lack of planning, coordination and exchange of knowledge between bricklayers.

What accidental evolutionists propose is similar to the later case: They propose that *dumb chemistry* accidentally kept building complex physiological organisms one layer at a time. Somehow, through sheer luck, these dumb chemicals ended up building the complex multi-cellular organisms around today.

> *Without purposeful design, planning and collaboration we are left with scattered, disjointed, and faulty construction.*

In the case of such a building, how could such a huge building be built without a good design and knowledgeable builders?

Consider if, as current accidental evolutionist thinking goes, just one favorable accidental mutation could take between a million and a billion years to take hold among a species. *This is only one mutation.* The number of mutations it would take to get the amoeba to a human body is currently unknown but *trillions* of mutations would not be outrageous.

Using some genetic scientists' calculations, consider the likelihood of only *one* accidental favorable mutation occurring:

One chance in

1,000,000,000,000,000,000,000,000,000,000,000,000,000,000,00
0,000,000,000,000,000,000,000,000,000,000,000,000,000,000,00
0,000,000,000,000,000,000,000,000,000,000,000,000,000,000,00
0,000,000,000,000,000,000,000,000,000,000,000,000,000,000,00
0,000,000,000,000,000,000,000,000,000,000,000,000,000,000,00
0,000,000,000,000,000,000,000,000,000,000,000,000,000,000,00
0,000,000,000,000,000,000,000,000,000,000,000,000,000,000,00
0,000,000,000,000,000,000,000,000,000,000,000,000,000,000,00
0,000,000,000,000,000,000,000,000,000,000,000,000,000,000,00
0,000,000,000,000,000,000,000,000,000,000,000,000,000,000,00
0,000,000,000,000,000,000,000,000,000,000,000,000,000,000,00
0,000,000,000,000,000,000,000,000,000,000,000,000,000,000,00
0,000,000,000,000,000,000,000,000,000,000,000,000,000,000,00
0,000,000,000,000,000,000,000,000,000,000,000,000,000,000,00
0,000,000,000,000.

This is *one* progressive mutation. Among organisms, trillions of such single variations would have had to occur in order to accidentally create just a few progressive complex improvements. Consider that with each progressive mutation, the complexity of the creature increases by only one small variation. This would be like saying that each single bricklayer not only didn't know how to make or lay a brick, but the chances of them actually getting *one brick* in place was one chance in 10^{3000}. Could such a building ever get built with these incredible odds against it? As you stack each progressive mutation necessary upon the other, the time required simply does not compute to any logical time frame—certainly not within the speculated age of the earth. Nor does it fit within the range given by the fossil dates of various species or the suspected age of the earth. This point has also been debated by a number of well-known accidental evolutionists. Some have proposed the solution of the *directed panspermia theory* as discussed earlier. Again, this theory suggests that life on earth was seeded from a distant planet because not enough time was available. This of course bears the question of which planet that was, and how did life develop on that planet.

In reality, accidental evolutionists *do not know* how long these supposedly accidental mutations might have taken. They do not know how long improvements developing into complex organs might take. No one has yet to see a fish mutate to a mammal. This means quite simply that they are *guessing.*

Accidental mutation renders likely destruction.

At the bare minimum, accidental evolutionists seem to be asking us to believe simple chemicals somehow had the ability to develop into increasingly complex life forms accidentally. Accidental evolutionists ask us to believe that a string of nucleotides along a phosphate-sugar helix (DNA) has the ability to keep accidentally rearranging progressively, without any ultimate purpose. This also implies that trillions upon trillions of rearrangements happened, and only a few allowed survival.

As we have seen with destructive viruses and other dangerous mutations like cancer, just one misplaced nucleotide could result in a deadly mutation which could easily wipe out an entire population—or all life on earth many times over. The question arises: With these kinds of odds (one chance in 10^{3000}) why would living organisms still exist? With such a low probability of progressive mutation, the inverse results in a high probability of destructive mutation. How could accidental life have survived through all those more probable destructive mutations? There is simply no logic for *continued accidental progressive* mutation. It is a virtual impossibility and improbability. With so many accidental mutations possible and so many billions of accidental mutations supposedly taking place, a scorched-earth scenario should have squelched life long ago.

Dog genetics reveal behavioral link.

Accidental evolutionists have had a rough time with things like why there are so many breeds of dogs:

> *There are big dogs, little dogs, hairy dogs, skinny dogs, dogs with floppy ears and dogs with pointed ears; dogs who bark loud but don't bite and dogs that don't bark much but bite hard. There are red dogs, white dogs, brown dogs, spotted dogs and all sorts of other color mixes. There are dogs with flat faces, dogs with pointed noses and dogs with long wiener-shaped bodies. There are bald dogs with smooth skin, skinny dogs with curly white hair, and big hairy dogs with muscular, large bodies.*

For what practical purpose did all these mutations take place? Biologists seem to be determined to link all of these various dog breeds to one master-dog—the wolf. Biologists have had to conjure up a strange accidental evolutionary process lasting a mere 10,000 years to explain how all these various breeds all mutated from the wolf. Biologists have tried to explain how the wolf was gradually bred by humans into more and more domesticated versions, accidentally yielding such crazy mutations like dachshunds (some call this *pure-breed* a "wiener dog"). How and why did this nutty-looking dog develop these characteristics? Why would these dogs mutate so quickly, and select these various features? Certainly the features didn't help them survive longer or better. In fact, in many cases these pure breed dogs actually die sooner than normal dogs, with ailments caused by malfunctioning organs inherent in that breed.

In the 1950s a wolf dog breeding experiment was directed by Dr. Dmitry Belyaev of the then-Soviet Union's Institute of Cytology and Genetics in Novosibirsk, Siberia. The intent of this long-term study was to determine the genetic role humans played in the domestication of animals. Most importantly, he wanted to study how contact with humans might bring about not only new behavior but also changes in body features and physiology. The prime subjects of the study were silver foxes, who were cruelly caged while they and their offspring were put into various degrees of contact with humans.

This breeding experiment continued over forty years and the results were revealing. After over thirty generations of foxes were handled and petted by humans a number of subtle changes were apparent when compared to undomesticated control groups. One of the few apparent physical changes was the development of droopy ears among the domesticated foxes. Rather than the perky upright ears seen among so many wild wolves and foxes, these domesticated foxes had developed floppy ears over the generations. One cannot help but be reminded by the sight of domesticated killer whales, who also mysteriously tend to develop floppy dorsal fins during capture and domestication in public aquariums.

Other observed effects of domestication include the fact that the domestic foxes developed rolled up tails rather than tails pointing straight up. This seems analogous to the floppy ears. Dr. Belyaev speculated that the pointed ears and tails were possibly used for defense purposes (to stand tall against challengers) and to sense the external environment in a more defensive manner. During captivity within the protective dens provided by humans, these facilities were not necessary for survival.

Differences were also seen in circulating neurotransmitter and hormone levels among the foxes. Domesticated foxes had significantly higher levels of serotonin in the bloodstream, and their corticosteroids would cycle differently at different levels than their wild relatives.

Behavioral changes were also observed as the foxes became domesticated. Over the generations, they became increasingly relaxed and comfortable around humans, responding positively to petting and other touching. Their ability to respond and communicate with humans also increased over the generations as well.

This research indicates a connection between changed consciousness and the alteration of the physical body. When we consider the central difference between the domesticated environment and the undomesticated environment, the central difference outside of the fear of attack was the being in the company of an organism (humans) of higher consciousness. The humans expressed companionship through petting, talking and feeding. These are all expressions of higher consciousness. Note also that decreased fear from attack is also related to consciousness.

The physical and behavioral alterations followed the foxes being in the proximity and care of humans. We should logically connect these physical alterations of the floppy ears, curled tails and altered hormones to their increased contact with humans. Because human consciousness is different from fox consciousness, we can readily make the association. We can connect physical alterations to alterations in consciousness contact.

Dr. Belyaev's assumptions that the changes were completely due to the animals not having to defend themselves is short sighted. He has ignored the *consciousness element* staring him in the face. To ignore the exchange between the humans and the animals is typical of the sterile view accidental evolutionists have about the living organism. Those foxes were not chemical robots. They were living beings.

Still we can partially agree with Dr. Belyaev that not having to defend themselves should have played a definite role in the physical changes of the foxes. Instead of being left to their own devices defending themselves in the wild, the foxes were protected and fed daily. Instead of them fearing for their survival, they were petted and cooed as a pet might. However, as the foxes gradually got closer to humans, and began relating with their human handlers, changes began taking place. Their bodies and behavior—reflecting their new surroundings and contact with humans of higher consciousness—were adjusted.

Although we all accept readily the physical changes caused by a changing environment, the critical issue here is the *consciousness element.* While we can all accept that a changing environment will create alterations, this alone—as we have discussed—does not explain the various species and the definite distinctions between them.

Note the increased hormone levels among the foxes came as a new twist on the accidental evolutionary theory. Suddenly accidental evolutionists were trying to blend in this information with the standard theory. The existence of many of some of these neurochemicals only became known in the mid-twentieth century.

These researchers appropriately connected the increases in neurochemistry to human contact: petting, feeding, and other emotional expressions of consciousness. In other words, the human contact drove biochemical alterations. The inclusion of behavior and emotion with genetic diversity opened a new factor for accidental evolutionists to wrestle with—*like maybe the living being.*

The body reflects consciousness.

Consider for a moment how our bodies can change and adapt to a change in consciousness:

> *An overweight person decides to make dramatic changes and improve his health. He becomes a long-distance runner. After*

several years of running, his body has become slender, with well-built calves and thighs.

Over time the DNA in the cells also begin to mutate, making the cell more efficient in utilizing glucose and oxygen. The cell's metabolism will increase, and various other physiological functions adapt to adjust. Expanded lung capacity, larger heart muscles and other changes will take place in the body. On the other hand, a person who likes to eat and does not exercise much will probably develop a larger stomach, enabling more eating. Their metabolism will decrease, adapting to that behavior.

Certainly the physical body changes as a result of particular activities. However, prior to the change in activities came a *decision* to change that activity. This decision arises from consciousness. For this reason, the shape of our body and our activities will reflect our consciousness.

Should we decide to become a boxer, we will probably end up with a broken or twisted nose and a puffy, scarred facial countenance. Likewise, a hardened violent criminal will probably have a number of scars and injuries as a result of his or her choices in life. His body may also end up dead because of his consciousness. On the other hand, an accountant will probably have more delicate physical features, and probably smaller, weaker muscles as a result of his or her choices and activities. An athletic accountant will probably have a longer life than the violent criminal will as well.

We can easily see how our physical features reflect our consciousness in so many different ways. Considering our consciousness to be a combination of our current desires and past behavior, we can see how our accumulated situation reflects either decisions we may have made in this lifetime or a past lifetime. As our consciousness changes, so does our body. We can thus scientifically and logically conclude that our bodies (and species) reflect our own personal consciousness. And as that consciousness evolves, so do our bodies.

This research on wolves and dogs set out originally to dispel the doubts regarding dog ancestry in support of accidental evolution. It unintentionally resulted in a practical display of how every living organism contains a living being. It showed how living beings have relative states of consciousness depending upon the body they wear. It showed how contact with higher organisms will result in increased consciousness and subsequent physical reflection. The bottom line is that all creatures display consciousness because *all living organisms contain a living being:*

Even the smallest creatures such as bacteria show the same survival and adaptation responses larger creatures do. In numerous studies and observations, researchers have observed that bacteria respond to various stimuli in much the same way that any creature does. They are attracted to elements that bring physical comfort and are repelled by elements that cause discomfort, pain or a threat of death. Furthermore, they have a memory of what caused pain or comfort in the past, and they can thus respond appropriately. Their basic responses are no different from other living organisms. This is evidenced by pathogenic bacteria learning to adapt to medicines like antibiotics.

Because these creatures are physically different, we often do not consider them living ***being*s**. Yet they respond to challenges and adapt the same way most other creatures do, including humans. When a bacteria or insect physically adapts to a new threat this is obviously an attempt to survive and avoid pain. The threat creates a challenge to survival. Since these organisms are alive, *they are conscious.* Since they are conscious, they avoid pain and death. In the same way a human might don a camouflage outfit to outsmart an opponent, a bacteria or insect might develop new physical traits to resist a particular poison. They cannot quite change species, but they can adapt within limitations. These adaptations are merely different ways organisms express their consciousness of being alive and their intent to become happy.

Love and sacrifice are not errors.

The *'survival of the fittest'* and *'natural selection'* theories do not explain the various complexities of families. If a chemical machine was intent to simply survive, why consider ones future descendents? Why consider the health and survival of offspring? Future descendents will not increase an individual's personal survival chances. Having and protecting offspring is simply a burden, slowing down ones chances of personal longevity. While we might consider the possibility that stronger offspring might one day protect the parents, this requires a complex outlook into the future that includes the assumption that the offspring will stick around. The accidental evolution theory is quite vague on this subject. Most accidental evolutionists will mumble that some strange accidental genetic mutation created an instinct within physical organisms to promote the survival of their own clan. If one asks where this instinct came from, more mumbling about random accidental genetic mutations will probably result. This is because accidental evolutionists *do not know where instinct comes from.*

Let us examine the *'survival of the fittest'* doctrine a little closer with respect to practical life on our planet. Humans throughout history have sacrificed their survival on behalf of their mates, their family, their country, or their relationship with the Supreme Person. Others may risk their lives for the sake of achieving respect and love from others. Consider a mountain climber who risks his life to get to the top, thereby gaining the respect of others. Animals also make similar sacrifices. They are often seen defending family or fighting to increase their pecking order and the respect of peers.

How would these types of behaviors translate to the *'survival of the fittest'* theory? Love and sacrifice would seemingly have to be considered errors of evolution. Loving another or sacrificing oneself for another would require a feeling that others are more important than ones own survival. Risking ones life for the love or respect of others means that gaining love and respect are more important than survival. This conflicts with the assumption that creatures have evolved through motives of pure self-preservation. In other words, have these humans and animals who act out of care for one another become genetically crazy? Are those who value family, love, honesty, beauty, humility, gratitude, and sincerity above their own lives just irrational mutants? Accidental evolutionists seem to be saying that an accidental *family gene* somehow developed, connecting ones family's survival to the survival of the species. This would seem to be quite the intricate accidental gene mutation—but it does not explain the more complex activities related to love and sacrifice.

The *'survival of the fittest'* theory assumes living organisms are essentially self-centered, self-motivated chemical machines. Love and sacrifice confounds this theory, because *'survival of the fittest'* should result in only cruel, selfish actions. In the true *'survival of the fittest'* world, activities of love and sacrifice simply would not exist. This is because the living being is by nature *not* a selfish creature. Though we display quite a bit of selfishness within this dimension, caring for ones family and sacrificing for noble concerns reflects that living beings are loving creatures by nature. It reflects that living organisms are simply not chemical machines.

Anatomical change reflects a search for fulfillment.

Making physical changes in response to environmental stress is the living being's search for happiness reflected physically. For example, the immune system of an organism will deter invaders, developing new antibodies to increase the likelihood for physical survival. This is the same as actively fighting off predators. All living organisms try to avoid physical destruction in an attempt to keep their physical bodies as comfortable as possible. This is in hopes that the physical body will generate some ultimate fulfillment. Meanwhile an organism focuses upon relationships with family and friends as another means for potential fulfillment. The commonality among the various creatures is that within each physical shell is a living being who is searching for fulfillment within the temporary physical dimension. As a result, the living being's desires will cause a manipulation in its physical shell. This manipulation of the physical shell is common among all organisms that contain a living being. At the end of the day, both the physical shell and the attempt to manipulate the physical shell is a reflection of the living being's desires and consciousness.

> *Just as one might improve ones house in order to become more comfortable; changes to ones physical body are outward reflections of the inner self's ongoing desire for fulfillment.*

Accidental evolution theory eliminates life.

The primary rationale for the accidental evolution theory has always been observations noting the similarities between various species. As one examines the physical body of each species, it is not hard to notice what motivated the widespread acceptance of this speculative theory. This simple observation, without a better explanation, seems outwardly logical. That is until the complexities are examined as we do here. It is one thing to notice that creatures can change and adapt their physical forms in response to environmental stress. It is wholly another to concoct a speculative theory where one small original creature accidentally evolved into the diverse complex of creatures we see today.

Certainly a living organism can make physical adaptations to their environment and carry on those adaptations to successive generations. We do not debate this. However, an organism will only make changes within a narrow bandwidth and under certain guidelines. As a result, we see various environmental controls regulating the various species populations: We see predators keeping populations in control, illustrating just one of the governing systems among organisms.

The central failing of the accidental evolutionist theory is that it does not distinguish between life and matter. It cannot explain where life came from. It is not able to explain consciousness; the recognition of life; a living organism's will to survive; nor an organism's tendency to treasure love more than survival.

Furthermore, the accidental evolution theory is full of gaping holes: A lack of evidence exists for transitional species, deceased variations, spontaneous generation, accidental DNA or RNA creation, and random mutations. These shortcomings of the theory have made it subject to a variety of fixes over the years. This is because the accidental evolution theory was and still is simply an imaginative, speculative guess, based on a thin set of observations, patched together with allegory and supposition. The accidental evolution theory creates more questions than it solves, leading to side-theories and continued controversy.

The central question is: Why do the various species appear so similar? Could there be any other explanation for the similarities between different species? What if there was a better explanation? And what if this explanation also explained all of the other problems currently resident in the accidental evolution theory? What if this also explained the individuality, spirituality, love and the quest for fulfillment and survival among species? What if this also explained the ability of a particular body to adapt to new challenges, and explained such anomalies as the many species of dogs?

There is a more scientific explanation.

We accept a more practical and logical explanation for the development and existence of living organisms: It is the *living being* who is evolving. The physical body each living being dwells within merely *reflects* that evolution. Thus, the physical forms which living beings inhabit evolve *around* the consciousness of the specific living beings who dwell inside each form. An adaptive and organized mechanism enables living beings to be incorporated into changing physical bodies that reflect their desires and consciousness. This mechanism guides living beings through a learning process in order to achieve greater or lower levels of awareness, depending upon the specific desires and consciousness of each living being.

The living being is superior to physical chemistry. The living being is manifest with personality, individuality, a quest for truth and goodness, and the need for relationships. Through an arrangement of design, this superior living being (each of us) is able to influence physical chemistry through will, desire, and intention. As a result, the living being is able to indirectly adjust the physical body within certain designed guidelines, through the ongoing status of the living being's desires and past activities. This influential role of the living being on the body renders the physical body a reflection of the specific consciousness of the living being utilizing it.

The living being has an ultimate reason to survive.

Every living organism struggles to survive. Attempting to avoid death only illustrates that the living being has an ultimate *reason* for living. Living beings all innately want to remain living. Why would any creature desire to avoid death unless its central characteristic was being alive? Survival is hard work. Creatures work very hard to eat and drink enough to survive every day. In terms of energy expended, dying would certainly be much easier. Living organisms all pursue survival because there is an ultimate reason for living.

The missing link within the concept of survival and evolution is an understanding of *who* desires to survive. If we accept that in order to distinguish life from dead chemicals there must be an awareness of life; the question becomes: *Who* is aware of being alive? *Who* distinguishes itself from non-life? Distinguishing between life and non-life requires an entity who must be conscious of being alive, and who must value life. Without valuing life there would be no quest to survive, as dead chemistry would preferable since it requires no effort to remain alive.

If we accept the existence of a being who in every living creature desires to survive, then we must ask, for whose benefit is survival? If the living organism dies, which all living organisms do, then who is left to benefit from the that species' longer survival? Why would a bag of chemicals adapt so that the next generation could survive better? What would the purpose of that extended survival be?

The living being, relative to its current level of consciousness, has specific desires, goals, and a basic quest to survive. The living being is capable of love, fear, anger, compassion, and consciousness because the living being is alive, and these elements are characteristics of living beings. As components of living beings, these emotions translate and reflect through each physical species in one way or another. The living being is the source of the energy and personality residing within each physical body. Whether single-celled, human, animal or plant, every living organism is powered by a distinct living being. Without a living being inside, the body is lifeless and there is no quest to survive. Without the living being's continued quest for survival, there can be no functioning DNA, nor any altering of DNA.

With the physical eyes of our physical bodies, we cannot perceive this living being. This is because the living being is nonphysical and transcendental to the body. With this understanding of the living being, we can begin to make sense of how and why the living being evolves, and why the particular species reflect that evolution. We can also understand why species are so similar.

We might first clarify the elements that provide the foundation for the *evolution of the living:*

- ***The body is constantly changing:*** The physical body is a moving, changing structure. It is constantly undergoing molecular and biological transition, as it exchanges molecules, cells, and form. The physical bodies we wear now are not the physical bodies we wore even a year ago. Within five years, every molecule has been exchanged for a new one, and we are wearing a completely different body.

- Each living being displays emotion: As evidenced by experiments on plants, bacteria, and other types of animals, all species have the capacity to exhibit emotions. Each living organism exhibits the will to survive and avoid pain. Through these exhibitions, each organism seeks relative happiness.
- ***Each living body contains a distinct living being:*** All living organisms, including humans, animals, plants, bugs, amoebae, etc., each have within their respective physical shells a distinct individual living being.
- ***Each living being is transcendental by nature:*** The living being cannot be measured, quantified physically, nor perceived by the physical senses. It is of another dimension. The living being's *actual* nature is transcendental—outside of the physical dimension.
- ***Each transcendental embodied living being is prone to misidentify with the body:*** The risk of being embodied is mistakenly assuming that identity. The living being mistakenly identifies itself as the physical body, seeking satisfaction through physical means.
- ***The physical shell of each living being adapts to environmental challenges:*** The living being, seeking fulfillment through physical embodiment, stimulates an adaptive physical response to environmental and internal challenges. This is an attempt to improve physical conditions—increasing the likelihood of physical happiness—just as the man improved his house to suit his liking.
- ***The current physical shell of a living being reflects the consciousness and prior activities of the living being within:*** Each species of physical body allows different capabilities of expression and consciousness. Some species have greater capabilities for awareness while others have less. The distinct capabilities of each physical body of each

species reflect the graduated consciousness (or evolution) of the particular living being occupying that body.

- ***The mind is a subtle body covering the living being, forming the platform upon which the gross physical body is formed:*** We shape the mind by our various desires and sense activities. The mind thus creates the basis for the type of senses and the type of physical forms we take on.

The human form of life is capable of greater awareness and thus has greater responsibility for the decisions made by living beings within these forms: The human form of physical body has a greater awareness of life and the consequences of activities. The human form is a life of greater responsibility. The human form is a lifetime at the crossroads.

We should discuss some of these points with a bit more detail:

Each living being is independently evolving.

Again, it is the living being within the body who is evolving. The physical body each living being inhabits merely reflects this evolution. Consider that each physical lifetime of each species allows for a range of learning experiences at a specific level. Each of these experiences teaches us various lessons, depending upon what we need to learn. We are all learning, growing and evolving throughout our lifetimes; each learning at different rates. The bodies we dwell within change as we grow and learn, and thus our bodies reflect our growth. While the lower species are learning lessons that relate to survival and fear, the higher species have greater capability to influence others, and thus can learn lessons related to love and compassion; understanding how our actions and decisions can affect others in a deeper way.

Evolved species have a greater capacity to learn.

More evolved species have increased intellectual abilities. As a result, the evolved species have greater capacities for learning.

Simple observation tells us that humans have the highest intellectual abilities within our visible environment: we have greater awareness, giving us a greater capacity to learn. We can use this also to measure the relative consciousness hierarchy among the various organisms we see around us. We can teach higher species how to cooperate with us, while lower creatures simply run from us in fear. We can teach a monkey to do things we could not teach a dog to do. We can teach a dog to do things we could not teach a mouse to do. We can teach a rabbit to do things we could not teach a lizard to do. We can see by the organism's ability to learn and communicate what level of consciousness that species has, and what stage of evolution the living being within that body is at. As a result, we can see a hierarchy among humans, animals, birds, fish, plants, and the lower forms, with regard to the consciousness of the particular living beings inhabiting those particular physical forms.

An elephant could easily hurt a human being but since it displays a greater consciousness, it has a greater capacity to cooperate with humans. As a result, elephants have become great friends with humans, as have dolphins, horses, cows, and other more evolved animals. The living beings in these species have the capability to learn greater lessons with respect to the exchange of relationships than insects or small fish might. An insect cooperating with a human, for example, is simply not practical, as its consciousness is centered around survival and fear.

Over recent years, some scientists have begun to accept that animals and plants display emotions just as humans do. A number of studies have observed animals having many qualities thought previously to be exclusively human: honor, compassion, fairness, empathy, envy, even morality. For many years, most scientists assumed that animals had none of these qualities. Many animals—including rats, dogs, monkeys, birds, penguins, dolphins and others—have since been studied and observed at length. Dolphins display complex behavior related to helping their mates, even other species. Monkeys show complex behavior associated with cooperating in the gathering and sharing of food with less fortunate monkeys. When playing, an older rat will allow a younger rat to win sometimes. When dogs play, they pretend to be angry but are careful not to hurt their playmate. If they were to hurt their playmate, the playmate would lose trust and may not play next time. These observations illustrate that living organisms have various levels of consciousness, reflecting the living beings within.

Our physical bodies reflect our minds.

The mind is an instrument that records sensual activities and assists the living being in concocting various ways to attempt to enjoy in the physical world. Because of these features, the mind reflects the desires of the living being together with the various sensual inputs. For example, if we see a movie, that movie is now recorded into the mind, and all of those images in the movie are now images the mind holds. Because we desired to see the movie in the first place, the recording reflects not just the images, but also the self's desire to see the movie. Not only does the mind reflect every movie image, then. The mind retains the initial concoction set up by the living being: *I will enjoy watching this movie.* In this way, our minds have a combined *database* of sensual images and the various concoctions we have developed—some of which have been achieved and some of which have not. Those concoctions that have been achieved may provide learning experiences for us, providing some wisdom. However, those concoctions that have not yet been achieved are quite dangerous. They will shape our future bodies.

The instrument of the mind is incredibly precise in its ability to record, yet we have conscious access to only part of it: the conscious mind. The unconscious part of the mind contains the recordings and concoctions of everything we have ever experienced.

Because the mind contains both concoctions and images, the combined status of our mind is the sum of our activities and desires. Our gross physical body reflects this status of our mind. Therefore, the contents of our mind will be reflected by the type of body we have on: our concocted desires for sensual enjoyment combined with our recorded sensual activities determine the kind of physical senses we develop. Thus, the types of physical characteristics we have now were determined by the characteristics of our mental status in the past. These characteristics include our history of relationships, activities, and desires. The mind can be considered the primary vehicle we travel within throughout our journeys through the physical world: It carries us through various experiences and lifetimes, all the while accumulating these experiences and concoctions, constantly reflecting them through gross physical forms.

Our physical bodies reflect our relationships.

Consider how humans, after living with a particular animal such as a dog or cat, may begin to take on physical features of the animal and vice versa. As a result, many dog owners share similar features and characteristics with their dogs. These outward similarities are a result of two basic elements: Initially the two living beings are drawn to each other as they share common personality and physical traits. Then, as they spend time together—sharing emotions and communication—they both begin to take on some of the other's mannerisms and physical characteristics. The living beings we choose to live around *affect* our consciousness while the body we wear *reflects* our consciousness.

This is also apparent when observing couples who have been together for thirty, forty, or even fifty years of marriage. Over the years of close proximity with each other, both gradually develop similar mannerisms and lifestyles, which eventually become reflected in their physical features and activities. They may begin to use similar language, walk similarly, have the same physical build, and sometimes even begin to have similar facial expressions. It is uncanny how our physical body, as it evolves during this lifetime, becomes shaped around the consciousness of the living beings we share time with.

Recently it was reported that human genes were surprisingly very similar to those of dogs. This has created quite a stir among accidental evolutionists who have attempted to explain this through the accidental evolutionary theory. The simple understanding for this related DNA lies in the fact that the commingling of living beings in dog bodies and living beings in human forms have mutually affected these living beings' physical shells and thus their DNA, due to their relationship exchange. Dog bodies have become more human-like, and human bodies have (unfortunately) become more dog-like over the generations. This of course, relates to the genetic/neurochemical research on wolves and dogs we discussed earlier.

Our physical bodies reflect our past choices.

During our current lifetimes, our bodies and environments reflect our previous actions. For example, a person who makes violent choices—inflicting pain upon others—will typically develop physical features reflecting that mean, violent lifestyle. They may develop strong arms and fists, and abilities to fight more efficiently. They may also develop facial features such as mean eyes and scars, effectively imparting fear upon any person who may challenge them. In this way a violent person will physically reflect their prior violence. A violent person will also eventually experience the pain they inflicted upon others. They may be thrown in jail where other violent people are, for example. This allows the violence they initiated to be experienced.

Similarly, a person who wants to run fast over long distances may develop, after years of training, a body resembling the build of a greyhound, antelope, or racehorse. The physical body thus provides the capabilities desired by the living being. Likewise, a person who loves to overeat may take on physical characteristics enabling further overeating, such as an extended stomach. Physical changes thus reflect the living being's desires and activities, outwardly expressing the living being's various attempts to become happy in the temporary physical world.

Once the temporary physical body dies, if the living being has continuing desires to become happy within the physical world, the living being will become embodied into another physical body; picking up where the last body left off; again perfectly reflecting that living being's consciousness and past activities.

Our sum consciousness determines our future.

As the living being travels through the physical dimension, its *actual consciousness* is covered up by the accumulated physical relationships, images, and concoctions. This creates what we will call the *covered consciousness.* Our currently developed *covered consciousness* is partly a reflection of the results of our actions and partly a reflection of our various desires and goals. In simpler terms, it is *what we want* combined with *what we have done.* Our covered consciousness might be compared to a sort of *dossier,* or file containing our track record of past activities together with our desires and goals for existence. Assuming our goals remain focused on our own enjoyment within the physical world; this covered consciousness will shape our future physical environments and physical forms, from the family and country we are born into, to our body's DNA arrangement.

As each of us progress through our lifetimes, our desires, activities and relationships accumulate to develop particular tendencies. As these tendencies gradually become reflected into physical attributes, they will lead us to further tendencies:

> *As a river moves along the shore gathering the stems, leaves and branches of the plant parts which fall into it, our physical forms gather the various effects our choices and lifestyles have created.*

As one physical body ages and becomes useless, the sum of our covered consciousness will determine the next physical form we embody. The sum of our covered consciousness at the time of death will thus determine the next species we embody, the next family we become a member of, and the next environment we will live within.

The similarities between the various species therefore result from the gradually changing consciousness of the living being. As our tendencies gradually develop, reflecting our consciousness and prior activities, we step from one physical form to another. Like a cascading river which winds and bends through a forest, one change typically yields another in the same direction, flowing with connected behavior. This effect can also be seen in our current lifetimes as our bodies gradually change through the years.

If we were to choose to live an animalistic life, focused upon eating, sleeping, mating, and defending during our human lifetime, without any development of higher consciousness and awareness; after our human life we may first take on a higher form of animal species most closely reflecting our consciousness. Then as those animalistic tendencies develop further while in those forms, we may gradually sink deeper into the lower species. Meanwhile our prior concoctions to enjoy drive us further into sensual activities, while our past activities drive us into fearful situations where we directly experience the effect our prior activities had on others. In this way, we will directly and perfectly experience the results of our choices and activities made when we had the greater consciousness of a human form.

Should our focus remain attached to the accomplishments of the human existence, after the death of this body we will transmigrate to another human form, albeit in another family and environment. Again, however, we will be put in an environment perfectly reflective of our decisions. Should we have been hurtful in a specific way towards others, we will likely experience that same activity punished upon our own bodies. Should we have aided others in particular ways, we will likely be aided in that same way.

Hypnotherapy research over the past twenty years has accumulated quite a bit of evidence that the living being has occupied previous physical bodies. The procedure is called past-life regression, in part developed by Dr. Ian Stevenson, a Medical Doctor and professor of research at the University of Virginia, Department of Psychiatric Medicine. Dr. Stevenson and various other researchers documented how they would clinically put a subject under hypnosis and draw them into a recall of a previous lifetime. In preliminary research, this result was discovered by accident (as Dr. Stevenson had no prior belief in the self's transmigration). Quite often the subject described in detail a previous lifetime as a particular historical person, describing events which occurred at that time with a clarity and experience only possible from having been personally in that situation. The research did not stop there however. The researchers then researched the historical accuracy of the statements heard during hypnosis, to confirm whether 1) the subject could have known these facts otherwise; and 2) whether the facts can be confirmed as being historically accurate.

The research has been thorough and clinically supported. Some thirty scientific books and hundreds of scientific papers have been written to document studies by various credentialed hypnotherapists, some of whom are Medical Doctors and licensed Psychiatrists. Dr. Stevenson's research itself spanned over thirty-seven years, and he documented hundreds of cases of previous life recognition by children who remembered their past lives. His research indicates that past life recollection fades by about age seven. Before that age, children will often speak spontaneously about their previous lives as historical individuals, recalling historical details decades' old and otherwise unknowable. Dr. Stevenson and his various associates meticulous documented these recollections along with the research confirmed their historical accuracy. He has written several books on the subject, presenting the evidence in a clinically rigorous and scientific manner (Tucker 2005;

Stevenson 1975, 1977, 1997, 2003). A number of other psychologists and hypnotists have also documented regressing patients into verifiable past lives, including Dr. Helen Wambach (1978), Dr. Morris Netheron (1978), Dr. Edit Fiore (1978), Dr. Bruce Goldberg (1982), Dr. Joel Whitton (1986), Dr. Brian Weiss (1988), Dr. Christopher Bache, Dr. Winafred Lucas (1993) and Dr. Marge Rieder (1995; 1999) among others.

Interestingly, Dr. Rieder documented regression sessions with a range of subjects that revealed historical information regarding Millboro, VA, a village once in the midst of the Civil War. Dr. Rieder's patients accurately described the historical aspects of the war and the town, including the uncovering of previously unknown hideaways and tunnels used during the war.

We can add to this the research of Dr. Michael Newton, a psychologist and master hypnotist who regressed patients into the period between their last life and the current one. Dr. Newton's patients consistently tell of interlife judgement scenarios, karma and other topics in his 1994 *Journey of Souls: Studies of Life between Lives,* and his 2000 work, *Destiny of Souls: New Case Studies of Life between Lives.* Dr. Newton was a clinical specialist in pain management who stumbled into the reality of past lives while treating patients for pain. His texts document some fifteen years of clinical research.

The evidence presented by these scientific explorations is clear: Throughout our physical lives, we are evolving (or devolving) through lessons provided by the design of the physical realm. After we work through the dilemmas and challenges of this physical lifetime, we transition to physical embodiments. These progressive embodiments reflect our particular consciousness, reflected by decisions made. As documented in some of Dr. Newton's studies, confirmed by many ancient texts, should we raise our consciousness to a transcendental level, we will graduate beyond the recurring embodiment process.

The human form has greater responsibility.

With the human form's higher level of awareness comes greater responsibility. The human form brings the living being greater responsibility because of an enhanced ability to determine morality. Future shells we may embody after the death of this human form will be determined by the actions we take while in this human form. Tendencies towards cruelty and pain in the human form can thus send that living being into an entire array of vicious physical forms, starting with vicious animal species, followed or preceded by a descent into bodies of weaker animal species that in turn are eaten by other vicious organisms. In this way, we will not only become embodied into organisms reflecting our consciousness, but we will directly experience the results of activities made during our responsible lifetimes. The mechanism is designed perfectly, allowing direct learning experiences for actions taken during aware lifetimes.

Likewise, choices we make in kindness to others will be reflected into progressive lifetimes of greater consciousness and responsibility. Just as a worker who performs his job steadily and honestly is rewarded by promotion, the living being who proves to be responsible during aware lifetimes gains higher awareness, leading to greater transcendental growth.

The human form has the potential of greater intelligence. With greater intelligence comes a greater opportunity for decision-making and the ability to solve the problems of life. Seeking the transcendental solution to life's questions can lead to our ultimate exit out of physical embodiment. This opportunity comes with greater responsibility as well:

> *A person who holds the position of captain of a ship has the authority to change the direction of the ship. Therefore, the captain retains the responsibility for the ship's course. If the ship crashes into a rock, it is the captain who is held responsible. He was the person who ultimately had the ability to direct a change in course.*

Awareness can either be utilized or abused. With the capability of awareness comes responsibility. A person wanting to escape awareness, for example, might drink, take drugs, or escape into sensual activities. These actions will allow a person to gradually lose the ability to be aware. This will eventually lead to taking on physical forms that allow *more* forgetfulness. Unfortunately, the byproduct of these physical forms is that the being's consciousness will be geared towards the struggle for physical survival. The opportunity for higher awareness will be gone, being replaced by an overwhelming fear of pain and death.

Our choices determine our direction.

The choices we make while in the human form of life have a great impact upon our future direction simply because we are more aware of the consequences of those choices. Should we choose to ignore this awareness, then the depth of our slide into the various species of life will rely upon our various activities and lifestyle choices. The decisions we make when we have more awareness and thus a greater understanding of the consequences will have an impact upon us for many lifetimes in the future. This is to promote learning. While many of us pride our human species for having the ability to make moral and ethical decisions, we must understand that should we misuse this ability, we will lose it. Those lower species that do not have these abilities are not merely *ignorant* creatures; they are unfortunate living beings who have in the past chosen not to utilize those abilities when they had them. Thus, they have to learn through experience when they could have had those realizations when they had greater awareness.

This is a common scenario during our everyday lives as well: Often parents tell their teenage children that if they do not listen and learn now, they will be forced to learn those lessons through the *school of hard knocks.* For example, a parent may tell a child not to steal, but if the child doesn't listen and learn from that, then they will end up being arrested for stealing and learning the *hard way* that they shouldn't steal.

The depth and path of one's gradual decline into the lower creatures is determined by the choices the living being made during any lifetime in which there was the ability to understand moral consequences. As a result, living beings who chose to be cruel as humans—inflicting pain upon others—will be carried through enough painful lifetimes to *work off* the suffering they chose to inflict when they had the moral understanding to make a choice. The lower life forms give the living being the opportunity to reap the results of those actions, all the while learning lessons that gradually accumulate, resulting in greater awareness of proper action.

Once a person has descended through enough forms to *work off* their past deeds and choices, they again may have the chance to rise through the life forms and arrive at another human lifetime. Each successive life form offers positive learning experiences to allow for another chance to evolve ones awareness. The living being may have another opportunity to become embodied into a conscious human body. This gives the living being another *rare* shot at developing greater awareness and the ability to redevelop our transcendental *actual consciousness.* Should the living being begin the path towards transcendental awareness while in a human form and not achieve complete success, they may take on another human form in order to continue that path. Should they reject the path towards greater consciousness, their journey may again descend into the lower species.

This descent and evolution through gross physical forms can be extremely difficult for the living being—enduring many frightful experiences through many lifetimes. Unmistakably, the path through the lower species of life is a *hellish* existence, and the loop can involve thousands of lifetimes enduring physical discomfort, varying degrees of distress and constant threats from other organisms. In the better case, evolving into another human form will give the living being another shot at transcendental awareness. This is not a matter to take lightly though. Our advice is to seek and try to complete transcendental awareness in this lifetime, while the opportunity is available.

'Natural selection' has a greater meaning.

It is this gradual descent or evolution of the living being through the life forms that creates the physical similarities between one species and another. As the living being gradually evolves or devolves through the species, each physical form displays a similarity to the previous physical form the living being inhabited. As Darwin saw this similarity between species, he could not help but think that there was some evolutionary system and some kind of *natural selection* going on. It is certainly true that we are in essence selecting our next physical forms by our current choices. In fact, our *natural selection* process is so *natural* it might be compared with the changing of ones clothes:

> *Before changing clothes, one must decide what kinds of clothes are needed for the day. Consideration of the desired tasks to accomplish will determine which clothes will be chosen, to the limit of ones wardrobe. A business meeting in a corporate environment might require a grey suit with a standard tie or a conservative dress. A casual day at work may require jeans and a Hawaiian shirt. If one is working in the garden, overalls and a t-shirt might suffice. Ultimately, the decision is based upon what is needed to accomplish that day, combined with how one wants to appear.*
>
> *Once a decision is made, ones current clothes are quickly changed, but through several steps. The shirt might come off first, leaving the undershirt, pants and socks. Once the undershirt is taken off, the new shirt can be put on. Then the old pants and underwear will have to come off before new pants can be put on. Eventually one will make the complete change, but a number of graduated steps will be required.*

In this same way, we step through physical changes in a graduated way. Each new form is similar to the previous form—making stepped changes in features and mannerisms. These changes all take place through design, but are ultimately determined by the conscious decisions we make while in forms of greater awareness.

Some accidental evolutionists argue that one of the faults of the *'intelligent design'* theory is that there seem to be many imperfections and shortcomings among the specimens of the creation. They report of theoretical *ugliness* evident in the various physical forms. *What intelligence would have designed these flaws?* they challenge. This is not a problem for the *evolution of the living* process because the living being's *own* consciousness creates the flaws in our physical forms. Imperfect physical forms merely reflect the imperfections of the living being's misidentified and erroneous quests for happiness. We might say our *lack of intelligence* created these flaws.

Instinct illustrates prior existence.

For centuries, science has been trying to figure out why animals and even humans are born with instinctive behavior. Instinctively we trust our family members. Instinctively we fear outsiders. Instinctively we search for food and struggle to survive.

The fact is all creatures have instinct because all living organisms are driven by an experienced living being. This living being *has lived prior to being born into that physical body.* Because we existed prior to being born into our current body, we have accumulated various survival tactics learned from previous lifetimes. These survival tactics will not necessarily be consciously remembered by the physical mind, but they will nevertheless enable us to instinctively coordinate basic activities of survival. These are combined with tools taught by current parents, siblings and peers, along with the inner guidance system transmitted directly from the Supreme Being.

Since our current physical forms were developed based upon our past lifetimes, our current physical forms are synchronized perfectly to reflect our incremental growth or descent. The family we are born into, the beings surrounding us and the environment we're embodied into all flow naturally from the point we left off in the previous embodiment. This is why family and friends may seem so familiar to us: We tend to rejoin the living beings we have become attached to. This is why we should be wisely choose our attachments and relationships in this world. Should we become attached to a living being who is heading downward into the species, we may follow them.

There is a purpose for the evolution of the living.

What is the purpose of this evolution of the living being? Why are our tendencies and past deeds determining the particular type of bodies we manifest? Why do we struggle to survive through so many lifetimes?

As to the root cause of the *desire to survive:* Because the living being is transcendental and thus ageless, yet trapped inside a physical body, the struggle for survival is a basic response to misidentification. As the eternal living being mistakenly identifies with the physical shell, the illusion that physical death will threaten our existence is reinforced. We living beings, outside our natural element and stuck inside a temporary body can easily mistakenly identify ourselves with the body through the subtle facility of the false ego.

The process of the *evolution of the living* points to the existence of an ultimate purpose for our existence. What are we evolving for or towards?

Often people will debate the concept of *predestination.* Many propose that our destinies are predetermined and our paths are already chosen. It is true that our current situation has been determined by the activities and choices we have made in the past. However, our future path will be determined by our current choices. These we have control over. We have the ultimate ability to determine our futures. Our future is thus in our hands. While there is a design interwoven into existence that enables specific choices to have particular results, we can *customize* those results with customized choices. This is because, ultimately, the purpose of the *evolution of the living* is to teach us. If there was no flexibility built in to the design, the only lesson we would learn is that we were trapped.

Evolution of the living is a learning process.

As we journey through these lifetimes, we come to understand which choices yield positive results, and which choices yield negative ones. This is called *learning.* As we become more aware of the fact that we are learning, our awareness of *what we are learning* can increase:

> *During the first few years of school, children are being taught things without a realization of what they are being taught. In kindergarten, they may play games and have story-reading time, all in an effort to teach certain skills. As those skills increase, it becomes apparent to us that they must learn a particular skill such as* reading. *Only later will the child realize that the reason they learned to read was in order to function within society as well as be able to learn more. As the child graduates through the various grades, they gradually learn that the various lessons being taught in school are preparing them for surviving in the real world: either allowing them to get a college degree, or being able to qualify for a job so that they can eat. Should they not learn these lessons early, they may take school for granted, and only learn much later—often* too late*—that school was meant to help them.*

The living being also moves through various stages of learning through various lifetimes, hopefully graduating to a point where we realize what we are being taught and why.

As we have all experienced, a great process of learning is direct experience, but the wisest way of learning is experience combined with learning through the advice of an expert. We can all repeatedly learn through *the school of hard knocks* that something is not good for us. We may not learn exactly *why* that something is not good for us from mere experience though. If we should understand from an expert why something is not good for us, we should be able to graduate through the lesson without experiencing it repeatedly. Our experiences will thus be reinforced with wisdom.

Our learning is ultimately measured by the choices we make. Should we again make bad choices, even though we've had the appropriate experiences and even learned why, then we are required to return to the direct experiences which teach those lessons. Should we learn from those experiences along with wise counsel, and we follow up that learning by making the right choices, we effectively *learn* what the physical dimension is teaching us.

Love is the theme of the evolution of the living.

The Supreme Being has the propensity to exchange love, just as we each have that propensity. If we can accept that the Supreme Being has the propensity to love and exchange loving relationships, then we can understand how this Being would also have the propensity to exchange a loving relationship with each of us. Simply by looking around us we can see that very few living beings who walk this planet within the various physical forms are currently engaged in much of an exchange with the Supreme Being. Since most of us are not currently engaged in such a relationship, and since the Supreme Being has a propensity to exchange such a relationship, we can see how the goal of *evolution of the living* set up by the Supreme Being would be to teach us the *benefits* of exchanging such a relationship with Him. Since a loving relationship requires freedom of choice, such a system of evolution also allows us the option to make our own choices. If we did not have the option to choose, it could no longer be a loving relationship.

> *The object of learning is to regain our original loving relationship with the Supreme Being.*

The Supreme Being has developed a *process* to enable us to grow to a point where we each make a conscious, educated choice concerning our relationship with Him. He wants us to make our own decision as to whether we would like to take part in a relationship with Him or not. Any choice requires not only freedom, but information and knowledge of the options. This is why we first learn that we are learning something. As we gradually learn about our choices, this leads us to *why* we have these choices. Without learning about the choices and why we have them, we have no ability to make conclusively good decisions.

The important question thus becomes *at what point will we learn what we are supposed to learn?* How many times will we have to experience that we are lonely in this world without our Best Friend before we realize it and do something about it?

A relationship of loving service towards the Supreme Being is our actual consciousness. The *evolution of the living* process allows us a range of experiences from which to gradually learn to make an educated choice whether we want to resume that consciousness: Whether we desire to resume our loving relationship with the Supreme Being. Certainly, we can see how the physical forms of most other species do not have the conscious capability to make these kinds of decisions. This is because their actual consciousness is more *covered* than ours are, so their physical shells don't afford them this capacity. Why not? Because these living beings made a *prior* decision to be covered up. They have decided in some previous lifetime when they did have the capacity to choose, to further ignore the existence of the Supreme Person, and instead chose a life focused on eating, sleeping, mating and defending—all of which cover up the existence of our Best Friend by putting themselves as the center. They have chosen a life focused upon self-preservation rather than self-awareness. As a result of these choices, they have *devolved* to more covered physical forms which allow them not to have to consider the Supreme Being's existence. Their physical lives of fear and survival *cover* their actual consciousness. They can ignore their position as subordinate to the Supreme Being by pretending *they* are the center of existence.

One might wonder why we cannot consciously remember all of the various lifetimes we have lived before. Although there have been cases of people remembering their previous lives, and some hypnotized people who have regressed into previous lives, most of us do not recall our previous lives. In fact, most of us cannot even remember many of the events earlier in our current lifetimes, especially the painful ones. We cannot remember the pain of being born. We cannot remember the pains we felt throughout much of our infant life as our bodies were adapting to the stresses of the world. These painful experiences have conveniently been blocked out of our conscious minds. For example, while a physically painful accident during our youth is probably a blur, we can often remember many fun times that occurred before that event. In this way, the *evolution of the living* process has been graciously set up to remove painful experiences from our immediate consciousness. This does not mean they do not still affect us and we did not learn something from them. All of our past activities and experiences affect us in a deep, internal way—influencing our many decisions and directions into the future.

This selective memory process is designed that way for a number of reasons. Imagine how horrible it would be to consciously remember all of the various deaths that were experienced in our different lifetimes. It would be unbearable, and would make living in the current lifetime excruciating. Indeed, not having these conscious memories allows us to approach our current situation from a *new slate,* allowing us to make choices from a position of free will. This *forgetful* mechanism of the physical realm is linked to the false ego, which fools us into thinking that we are these physical bodies and they will last forever. The overall system of forgetfulness and misidentification is designed to enable us to forget painful moments so we can make a few important choices with free will: *do I want to be the master or do I accept the Supreme Being as the Master?*

The bottom line is that we each have the ability to decide whether we want to exchange a relationship with the Supreme Person. Living beings who make the decision not to exchange such a relationship, instead focusing their lives upon self-concerned activities; automatically choose descent into less consciousness. The less conscious physical form allows us the full capability to forget the Supreme Being, whilst a full absorbance into self-concern. This self-absorbing consciousness carries the living being into one less-conscious body after another, continuing our forgetful consciousness. Unfortunately, since we are not connected to Him, we are forced to become connected *to ourselves,* resulting in our having to suffer through the experiences that result from our desires and past deeds.

Once through the learning cycle taught by the results of our covered self-consciousness, the living being may rise back through the different species, with each lifetime affecting a greater sense of awareness and learning. At some point, the living being may again have another chance to live within the human form, and have another chance to make an educated decision between self-enjoyment versus a loving relationship with the Supreme Person.

The Supreme Being does not easily give up on us.

We cannot predict when we might have this *second chance* in a human form. It may take millions of years of bouncing from one species to the next for another shot at the crossroads of a life of higher consciousness.

Despite original teachings to the contrary, many religious organizations at one time or another banned the teachings of the *evolution of the living*. The reason for this is that having a second chance to change can be a problem to organizations striving for membership. Still, we can see direct and indirect references throughout many scriptures supporting the *evolution of the living*.

The bottom line is that we can each make our own decisions about life, its purpose, and whether or not there is a Supreme Person. If anyone could force us, it would be the Supreme Being. Instead, He has created this perfect mechanism to give us each enough information to make an independent choice according to our respective desires. Even during this conscious life, a person can choose to avoid the actual lessons of life and instead focus on the attempted self-enjoyment of money, fame, and sensual pleasure. Or a person can choose to utilize the consciousness afforded by this life to explore transcendental knowledge, thus making a progressive decision regarding His existence.

The beauty in this mechanism is that we are supplied with just enough information to make the decision a difficult one: A decision that demands trust and commitment towards the Supreme Person. He supplies just enough mystery to give each of us the ability to make what appears to be a difficult but wise decision. This can be observed simply by talking to people. Most people are stubbornly confident about their particular speculations regarding the truth. Everyone feels that they have made a difficult but wise decision.

Because accidental evolutionists choose to ignore the evidence of the living being, they insist upon an accidental evolution of physical bodies. This allows them each the ability to ignore the Supreme Being and focus upon their own enjoyment. It does not matter whether or not the accidental evolution theory fits reality, or whether there are holes in the theory. On the other hand, those who choose to focus on the Supreme Being will transcend the *evolution of the living* cycle and go home, back to our actual transcendental home: the place where the Supreme Being resides.

***

Conclusion: *Having rejected the Supreme Being at some point, we wanted to enjoy the He does. So He gave us temporary physical bodies in a temporary physical realm to act out those desires. The physical bodies we are given reflect the status of our covered consciousness: our goals, tendencies, and developed desires, together with the results of our previous activities. After the death of one body, we will take on another physical body that precisely fits our ongoing consciousness. Each living being may embody various types of physical forms, each corresponding with our covered consciousness at the time of death of the previous form. This cycle will continue until we decide to raise our consciousness from self-interest to that of re-establishing our relationship with the Supreme Being.*

6

The Personal Universe

He walked a well-traveled path across a hard land. His back stiff with a heavy load, he trudged behind a fellow worker. He focused on trying to keep his burden balanced. He'd picked up too much again, he thought. His job was to haul food, balancing each load on his back while he wound down the path toward the city. Today's path led him along a flat wall of rock at the edge of a great barren desert. He walked silently in the dim light of the three suns. Year in and year out, he had done this hard labor, delivering food into the city. He was tired now. He was fifty and exhausted from a lifetime of work.

Today's journey was a bit more dangerous it seemed. The earthquakes were relentless. All season long the shaking had taken its toll on his nerves while taking the lives of many of his mates. During the dark cold season, there were typically no earthquakes, but during the light parts of the year, they could be more frequent. The earthquakes and the crushing storms were worse during the season of the three suns. During the third season—the season of the great single sun—the earthquakes and crushing storms were minimal, usually occurring in the early and late part of these seasons. The dark season was by far the safest for food hauling. He looked forward to the next dark season. He was less exhausted during the dark season.

As the three-sun season wore on, he was getting increasingly anxious. The quakes and storms were getting worse. As he walked this day suddenly an earthquake struck, followed quickly by a crushing storm. Several of his fellow workers were flattened. Dozens of his mates were also crushed, and everyone scattered off the trail, scrambling for their lives. Just as he turned to find an alternate trail, he saw a large storm surge crush about thirty of his fellow workers ahead of him. Now he was really scared. He'd never been this close to mass death before. As he was trying to figure out which way to go, he saw yet another group of fellow workers suddenly be crushed behind him. Uh oh, *he thought.* I hope the queen is going to be alright.

In the aftermath of this massive catastrophe, for a few minutes it seemed like things had calmed down. He had long dropped his load by then, and was anxiously returning to the trailhead to dash for the safety of the underground city. On his way, he checked a few of his crushed mates to see if he could help anyone. Nope—sadly they were all dead, outside of one who was being carried back to the city by a fellow worker. As he nervously scrambled for the path, a wall of liquid rushed over the ground and drenched him. It had a sickening smell. The warmth quickly turned to burning. The pain was excruciating. He writhed in agony as he began to feel numb. This is it, *he thought, as he twitched his antennae one last time, thinking* I hope the queen is alright.

What is the universe made of?

Many modern scientists seem to assume we are alone in the universe, surrounded by empty space and a few rocks still moving because of the big bang billions of years ago. They assume life forms have to be visible to our tiny eyes and our tiny instruments to be considered alive. These scientists seemingly assume life forms must live in the same dimension we do and exist at the same scope and breadth we do. They assume the lights that shine from the sun and the stars are accidental fires burning on lifeless rocks. They assume we are surrounded by empty, lifeless matter, randomly and accidentally producing the heat and energy to light and energize our world. Just as an ant may perceive indoor lights as multiple suns, people walking across the floor to be earthquakes, and people squashing them to be storms, modern science assumes everything around us to be impersonal forces of nature.

Over the past 400 years, physicists and other modern scientists have vigorously postulated and theorized about the makeup of the universe. As a result, a variety of different theories has been put forth. This branch of science is typically referred to as *theoretical physics.* It is called *theoretical* because there is no evidence or support for these theories. They are complete speculations, and the only practical application seems to be connecting each theory together to see if they fit somehow. Over the last century, theoretical physics has seemingly become a heyday for theoretical physicists wishing to toss their own speculations into the ring. As a result, there have been numerous theories proposed, with a handful of them garnishing enough attention to be published in science journals and textbooks.

The particle assumption

These various theories, each a speculative guess in an attempt to describe the substance of the universe, have gotten increasingly abstract and philosophical over recent years. With every new theory has come increasing complexity, creating more uncertainty. If one looks broadly at the theories and discoveries put forth over the last four hundred years, science is increasingly fixated with discovering the *next smallest* piece of matter: *"If we could just understand the next smallest unit, then we'll figure out what the universe was made of,"* physicists seem to be persistently telling us. This *'just around the corner'* progression has led modern physics from one theory and possible discovery to the next: From atomic particles to subatomic particles; from photons and gravitons to quarks. With every new theory of a smaller piece of matter, theoretical physics repeats its claim of being close to finally solving the mysteries of the universe.

Dalton's atomic theory, put forth by John Dalton in the early nineteenth century, stated that the tiniest indivisible pieces of matter must be *atoms,* and matter must be made up of these indivisible units. Furthermore, he suggested, each indivisible type of atom must be unique in its weight and numbered components. The later being more specifically its atomic number. The atomic number applied to each element was fairly arbitrary, and whole numbers were used for simplicity. The number selected was based somewhat upon a particular element's ability to marry other atoms to form the next level of matter, molecules. This new approach envisioned molecular compounds as combined atoms, brought together by an ability to share in common sub-atomic particles.

While Isaac Newton also theorized the atom centuries before, Dalton's theories—with his notions of the sub-atomic *electron particles*—brought a mathematical base to the aspect of these minute structures. In other words, how many electronic particles did each element theoretically have in its unsharing "ionic" state?

All of this was quite abstract until in 1897 English scientist Sir Joseph Thomson—who won the 1906 Nobel Prize for Physics—passed cathode rays through a slit within a vacuum tube. Using magnets, Thomson was able to bend the rays. This indicated to Sir Thomson that these rays must be particles since the rays could be bent. Sir Thomson went on to propose that Dalton's atom must be made up of these electrons—comparing them to plums sitting in a plum pudding. This theory became the *plum pudding model,* which was eventually abandoned in favor of Japanese physicist Dr. Hantaro Nagaoka's version, often referred to as the *Saturnian model,* and finally the *Bohr model* named for the work of Niels Bohr. This version eventually mutated to the *Bohr-Rutherford model,* which included Ernest Rutherford's concept of electrons orbiting the nucleus in classical orbital motion.

It must be clarified that this did not mean anyone had exactly seen an atom. For this reason, science is still debating: What is an atom? Newtonian physics models described atoms much like little solar systems with spinning particles circling a central nucleus. Eventually physicists like Bohr, Einstein, and Rutherford began to see the limitation of this 'billiard ball' view to consider another aspect about the atomic world: Atoms appeared to act more like waves than particles.

At the turn of the twentieth century, the realities of electrical oscillation began to unfold. A few physicists considered correlating atomic theory with the same energies observed in alternating currents and sunlight. Much of this was driven by tendency of atoms to be affected by radiation, and the tendency of radiation waves to be affected by magnets. Combining observations with calculations, Dr. Max Planck in 1900 theorized that the smallest unit of energy that could be absorbed or emitted at the atomic level was *characteristic* of light emission. To capture this idea of a unit of light emission, Planck called the fundamental unit of the wave-like particle as a *quantum.* From that moment, the connection between wave mechanics and the electron orbit of the atom was inescapable.

As new instruments of measurement developed based on these assumptions, theoretical physicists accumulated a complete array of characteristics linking sub-atomic activity with the elements of wave mechanics. While experiences with magnetism, polarity, and conductivity awoke nineteenth century physicists to the possibility of a tie between electricity and magnetism, radiation bombardment awoke twentieth century physicists to *electromagnetic oscillation.* As physicists like Bohr, Einstein and de Broglie began to consider sub-atomic units with waveform properties, the perception of particle electrons and protons became increasingly theoretical. The location of this theoretical sometime-particle-sometimes-wave soon was imagined as a range or even cloud rather than a specific spot. The orbit of the electron began to take on the form of a wide band of probable locations rather than the skinny circular orbit line of the Bohr-Rutherford model. Things were getting a bit dicey in the sub-atomic realm.

Science is guessing what the universe is made of.

The wave concept of light was first advanced by Thomas Young in the late eighteenth century. Young observed that if constant light passed through a slot within a barrier, it would expand outward from the slot. If the same light were shone through two slots, the resulting slot expansions would create both light areas and dark areas. As Young observed it, the light acted in the same way water does. Two different concentric waves interacted when light was shone through the two slots. As parts of the wave *interfered destructively,* dark areas were formed. The other parts of the two waves *interfered constructively,* forming brighter areas.

Tomson's work with the cathode ray brought these same relationships to bear with atomic matter. The problem is that like light beams of Young's test, these waves also acted as particles might by moving through one slit just as they moved through two slits. The incongruity of this was that for some reason, sub-atomic matter acts both like waves and particles.

After seemingly bombarding atoms with rays such as the cathode ray, Max Plank and Niels Bohr proposed that atoms emitted energy as electrons changed energy levels. They could also be influenced to change energy levels upon receiving energy in the form of light waves or other radiation. In other words, it seemed these tiny *somethings* were not working quite like particles circling like planets after all—they acted more like light and electricity.

Meanwhile Einstein's theories gave way to light acting in some ways like particles. This gave way to the *photon* theory, described light as *packets* of somethings.

In an attempt to unify these two vastly-different versions of matter, theoretical physicists concluded that these *wave-particle somethings* rotating around the nucleus of an atom behave like particles sometimes and waves at other times. The wave-particle theory gave birth to an even stranger proposal: that these *wave-particle things* were sometimes in more than one location at the same time. This *inconceivability* led to a new realm of physics which included *'quantum mechanics'* to try to explain our inability to comprehend the world around us. Along with the unlikely story of a world where sub-atomic particles are waves sometimes and particles other times, theoretical physicists have further tried to explain the unexplainable by saying these sub-atomic *somethings* are not *things* at all, but rather are *tendencies.*

'No, the next particle solves the mystery.'

This incongruous definition of the electron and the rest of matter including light did not prevent the continued quest for the next new particle. Various new theoretical particles were invented to be named, adding to the distortion between particles and waves. The nucleus was to contain a bevy of *neutrons.* To provide balance for electricity equations, the nucleus also was purported to contain *positrons.* Furthermore, another smaller particle, the *neutrino,* became identified as similar to an electron in that it orbited the atom, but did not carry electrical charge. The curious question about this foray into various particles is that not only had no one seen a particle, but there was little evidence that any particles exist. The preponderance of information pointed to matter consisting of waves.

Nonetheless, theoretical physics continued its search for the *next* particle. If we use theoretical physics history as our guide, locating such a particle will only point to yet *another* particle to discover:

Like a rope with no end, each pull finds only more rope to pull.

One might remember that not so long ago the *'cracking'* of the *'genetic code,'* was hailed as the key to understanding the universe. Unfortunately *'cracking the code'* seems to have only created more questions. Modern scientists have yet to figure out just how DNA and RNA become so extensively coded, and how it maintains such precision and holography within the context of a living organism.

As these theoretical scientists look closer into the nature of the universe, they seem to discover only further complexity. As they look deeper into the universe with increasingly technical instruments, the universe looks increasingly difficult to understand. This is because humans do not have the physical capability or the scope to determine the functional nature of the physical universe. The various speculative theories to explain characteristics of matter are just as shortsighted as our ability to see it physically. Postulations of electromagnetism, gravity, strings, membranes, waves, photons, quantum mechanics, parallel universes and others abound as a result. Theoretical physicists seem to think if we can just figure out a few *sections* of the universe, at some point we'll be able to join the sections together like a puzzle and get the bigger picture:

> *Several blind men analyze an elephant: One feels the tail and says "it's a snake," while another feels the ears and says "it's a blanket." Another feels the legs and says "it's a tree."*

Werner Heisenberg illustrated the incongruity of the situation when he showed the mathematical impossibility of determining the simultaneous position and momentum of a sub-atomic particle. This famous proposition was termed the *'uncertainty principle.'* The principle was later ascribed to be the situation between all the major quantum numbers—driven by the atom's wavelike and nonparticle-like qualities.

Over the past 25 years, physicists have attempted to combine various speculative theories into *'unified'* theories. An example is the *'wave-particle unification theory,'* and more recently the *'theories of everything.'* These attempts at unifying disconnected theories have resulted in further testaments of *'inconceivability.'* Yet despite these admissions, we find such *unified theories* in science textbooks confidently portrayed. This appears to be related to the unacceptable alternative: refuting previously published speculative theories as new speculations are postulated. Declaring a previous theory wrong could severely damage the credibility of the entire institution of science. It could force the institution to use those three dirty words: *we were wrong.* This would of course leave any new theory subject to increased doubt and if repeated, could ruin any confidence the public has regarding theoretical physics. *Unification* of two or more theories is a much more appealing alternative, even though unifying the theories can also result in the *'inconceivable'* portrayal—as has been attributed to the wave-particle unified theories:

After all, couldn't it be a snake, a tree and a blanket all at the same time?

The real problem here is that both the old and the new theories are speculative and thus *both wrong.*

Still the hunt for the elusive *mystery particle* has gone on. Gluons, prions and other have become the vogue in the ongoing magic particle hunt. Over the past few decades, some theoretical physicists have looked to a supposed mass-emitting particle as the mysterious building block of the universe. This particle, postulated a number of years ago, has been hailed *'the God particle'* because of its supposed ability to lend mass to other particles.

Inconceivable theories limit the abstract.

An inconceivable theory obviously cannot be proved. It also cannot be proven wrong. One might ask why the various theories have been categorized as *science* if they are inconceivable and cannot be proved. Are these theories philosophy or science? This point also has been debated along with the various theories, as the distinction between philosopher and scientist has become blurred. Since physicists do not like to admit they have become philosophers, a mathematical-looking proof or the semblance of an equation is necessary to cloak the theory as science.

As we examine the theories and formulae of *quantum mechanics,* we can see how the pursuit to assign particle or unit attributes to an abstract characteristic can push the limits of the abstract. Not only does the assignment of a *quanta* or unit designation create the illusion of understanding, but it accompanies a need to satisfy further problems with additional theoretical units to fill the gaps.

In the 1960s, a Caltech physicist Dr. Murray Gell-Mann built upon the Planck-Bohr-Rutherford nuclear *quantum* concept and proposed the existence of yet smaller particle contents inside protons and neutrons. Assuming these protons and neutrons were particles, then their activities during collision scattering and separation into parts indicated sub-particles. These tiny sub-parts were labeled quarks. As the plugging of variables indicated some probability for the existence of these theoretical portions, the appointment of characteristics to these particles provided further theoretical abstraction into particulate matter. While these supposed units were admittedly too small and too uncertain to be proven, they nevertheless neatly fit the results of nuclear accelerator collision observations.

The four basic quantum numbers as developed by Erwin Schrödinger, provided the baseline for this uncertain realm: The first is the principal *quantum,* describes sub-atomic elements as having singular qualities. Without first defining an electron (or other sub-atomic particle) as a distinct single unit, no further estimations could be possible. The second quantum number is based upon the orbital qualities of the particle-wave, notably its *angular momentum.* This is also sometimes referred to as the second sub shell quantum. The next basic feature and third quantum number developed was the *magnetic projection of that angular momentum.* This is the magnetic field that theoretically projects from the electron, being perpendicular to its aspect. The final of the four quantum numbers is the *spin* quantum. This spin characteristic theoretically provides the third-dimensional view of the orbital qualities of the wave-particle.

These main four quantum numbers allowed the waveform characteristics of matter to become at least theoretically quantified. The quantum mechanical theory was soon expanded by Gell-Mann and others to present probability parameters for other possible tiny sub-atomic parts: *Quarks, leptons, gluons, bosons,* and *antiquarks* have been added to the bevy of theoretical sub-atomic particle anatomy. These quantum particle portions have been further described with various theoretical characteristics such as *charm, upness, color, downness, strangeness, bottom, hyperchange, top,* and let us not forget *flavor.*

Using linear accelerator observations of particle collisions and subsequent formulae, it was proposed that quarks are thoroughly disconnected from each other, as any particle might. They also apparently contained no charge. This circumstance presented a problem: Since quarks were conceived as indivisible units without charge, then they should be able to separate from the proton quite easily. What was keeping these units apart yet still within the proton?

It was later proposed—following further accelerator collision results—that quarks must be confined within the proton. There must be another force keeping the quarks within the proton and neutron then. This proposed force was called the *strong force:* The force holding the quarks, protons and neutrons together within the nucleus. This strong force had to be mediated, it was thought. A mysterious new quantifying unit was configured for this purpose: The *gluon* was proposed as a mediator or transfer agent for this strong force within the *hadon* (proton or neutron). It was subsequently proposed that quarks could be *colored* (or given these strong charges) by these gluons—themselves colored particles.

The puzzle this presented was a picture where quarks are moving around freely yet contained within the proton. There must therefore be another weaker force keeping these quarks from launching out of the proton they were confined within. This force was labeled the *weak forces.* It was suggested that these weak forces were mediated by the existence of yet another sub-atomic unit, the *boson.* Bosons were assigned to the display of activities such as nuclear decay and neutrino function. Instead of exerting a color like in the case of the gluon, bosons theoretically transfer an effect called flavor to sub-atomic matter.

Through this effort to quantify energetic wave-like behavior using abstract and primarily symbolic unit representation, physicists have successfully constructed an abstract basis for providing measurement for various nuclear activities. Whether these units actually exist as described is besides the issue: The assign units to the abstract.

> *An indigenous man must tell another how tall his house is, but has no way to measure it. He forages a stick from the bushes. He tells the other man the house is twenty-five sticks high.*

Despite not being directly observed, the quantification of virtual objects fit nicely within the theoretical application—describing theoretical and minute forces of nature.

Early on, as quantum mechanics appeared to fit a number of practical circumstances and observations, there was heady disagreement between theoretical physicists on how atomic quantum characteristics were cast and retained between particles, especially as these various particles were observed from different perspectives. One of the most famous arguments set forth by Albert Einstein was the quantum concept that *"God doesn't play dice...."* This comment later was later characterized in a 1935 paper presented by Einstein, Boris Podolsky, and Nathan Rosen as the *"EPF Paradox."* This statement argued that either the theory of quantum mechanics was missing critical elements (termed "local hidden variables") or there was a broader *non-local effect* allowing particles to retain and respond consistently—even at great distances. A non-local effect is some force acting outside of the system.

This argument was embraced by Irish physicist Dr. John Bell in the early 1960s, who attempted to explain the existence of a non-local effect pragmatically. The basic assumption in the now-famous *Bell's Theorem* states that the various predictions of quantum mechanics could not possibly be due to local hidden variables. As this theorem was tested and *Bell's inequalities* became present when quantum mechanics was applied to two particles split off from each other. It turns out these two types of particles would probably end up either neutralizing each other or continuing to reflect each other in some way. This implies that their relationship continued far beyond any type of quantum mechanic. This led to an interpretation that all particles are able to instantaneously exchange information from all others. This is often referred to as the *Bohm Interpretation,* and sometimes as the *seamless whole.*

All of these abstractions are based upon the problem of trying to define something that is outside the realm of perception. There are problems with attempting to image and measure theoretical electron cloud orbitals, for example. They are seemingly held to the nucleus not in circling orbits, but more like standing resonance waves. These resonance waves would relate the wave-like construction of the electron synchronizing with the other electromagnetic fields within and surrounding the atom.

Inconceivable theories cannot be disproved.

The substantiation of quantum physics and the further quark-particle view has been only that quantum physics has successfully described various functions that occur at these small levels. Certainly this would be the case with this sort of abstraction. A theoretical formula can merely be manipulated with new variables to fit the observations:

> *Consider a particular observation that yields five as the result and the only two visible contributing elements each have a value of two. Since 2 + 2 does not equal five, there must be an unknown contributing factor missing with a value of one. Out of necessity a new factor called "variable1" (where v1=1) can be created to complete the equation. Then consider another observation is made, but this time the conditions dictate that twelve is the resulting value, while the*

only observed causative elements in this situation are again the two 2s. At this point either variable1 can be given a range of values of either 1 or 8 (or v1=1, 8) or another variable we can call "variable2" (where v2=7) can be created to fit the observation in addition to v1. Thus the resulting formula can either be 2 + 2 + v1 = result, or 2 + 2 + v1 + v2 = result. In either case, the formula will naturally be proven by the observation because it was conveniently designed to fit the observation or range of observations.

Though an unknown factor can be plugged with a variable with range values rendering the observational result, this tells us very little about the actual nature of the unknown factor. This is precisely the situation in the case of the various particles and quantum variables utilized in theoretical physics. Examples of such variables include the quark; the boson; the gluon; the quantum numbers; as well as the strong and weak forces. Even the basic units created by Dalton, Bohr, Rutherford and others such as electrons, protons, positrons, neutrons, neutrinos, gravitons and photons are all arbitrary particle names to fit unknown variables plugged in to satisfy observation. With the variables created to fit the observation, certainly the formulae using these variables will be functional. This hardly means we know any more about what those variables are, however.

'Theories of everything' assume nothing.

Even with all of this quantification of the abstract, a constant dilemma has seemingly plagued theoretical physicists. On one hand, the theories regarding gravitational forces and relativity worked when larger elements such as planets and solar systems were observed. On the other hand, theoretical forces related to keeping atoms together—such as the *'electromagnetic'* forces keeping electrons spinning around the nucleus, the *'small'* nuclear forces keeping protons and neutrons together, and the *'weak'* nuclear forces that convert neutrons to protons—are considered very different from gravitational forces. As a result, electromagnetic forces and gravitation forces have not been able to be tied together or *unified.* This problem has haunted theoretical physicists for many decades. Why such a quest to unify? Beyond not wanting a various *erroneous* theories floating around, a common vision pervades from deep within every scientist and every living being: that *underlying all things is one basic principle—one Truth.*

In an attempt to somehow unify and explain not only the *inconceivable* unified wave-particle view of reality, but the dilemma created by the lack of unification among the electromagnetic/nuclear forces and the gravitational forces, a number of unification theories have been postulated over the past few decades by theoretical physicists. These new theories are often captured under the hopeful goal of arriving at the highly esteemed *'theory of everything.'*

One theory speculated by an astrophysicist a few decades ago has been called the *'zero point theory.'* The *'zero point theory'* refers not to the actual particle/waves that supposedly make up the universe, but the *space* between and around these particle/waves. As the theory goes, within the space between the wave/particles, is a *'field'* having electromagnetic and wave-propulsion characteristics. This field would supposedly connect all particles in the universe together within the same medium. It has been compared to a sea of water, connecting waves together as they move through the medium of the water.

Numerous other theories have also been proposed. Several of these have been grouped together as the *'string theories.'* These theories variously propose that matter is made of connected, vibrating 'strings.' (Some have presented these as hoops.) While these 'strings' supposedly connect everything together, their vibrations are supposed to produce the various activities of nature. Most of the *'string theories'* proposed the existence of not just three or four dimensions, but not more or less than either ten or eleven dimensions. Note that a number of string theories were floated, and no less than *five* different string theories gained prominent attention within the scientific community. These string theories may have had similarities, yet they were nonetheless rigorously debated on details such as whether there were ten or eleven dimensions. These debates between theoretical physicists embarrassingly ensued for several years, until a compromise theory was settled upon.

This compromise theory was called the *'M theory,'* or the *'membrane theory.'* This theory, related to the *'zero point theory',* said that matter is made up of numerous *membranes*. After some additional debate, theoretical physicists agreed that the revised *'M theory'* also included eleven dimensions. Today this *'M theory'* is theoretical physics' most fashionable and published theory on the make up and origin of the universe. This theory has also promoted speculation that instead of there being just this one universe, there are innumerable universes, including some parallel to ours, existing simultaneously. Things have gotten so abstract that one theoretical physicist is now attempting to create a new universe in his university lab.

Non-life pervades these theories.

Not only are these various speculations of the universe theoretical and uncertain, but they paint a picture of a universe with no living substance. When consideration is given to the ramifications of wave-particle theories, quantum mechanics, string theories and membrane theories, it becomes apparent that what is being postulated is a world of lifeless particles, waves, radiation, membranes, or other *stuff,* connecting and bouncing off each other without reason or purpose. While our eyes may paint us an illusion of a world full of solid objects, physicists paint a picture of random energies that accidentally developed rules of engagement and precise functionality. The bottom line is that neither the solid objects our eyes see, nor the lifeless theories the physicists give us are the actual reality of what our universe is made of.

An example is how we perceive our planet. Most of us consider planets to be dumb rocks rotating around another burning rock.

The earth as a living being has pervaded the ancient sciences in almost every early society, including early cultures of ancient China, India, Japan, Egypt, Greece, Rome, Mayan, Polynesia, and many other indigenous peoples around the world. The idea of consciousness within a larger level of existence made sense to these early peoples because they were tuned into the natural world. They lived intimately with the natural elements and saw them exhibiting motion implying consciousness. They also observed the limited scope of lower species and logically assumed their own limitations. Aristotle said in 354: *"The earth is an organism that is born, lives and dies. Its convulsions, earthquakes and volcanoes are bouts of fever accompanied by gasping and spasms…."*

In the last millennium, we find the Scottish geologist James Hutton—considered the father of the science of geology—saw the earth as an ancient evolutionary creature. However, as the dark clouds of the industrial age came upon civilization, the concept of larger consciousness among the universe slowly died.

In the 1970s, the concept of a living earth was revitalized by James Lovelock in a number of well-received scientific papers and an eventual book entitled *Gaia: A New Look at Life on Earth.* Lovelock's published exploration of this concept illustrated the earth's many systems of self-regulation and circulation among the nutrients of the oceans, soils, mountains, and atmosphere. He termed this nature *geophysiology.* Lovelock illustrated the earth as being a complex living organism.

Dr. Lovelock pointed to a number of pieces of evidence to support this theory. He pointed to the fact that although the sun's energy has increased by at least a quarter over billions of years, the planet's surface has maintained a relatively constant temperature—exhibiting homeostasis. Lovelock explained that although mineralization from rivers and other land sources should have increased the ocean's salinity, the ocean's salt content has remained a little over three percent for billions of years—long a mystery to ocean researchers. Another point he cites is the ability of the earth to maintain a steady mixture of gas in its atmosphere despite various reactive elements around the planet, such as methane—which should be combustible with oxygen. Lovelock extensively cited the various regulatory loops the earth maintains in its recycling of carbon dioxide, calcium carbonate and so many other constituents—activities again illustrating the case for the earth as a living organism (Lovelock, 1988).

While we spend billions of dollars endeavoring to other planets in search of life, we have overlooked the most obvious living organism—the earth itself. Showing every sign of a life form including growth, digestion, reaction, survival response and response-stimulus reactivity, there is every reason to believe the earth is a living organism, only living on a much larger scale than we do. Perhaps the situation is not much different than that of a ant walking across the floor of our kitchen. The ant simply does not have the scope to understand the presence of humans walking in an out of the kitchen, turning on lights and squashing entire groups with one stop. The ant's sense perception cannot perceive in that larger realm. Its eyes are simply too limited. Proud of our tiny brains and "advanced" culture, humans may well be missing the bigger picture much like the ant in our kitchen. While we observe thousands of species of simpler living organisms not having the scope to perceive even our existence let alone the larger environment we see; why should we assume that only *our* scope and perception gets the real picture?

Transmission broadcasting is a natural occurrence.

Broadcasting internet, television, and radio may seem fantastically technical, but it is nothing new to nature. All living entities code, transmit and receive signals. Dolphins and orcas for example, can not only code and transmit, but they can utilize their signals to obtain three-dimensional pictures of the objects they send their sonar to analyze. This allows them the ability to analyze the object's shape and movement from very long distances. Recent research has indicated that dolphins and orcas may also have the ability to sense even the feelings and emotions of other animals during these complex transmissions. Even ants communicate through a complex coding system by touching each other's antennae with certain signals. Other animals can broadcast their various reports over many miles, reporting not only their territories, but also the state of affairs within their domain. For example when one dog is faced with a threatening situation, he can broadcast that situation out to other dogs in that area, who can in turn broadcast it out to other regions. Theoretically, a large area and population of dogs can know about one single dangerous situation through these relayed communication transmissions.

The technology associated with broadcasting and receiving electronic frequencies is an extension of the same process our bodies use to interpret sensory input. The ears for example, are equipped with a converting mechanism in the form of the bones of the ear and the cochlear hair, which translate frequencies traveling through space into nervous impulses. These impulses are converted to messages specific cells in the brain connect to. The brain cells can then translate the signals into representations of sounds the person's mind is trained to convert.

The discovery and utilization of electromagnetic frequencies has seemingly enabled humans to successfully communicate sounds and images with accuracy over long distances. The technology has enabled pictures and sounds converted to electronic code to be broadcast to a receiver from distant transmitters, for example. Once received, the code is converted back to sound or pictures by the radio or television unit. At first glace this may seem incredibly technical. In reality, these transmissions are part of our natural world. From early experiments of inventors using crude wiring and vibration transmission, humans have been able to build upon a natural technology through trial and error. Our speculations on how this technology works have been adjunctive rather than necessary for its use. In fact, theoretical physicists are still debating over exactly *how* some of these technologies work.

Electronic transmission can be compared to the tapping of Morse code onto a pipe, allowing another the ability to translate the taps into the intended communication. As long as each party agrees on how the code is to be translated, the taps can be used for extensive communication. A television set is such a converter, translating electronic *taps* coded and transmitted from distant broadcasting stations into sounds and pictures. As long as the receiver is set up with the code used in the broadcast signal, it can convert the signal into the right image and sound instructions.

Hearing takes place, as all transmissions do, through the reception of vibrational frequencies. Our world is pulsing with vibrations. We can easily assemble various facilities to generate and receive vibrations. Tuning forks, musical instruments, and electronic instruments all serve to receive and convert energy to various frequencies. These technologies are no more complex than tapping our feet or snapping our fingers. They are simply mechanisms of capturing and manipulating vibration.

All matter is pulses with rhythmic transmission.

Light, sound, tactile vibration and all other sensations are merely the reception of vibrations moving through matter just as waves move through water. Vibrations are pulsing throughout the physical world, connecting everything together in much the same way that communications connect people.

Every chemical element and every molecular combination emits a unique frequency. These signature frequencies translate to each element giving off a unique visual experience, which is why gold appears shiny yellowish and silver appears shiny whitish. Specific wavelength measurements have been made possible over recent years through the use of various instruments. Gas chromatography and mass spectroscopy are methods typically used by chemists to identify different compounds, for example. This is because these instruments are sensitive to the particular frequencies that are given off by chemicals. Over years of looking at the frequency emissions of various compounds, chemists have cataloged frequency levels with particular compounds, allowing chemicals to be identified by their frequencies. This is all possible because each type of molecule emits a precise and measurable signature frequency.

Because mass and density of physical matter relate to the frequencies different compounds vibrate at, what we perceive as solid permanent objects are rather transitory vibrations that trigger those perceptions upon our holographic mind. Meanwhile observations have indicated that while matter vibrating at slower frequencies relates to more gross physical matter, matter vibrating at faster speeds relates to the more subtle layers.

Signature frequencies can also be seen across great distances. For this reason, we have been able to identify a number of different types of elements existing in space and on other planets. Of course the accuracy of these measurements is limited to the scope of the equipment and our perception capabilities, but these observations nevertheless illustrate how precise vibrational waves pulse throughout the universe.

Over the past few years, astronomers at large array radio telescopes have been tracking the existence of persistent intergalactic vibrational pulses. One of the most puzzling is the *gamma ray burst*, a consistent signature vibration discovered over the past few years. The cyclical yet persistent gamma ray vibrations are puzzling to modern scientists because they stream through the universe from the most remote regions of space, yet they maintain consistent pulse strength throughout that range. Cosmologists have difficulty with these gamma ray bursts because their extreme energy spikes do not seem to be related to a known *physical mass.* This point is critical to these scientists because the famous postulation of $E=mc^2$—relating energy to mass and the speed of light—would be contradicted should there be no physical mass related to these intergalactic vibrations. As a result, cosmologists cannot explain these tremendous vibrational energies pulsing through the cosmos, opening the door to various speculations about their origin. Regardless of these speculations, the fact remains that gamma ray bursts are persistent vibrational pulses occurring on a macrocosmic universal level, just as our heartbeat, brainwaves, and nerve firings are vibrational pulses intelligently connecting different parts of our body.

Cells emit signature waveforms.

In the 1920s, Russian scientist Alexander Gurwitsch picked up a weak photoemission from living tissue. The emissions appeared stronger during cell division (or *mitosis*), so he termed these UV-range wavelength rhythms *mitogenetic rays.* This presence of living radiation among dividing cells was confirmed shortly thereafter by some German researchers but their conclusions became overshadowed by skeptics. Ongoing biochemical experiments continued to confirm a link between cellular division and radiation at various wavelengths. Why was radiation so intimately involved with cell growth and division?

The topic did not gain much additional research attention until after World War II. European research teams from Italy, Germany and Britain independently worked on the living photon research. Each confirmed picking up rhythmic frequencies from living cells, which they gave several different names, including *low-level luminescence ultraweak chemiluminescence.* The prevailing opinion of these was the radiation originated from oxidation from free radicals.

In the early 1970s, German researcher Dr. Fritz-Albert Popp was engaged in cancer cell research at the University of Marburg. In one particular trial, he discovered weak emissions coming from both living cells and multiplying tumor cells at wavelengths of 260-800 nanometers (Popp 2003). Fascinated and after confirming this phenomenon over repeated assays, Dr. Popp focused his research on these emissions for many years thereafter. He published many scientific papers and wrote a number of books on the topic. He called these weak rhythmic emissions *biophotons* because of their resemblance to the properties of light radiation. As for cancer cells, Dr. Popp was able to correlate greater emission levels in expanded cancer cell growth and lower emissions during slower or no growth. His tests also indicated anti-carcinogenic remedies had the effect of lowering emission levels, indicating reduced tumor growth (Popp 1976; Popp and Chang 2002).

Dr. Popp, Dr. Chang and fellow researchers (1976; 1997; 2000) found particular frequencies and waveforms among healthy and diseased cells: Cancerous cells emitted different frequencies than healthy cells. He found cells responded to specific frequencies of light by repairing themselves. Especially productive were the emissions from other cells. There appeared to be a low-level communication occurring between cells. Every cell of our body apparently emits specific waveforms, and each living organism emits unique waveforms. Just as everyone has a unique fingerprint, this research showed that every living organism also emits unique rhythmic frequencies (Popp and Chang 2000). This use of identification revealed methods to create cellular *fingerprints,* using the signature frequencies and specific amplitudes to differentiate one from another. This concept also correlates with the differentiated DNA sequencing among cells as revealed by a number of researchers over the years such as O'Brien *et al.* 1980 and Thacker *et al.* 1988.

Research led by Professor Franco Musumeci at the Institute of Physics of Catania University in the early 1990s confirmed the existence of these weak emissions. Professor Musumeci studied cancer tissue systems and confirmed the existence of these ultraweak rhythms among growing tumor lines (Grasso *et al.* 1991).

He and his associates (Grasso *et al.* 1992) also compared normal tissues with cancer tissues, confirming consistent variances between the two. In 1994, Professor Musumeci and his associates analyzed food for biophoton emission, finding higher emission levels in freshly picked food than in older storage-bound food. While early-picked tomatoes might have the same red color as ripe-picked tomatoes, they could be distinguished only by a lower biophoton emission—or naturally by tasting (Triglia *et al.* 1998).

Professor Musumeci's research also focused upon yeast growth and soybean germination: Measuring weak photon emissions during germination. In the yeast growth studies, he discovered a consistent increase in photon emission levels with increased yeast growth. His soybean germination studies yielded some very interesting results as well. Both active (vital) soybeans and devitalized soybeans were tested together, and their photon levels were measured over time and against mass increase (growth). Consistently the active germinating seeds displayed higher sustained photon emission levels than the devitalized ones. The devitalized soybean seeds had higher initial emission levels however. These decreased over time, while the vital germinating soybeans had increasing emission levels through germination until they leveled off as they matured (Grasso *et al.* 1991).

Between 1986 and 1991 Dr. Humio Inaba, a professor at the Research Institute of Electrical Communication at Tohoku University led a research project focused on these ultra-weak photon emissions. His research revealed that these photons apparently originated somehow from the biochemical activity within cells and not as a response to external light. Although external radiation has been shown to prompt a delayed response, these ultra-weak emissions were unique. Dr. Inaba's work utilized a single-photon counting device with an amplification system to enable photon-counting images with narrow photon ranges approximating single waveforms. With this system Dr. Inaba's research revealed photon emissions from germinating seeds of soybeans and other plants, spinach chloroplasts, sea urchin eggs, and mammalian nuclei (Inaba 1991).

Waveforms are transmitted between molecules.

The vibrational memory of a substance within water long after the substance's molecules are diluted away has been proven over the last 200 years of homeopathic medicine. Dilution factors of well-beyond one million parts to one—to a level where no molecule of the substance could remain—results in not less response but in a deeper and more lasting healing response. With millions of case histories and hundreds of clinical trials showing the effectiveness of diluted dosing, homeopathy illustrates how vibrational our physical existence really is.

The implications of vibrational memory have been expounded from the research of Jacques Benveniste, M.D. Using the latest technologies, Benveniste initially inadvertently observed that biochemicals apparently have some vibrational effects upon water molecules. This accidental proving of homeopathy—something he had initially not agreed with—led to his further research, concluding that decreasing the dilution factor of a solution to a point where the solution theoretically no longer contained the active chemical resulted in the water retaining an ongoing signature of that chemical.

Within a few years, Benveniste's research group figured out how to record the vibrational frequencies emitted by specific biochemicals as digital sounds. They soon observed that the sounds themselves would have the very same effects the original biochemicals had. For example, physiological reactions from the digital sound recordings of biochemicals such as acetylcholine and histamine were the same as introducing the biochemicals directly.

What quickly became evident—which is also displayed throughout nature—is conscious intent can be transmitted from one biochemical to the next through a subtle vibrational messaging system.

Living organisms transmit waveforms.

When we consider the ramifications of these studies, performed by a credentialed group of scientists and confirmed by others, it reveals how little we really understand about the world around us. Consider for example how the human body can physically respond so quickly to internal and external stimuli: The entire body—all of its organs, blood vessels, and other tissue systems—will almost instantly react to visual or aural perception of something potentially harmful. Through a miraculous network and transmission system, the signal of impending danger is passed instantly to billions of cells and muscle fibers throughout the body, enabling the body to immediately respond to such a threat.

Scientists have observed neurochemicals surging through the bloodstream and synapses during such episodes. As a result of these observations, some scientists have suggested that these neurochemicals are bouncing around like ping-pong balls, occasionally bumping into cell *receptors.* They propose that when a neurochemical happens to touch one of these receptors on a cell membrane, the cell is triggered into action. It is estimated that there is one protein molecule for every 10,000 other molecules in the body's fluids surrounding cells. Furthermore, there are about 200 trillion cells in the human body, and billions if not trillions of them are activated in a fear or stress response. How is it that these neurochemicals can weave through this dense maze of molecules and just happen to bump into all the needed cells with the right receptors instantaneously?

The sheer speed of the body's response to stimuli indicates a deeper energetic mechanism than physical chemical reception. The likelihood that physical molecules ping and pong that rapidly through the body to touch every necessary cell is remote to say the least. As these observations of the vibrational aspects of cells and molecules indicate, the instantaneous response of these cells and their tissues require an advanced intelligent signaling process. This intelligent signaling process allows for a flow of vibrational energy through these neurochemical messengers. They are obviously communicating messages *through* cellular reception as the neuroscientists postulate.

The means for the message delivery is not an accidental *bumping* process. Rather, these messages are transmitted through a complex and intelligent vibrational signaling process. We say intelligent simply because these signals and their messengers are designed and programmed to know exactly where to go and how to get there. The entire process uses technology that is beyond our physical range of perception.

Indeed, when we consider every response and movement within the physical body, we are seeing vibrational frequencies pulse through every physical layer. From the pumping of the heart to the various brain waves and muscle twitches, our physical body is pulsing with vibrational energy. Vibrational messages travel through the nerves, pulse through the blood, and signal through the endocrine system with orchestrated synchronicity.

Waveforms are communication transmissions.

Although we have been utilizing natural vibrational messaging throughout our physical existence with our sense organs, humans have increasingly figured out how to electronically manipulate vibrational energies. Various everyday appliances manipulate vibrational energy, such as the DVD players, sonar toothbrushes, electronic insect and rodent repellents, and so many others. Lasers (**L**ight **A**mplification by **S**timulated **E**mission of **R**adiation) are now being utilized in every hospital and many manufacturing settings. Our CD players utilize tiny lasers. Indeed, there are many other examples of how we manipulate natural vibrational technologies in our every day lives: Microwaves, x-ray equipment, radios, cordless devices, magnetic resonance imaging equipment, televisions, satellites and so many other devices utilize and manipulate natural frequency technology.

Over the past few years we have determined how many of these electronically manipulated frequencies can be damaging to our physical health. Electromagnetic frequency radiation emitted by electrical equipment and power lines has been suspected in a number of types of cancers, fatigue, and other disorders. This research indicates that some frequencies are beneficial to the body while other frequencies are harmful. For example, the radiation from sunlight is a beneficial frequency to most living organisms, while the radiation from uranium isotopes can be very harmful.

Why are some frequencies healthy while some are harmful? This question brings us to the issue of *resonance.* If a particular wave type or wavelength vibrates in such a way that resonates with the natural vibrations occurring within and around our bodies, that vibration would be considered beneficial, or at least neutral. However, should the wave type or frequency of a vibration interfere in a destructive way with our natural vibrations, then those vibrations could well be considered harmful or at least disruptive. We can easily see this phenomenon when we look at ripples or waves on the surface of water:

> *If a pebble is dropped into a still pond, precisely concentric waves will expand outward from the point of contact on the water surface. If a larger rock were then dropped into this concentric wave pattern, larger waves from the rock drop will collide with the waves from the small pebble. This will cause a disfiguring of the concentric design, leaving a host of angled wave collisions with disruptive patterns.*

This illustrates how waves can collide and disrupt other waves that are being vibrated. Some waves will not collide, but will vibrate in sync with the existing waves. This creates resonance. We can hear resonance when we hear musical instruments are tuned to the same key. Furthermore, when waves resonate in certain ways, they can also harmonize. When instruments tuned together play a song together with the same basic tones and tempo, they are said to harmonize. We can also feel harmony when we are together with friends that share positive feelings.

During our physical lives we can easily choose whether to generate harmony or conflict, simply by choosing what words to speak. The vibrations of our vocal cords can either reflect a harmonious consciousness of positive intention or they can reflect a conflicting consciousness based upon self-interest. Therefore, just as visual appearances are transmitted through vibrational waves the eyes translate, our words are vibrational waves the ears translate. In both cases, these vibrations are reflections of our inner self. They reflect the status of the living being within.

The waveforms of our universe are intelligent.

A vibration must have an original generator to begin the pulse. The vibrational pulses surrounding our physical existence reveal a source beyond our speculation abilities. There is a saying that *'truth is stranger than fiction.'* In the case of the natural universe, this is true because our minds cannot conceive the breadth, depth, and origin of all the naturally occurring vibrational energies, let alone their source. Most modern scientists perceive energy as merely a pulsing of dead electrons or ionic charges. However, this does not explain the functioning nature and *intelligent* activities that occur around the physical world and within our physical bodies. These intelligent functions cannot logically be stimulated by random accidents. Rather, intelligent vibrations reflect functional purpose and intention within every atom, every organism, and every universe. Because we can see that the arrangement and structure of matter is organized functionally and particular operationally programmed results are being achieved through vibrational mechanisms, we must recognize that these energies are not dumb. We must recognize the existence of an *intelligent mechanism* initiating these vibrational functions.

Around us and inside of us, the universe *we can see* is teaming with life. Even our physical bodies are inhabited by billions of living organisms. Living organisms called bacteria function as either beneficial or destructive populations within each and every human body. Some living organisms, such as yeasts and fungi, can be beneficial at some populations but destructive at others. Some bacterial colonies, such as probiotics, actually help our bodies digest food, excrete vitamins, and protect our digestive tract from invaders. Just as our bodies are populated with so many living organisms of different species, the earth is also populated with many organisms of different species. Some species are beneficial to the earth and some are destructive. Each of these organisms—bacteria and humans alike—contain consciousness. Each of these organisms has a distinct living being consciously operating from within.

Meanwhile, the earth also performs all the metabolic activities of a living organism. The movements of the earth's crust, the circulation of fluids throughout the various water ducts around the world, the dispelling of carbon dioxide and the converting of energy from one form to another all point to the earth also being the body of a conscious living being outside of our scope. Just as the earth is a living organism outside of the scope of our current perception, there are many other conscious living organisms outside of our scope. Consider even our scope in seeing organisms within our size range:

> *If the earth were a living being could we recognize it? Does the flea riding on the back of a dog have the scope to understand and recognize the existence of the dog?*

Life on other planets is a major concern among many physicists and astronomers. While we focus on beings living within the chemical and molecular structures of our planet's atmosphere, we recognize that each planet has different chemical and molecular atmospheres. We assume life within those atmospheres is visible to the physical bodies of our atmosphere. Is it reasonable to consider that an eyeball made for our atmosphere could see another eyeball made for another atmosphere? Is it reasonable to even assume that the two eyeballs were even of the same structure, scope or size? Put another way: does an ant have the scope to see a human? Will an indoor ant notice that the suns in his sky are actually table lamps we have arranged around the room? Indeed, life outside of this dimension is on another scope and range outside of ours.

A revealing observation is our recent imaging from Mars, indicating that at some point waters such as oceans and rivers flowed on the planet's surface. We assume this because we see topography that looks similar to water formations on planet earth. Is it not possible that Mars currently has a type of liquid flowing around it but our eyes and instruments simply do not have the ability to perceive that molecular structure of liquid? For all we know, the entire planet of Mars could be inhabited by beings we simply do not have the scope to visualize or perceive with the senses and perception tuned and trained to this atmosphere and scope.

Much of life occurs outside of our perception and comprehension. On our own planet, we see whales, birds and other creatures instinctively migrating to specific areas of the planet dependent upon the seasons. They do not consciously make this decision, and are not aware of the entire species migrating. Meanwhile insects will colonize into elaborate nests, and spiders will build elaborate webs with symmetry and skill well beyond their conscious awareness. In all living organisms, the living being inside is aware of only a small range of observations and experiences, while overriding forces move and orchestrate the physical world around us. All of this is outside the scope of each living being for a reason: the same reason we cannot remember past lives and many painful experiences of this lifetime: We are here to learn specific lessons, and experience certain realities based upon our past personal activities.

The totality of living energies around us is outside of our physical range of vision and comprehension. If we try to use our mind to speculate upon the energies of the universe, we will fail due to its multi-dimensional complexity. Real perception can only be developed through a generous dose of humility. If we can realize that our bodies were designed to perceive only a limited range and scope of reality, and were not designed to perceive outside of those, we can begin to accept information coming from informed sources. The physical senses relay only partial reflections from this tiny part of the physical universe we live within. Our memories are selective due to the design of the mind. We simply do not have the tools to comprehend the vastness of life around us. As a result, speculative understanding of the universe will always remain *theoretical.*

Over-confidence is a state of being where we are confident of something that should not bring that level of confidence. This sort of confidence interferes with awareness, because it blocks future opportunities to become aware. Awareness requires being open, while over-confidence promotes a hasty finality of ones own conclusions. Over-confidence in our abilities simply blocks our ability to learn. Furthermore, confidence can easily erode what we do know, as our pride replaces our remembrance and we either shrink or stagnate. A humble position of *"I don't know,"* or *"I was wrong,"* is a safer position because it allows us the opportunity to allow the correct understanding in. The position of *"I already know"* dooms us to our speculative conclusions.

Universal rhythms reflect purposeful organization.

To illustrate this point, we bring as evidence the personal effects the sun has upon our lives. Most of us consider the sun as lifeless burning rock in the distance. Research over the past few decades indicates otherwise. The pulsing cycles of the sun are mostly outside of our range of perception. However, in 1843 German astronomer Samuel Schwabe first documented observations of solar storm activity, noting that these storms appeared to occur repetitively and periodically. Subsequent research by numerous astrophysicists over the years since has brought the understanding that these solar storms occur about 11.1 years. Within this periodic behavior, astronomers also noticed a rhythmic nature within the amplitude of each cycle, and recent advances in the technology have revealed these flaring explosions—also called *sunspots*—move cyclically with respect to their intensity as well. When sunspots over more than a century are graphed, an repetitive "butterfly" shape comes into view.

In the 1920s, Russian scientist Alexander Chizhevsky charted the periodic incidence of various historical upheavals from around the world from 500 BCE to 1922. Amazingly, some 80% coincided with peak sunspot activity. Research from other researchers since Chizhevsky's work confirmed this correlation for events before and after 1922. While magnetism was thought by Chizhevsky to explain this, researchers yet to have a clear understanding of these seemingly *geomagnetic* mechanisms between the sun and human behavior.

Sunspot cycles also appear to affect human behavior and health in other ways. The Cardiology department of Israel's Rabin Medical Center (Stoupel *et al.* 2007) studied the occurrence of acute myocardial infarction with the timing of solar activity. They differentiated the effects of higher cosmic ray activity from periods of higher geomagnetic activity (magnetism from sunspot activity). This study found myocardial infarction rates inversely correlated with monthly solar activity and positively correlated with increased cosmic ray activity. Low geomagnetic activity days and higher cosmic ray days were both separately linked with significantly greater rates of fatalities due to myocardial infarction.

Marasanov and Matveev also reported in 2007 that among lung cancer patients having surgery, complications occurred more significantly during solar storm periods (geomagnetic storms) than for patients having surgery during geomagnetic "quiet" days.

Stoupel *et al.* (2006) also compared levels of immune system strength by measuring IgG, IgM, IgA, lupus anti-coagulant, clotting time, and antibody levels. These levels were correlated with periods and strengths of solar activity as measured by the U.S. National Geophysical Data Center. This research found the immune system biomarker levels significantly decrease with solar geomagnetic activity. This research confirmed research done at Canada's Laurentian University in 2004 (Kinoshameg and Persinger) which concluded that rats cruelly exposed to induced geomagnetic activity had immuno-suppression, and thus higher levels of disease.

Vaquero and Gallego (2007) confirmed the connection between immuno-suppression, outbreaks, and sunspot cycles in research studying pandemic influenza A outbreaks. In 2006, Yeung analyzed pandemic influenza outbreaks from 1700 A.D. to 2000 A.D. Significant correlations existed between outbreak periods and sunspot cycles.

A study published in 2006 by researchers from Kyoto University in Japan (Otsu *et al.*) reported that correlations between sunspot activity, unemployment rates, and suicides existed between 1971 and 2001. Both unemployment and suicides were inversely proportional to sunspot rhythmic periods.

Another study from 2006 (Davis and Lowell) using the birth dates of 237,000 humans found a positive correlation between the births of genetic mental diseases like schizophrenia and bipolar disorder and solar activity. They also found another rhythmic connection between diseases like multiple sclerosis and rheumatoid arthritis. These diseases were more closely correlated with being born in a particular season.

In another study done in Israel (Stoupel *et al.* 2006) 339,252 newborn births over a period of seven years was compared to monthly cosmic ray and solar activity. Significantly more babies were born of both genders during higher cosmic ray periods. Significantly fewer newborns were born during solar activity periods as compared with non-solar activity periods.

The Rabin Medical Center (Stoupel *et al.* 2005) also studied Down syndrome cases among 1,108,449 births together with solar activity. With 1,310 total cases of Down syndrome in the data, a significant inverse relationship between solar activity occurred. In other words, Down syndrome—a genetic defect—occurs more often during the periods between solar activity and less often during solar activity periods.

Researchers at the Universidad de Chile's Clinica Psiquiatrica Universitaria (Ivanovic-Zuvic *et al.*) presented a study in 2005 of hospitalizations of depressive patients and hospitalization of manic patients with solar activity. In this study, depressive hospitalizations correlated with periods of lower solar activity, while manic hospitalizations positively correlated with higher solar activity periods.

A study (Davis and Lowell 2004) at the Augusta Mental Health Institute in Maine established that both ultraviolet radiation from the sun and solar flare cycles were positively related to mental illnesses resulting from DNA damage.

It also appears from research as reported by Davis and Lowell (2004) that human lifespan correlates with solar activity. Chaotic solar cycles (as opposed to typical cycles) appear to cause increased mutation among DNA. Further exploration into lifespan and birthdates around solar cycles found disrupted solar cycles correlating positively with shorter lifespan.

In an Australian study (Berk *et al.* 2006) of suicides between 1968 and 2002, both seasonal and geomagnetic solar storm activity were investigated using 51,845 male and 16,327 female suicides. Suicides among females significantly increased in the autumn concurrent to geomagnetic storm activity. Suicides were lowest during autumn for males and lowest during the summer for females. The average number of suicides for both males and females were the greatest during the spring.

This seasonal and geomagnetic activity rhythm connection with suicide was also confirmed in research on 27,469 Finnish suicide cases between 1979 and 1999 by Partonen *et al.* (2004).

A number of studies have also correlated the moons rhythms with human behavior. Several studies have shown crime to correlate positively with full moons. Thakur and Sharma documented this in the British Medical Journal in 1984, relating the incidence of crimes reported by police stations in three different Indian towns from 1978 to 1982.

Intelligence and purpose requires consciousness.

Energy at the atomic level has been speculated by theoretical physicists to include electromagnetic and nuclear forces, yet there is no understanding of what might cause these forces. What is holding the subatomic particles together within the atom? What is holding atoms together within molecules? What force allows molecules to come together to structure the complex objects within the physical world? Furthermore, physicists are struggling to understand gravitational forces, and what makes these large bodies so magnetic.

We do not subscribe to the speculative process of gathering information and guessing. Instead we accept a descending process to explain the world around us. The various atomic forces which surge through every atom and every molecule, as well as the larger forces of gravity, planetary movement and time stem from an intelligent vibrational energy moving through the universe, not only holding the smallest parts of everything together with precision and intelligent functionality, but orchestrating all of the parts in a rhythm of synchronicity. For the purpose of this discussion, we will call these forces *conscious vibrational energy* or simply *intelligent vibrations.*

This *conscious vibrational energy* pulses through this universe, reflecting through matter while governing matter's movements. From a core intelligent pulse there are many reflective vibrations spread out in various forms, regulating every particular movement, while sustaining and distinguishing every part of the universe. Every physical object and every organism therefore either utilizes or converts these intelligent vibrations, producing an overall synchronization of behavior and structured motion. Furthermore, these energies emanate from a Conscious Living Source, *transcendental* to the physical universe.

Living organisms manifest a superior source of intelligent energy: the living being. Through each living organism, through each cell and every organ, intelligent vibrations pulse from this transcendental living being. We can easily see the reflections of this living being vibrating internally through metabolism, as well as externally through the actions, expressions, and character of the physical body. We cannot physically see this actual living being however, because the living being is transcendental to the physical dimension. The living being dwells within the *actual* dimension of life. This might be compared to an electrical current vibrating through the wires of a house. The electricity is different from the wires and the electrical parts: electricity pulses from an outside source.

Purposeful activities have meaning.

One of the main characteristics of intelligent energy is that it does not flow in a chaotic manner, but in consistent, measurable, and meaningful ways. This consistency is why we can develop complex mathematical formulas that represent the functionality of our mechanical universe. If the universe was composed of random, chaotic energies, then there could be no ability to apply a formula to consistently predict the flow of these energies. If there were no consistency in energy flows within this world, our physical bodies would not survive. If we did not have a constant supply of sun, food, water, and oxygen, our bodies—and all living organisms—would fail.

The universe is designed to allow vibrational energy to flow consistently with measured synchronicity. We can easily observe this by seeing the constant energy emission from the sun: As the sun's energy enters our *earthly system,* organisms utilize it for conversion to subsequent energy, nutrition, and movement. Without this consistent outside source of energy, the physical forms of this planet could not function. The physical forms do not send energy back to the sun: It is not recycled. The sun is providing a consistent flow of energy from an outside source into our earthly system, specific to the various organisms' needs for nourishment.

Some might look at the various characteristics of energy flows through our whole system and say that they are not *always exact,* so they must be chaotic. This suggests that energy is either rigid or random: One or the other. This view, however, is assuming that the universe is *lifeless.* It is assuming that the universe around us is either a machine or a random ball of confusion. Like a top that accidentally began spinning, most accidental scientists think the universe began through chaos and exists through chaos, yet somehow accidentally (and improbably), it created function and design.

The view that these accidental scientists have not considered, however, is the actual case: the universe is vibrating life coming from a *living Source.* A living machine would be differentiated from both chaotic confusion and the rigid machine because the function of a living system would reflect the purpose of a living driver. A living driver has consciousness and within consciousness comes choice and thus flexibility. Precision is one thing, but a system allowing for choice and reaction yet consistent behavior is created through conscious and meaningful programming.

Meaningful systems come from a living source.

What is the source of these vibrational energies which connect every atom in every molecule and every planet in every solar system to function in so many variable, yet precisely structured ways? Classical scientists correctly observed that the energy of an isolated system is conserved, and the only way to change the total energy of any system is through outside interference. If we consider the universe as one gigantic isolated system, then the organizing, structured energy that constantly flows through it logically has a source outside of the universe. Since the energies pulsing through this universe are reflecting *through* matter, and every physical object and organism is either transmitting or converting these vibrational energies, none of this energy could be coming *from, or created by* these physical forms.

Just as the intelligent vibrations of the living being pulsing through the human body are invisible to our physical senses, the conscious vibrational energies driving the universe's functionality are invisible. Consider for a moment how death will result in a disappearance of the intelligent energy of the living being. We cannot see the source for this energy. Notice how we cannot manufacture energy, but we can *draw* energy out of certain substances like natural gas or uranium. All life within the universe draws or utilizes energy from hubs supplied by an outside Source. Consider the analogy of television transmission:

> *To broadcast television, a camera and recorder are first required to convert a scene into digital codes representing the sights and sounds of the scene. These digital codes are converted to transmission signals and broadcast out using special broadcast equipment. On each television is an antenna and receiver, which together take in the transmitted signals. Once received, the television converts the signals into impulses that are fired onto a charged electronic screen, which simulates the scene visually.*
>
> *Both processes (the station and the television) convert, transmit and receive signals using electricity. Electricity is required to power the camera, the recorder, the converter, the transmitter and the television. Electricity is required to boost*

> *the signal enough to be broadcast out. Electricity is required to convert the signal, and electricity is required to power the cathode ray tube on the television.*
>
> *The source for this electricity comes from a power station external to both the television station and the television. Electricity is piped in using power lines connected between the television station, the home, and the power station. Without this outside source of electricity, there could be no signals to transmit or receive.*

In fact, the various signals used in television are actually manipulated electricity. The television digital or analog codes are flows of electricity that have been altered and arranged into series of differently pulsed signals. Hence, these transmissions are *modulating* the standard pulses of electricity vibration to create the appropriate coding.

The body of a living being is also a vehicle for energy transmission and conversion. It can act like a television station as well as a television. Inanimate molecules can absorb and pass energy on through to other inanimate molecules. Living organisms will convert energy into different forms using metabolism. The body housing a living being is a complex structure. Because it is energized by a living being, it has advanced capabilities—all driven ultimately by consciousness. Organisms with higher consciousness have greater complexity of metabolism. Higher consciousness living organisms will perform a greater number of complex energy conversions with a greater variety of byproducts. Human beings, for example, will use metabolism at higher levels, infusing greater intelligence and productivity into their energy output. We can also extend our energies into creating technical machines and other equipment to extend our physical capabilities. In one form or another, all living organisms metabolize and convert conscious vibrational energies into attempted enjoyment.

Living systems flow from a harmonic source.

The various symmetrical patterns and precise structures that make up the physical world vibrate with design and purpose. From the grand movements of the orbital arrangement of planets within the various universes, to the biorhythms that exist within our bodies, the *conscious vibrational energy* provides structure and organized function within a grand scheme. The universe around us is so precise that we can derive elaborate mathematical formulas from its various functions and movements. The ability to derive precise mathematical equations from natural events only illustrates a programmed intentional precision residing within these energies. There are no accidental movements. This is why scientists are continually observing *sine waves* repeating through the various vibrations in the physical world, and this is why we continually see proportions and dimensions like the *golden mean* and the *golden spiral* throughout the structures of the physical world.

Any vibration must have an original source and mechanism to drive the pulse. A voice is vibrated from the vocal cords. A car honk is vibrated from a horn. A heartbeat is vibrated from the heart. If a vibration is continuous, then whatever movement is causing the vibration must be ongoing. If a vibration is not only continuous, but it is rhythmic, producing consistent amplitude and frequency, then the source of the vibration is steady, consistent, and harmonious. Otherwise, the vibration could not be consistently rhythmic. Considering the steady harmonious and rhythmic nature of all the various vibrations of this universe, we can understand that the *Source* of these vibrations is outside the system. We can also understand the *Source* to be tremendously steady, consistent, and harmonic. In fact, *all existence vibrates to the rhythm and harmony of the Greatest Musician.*

Orchestrated harmony requires a conductor.

Over the past few years, modern scientists have claimed to have found the source for the biological clockworks residing within humans and animals. A set of cells called *suprachiasmatic nuclei,* or *'SCN'* cells apparently work together with the pineal gland to orchestrate the timing of the body's biorhythms. This system apparently works to signal the cyclic release of the various hormones and other functions within the body.

The activities of these cells are in fact driven by greater biological clockworks. The biological activities of these cells reflect the rising and the falling of the sun, the moon, and other rhythms synchronizing our bodies with nature. As the timing of the various celestial bodies synchronize our body clock cells, various neurochemicals are secreted to harmonize bodily functions with the rest of the universe. Therefore, these SCN cells are merely *tuning* the body to the larger clockworks of the universe. They are not the clock itself, as purported by some modern biologists. This means—like musical instruments—our bodies are being *tuned* to the rhythms of the Great Harmonic Source:

> *In a symphony orchestra, the violins, flutes, drums, oboes, trombones and many other instruments all play in synchronized harmony, interweaving their various melodies and beats to form a composition or musical performance. In order to play a specific part of the composition, each musician reads from a sheet of music written specifically for that instrument, enabling a coordinated harmony between each instrument and the rest of the orchestra.*

The human body vibrates to a similar type of orchestration: The heart pumps blood at one rhythm while the lungs take in oxygen and dispel carbon dioxide at another rhythm. The brain waves ebb and flow to another rhythm while the four ventricles of the brain pulse cerebral spinal fluid to yet another rhythm. The body's endocrine system releases cortisol, growth hormone, follicle stimulating hormone, insulin, vasopressin, rennin, oxycocin and many other activating hormones—all in rhythmic cycles. All of these various cycles flow and vibrate together in synchronicity, like instruments playing together within a tuned orchestra.

Through tuning devices such as the pineal gland and the SCN cells, the orchestra of our body is actually tuned to the greater vibrations of the Supreme Being. The body's vibrational activities flow in rhythm to His greater vibration because our body is not able to produce its own harmony—it relies upon a source harmony to tune to:

> *The instruments in an orchestra must tune to a standard range of notes and octaves before they can play. Once tuned, the orchestra is prepared to blend their harmonies together. These harmonies must be defined within the composition so that whenever that composition is played, each instrument is tuned to the correct key.*

In the same way, the functions of the living organism are tuned to the master vibrations expanding from the Supreme Being. Once tuned, the living organism plays a choice of songs written by the Master Composer. Should the organism not be tuned very well, it may function in a diseased state.

Ultimately, every living organism has a choice as to how well we want to tune in to the Master Composer and which song we want to vibrate. We have the choice to tune in or tune out of certain harmonics: we can choose to learn from the universe or run our own independent and conflicting courses. In all cases, the conscious vibrational energy will respond with particular arrangements—orchestrated though conscious intent to deliver His harmony back to the living being.

Precision communicates intention.

The various mathematical formulas derived from nature are a one-dimensional indication that conscious vibrational energy flows are intentional. A multi-dimensional perspective of these symmetrical and measured vibrations illustrates their personal and conscious nature. Each of us can see these conscious energy flows in our everyday lives. Although some try to ignore them, those who try to learn from life will see many congruent learning situations evolving throughout our personal lives. Sometimes these lessons occur symbolically and sometimes they occur practically. Sometimes we can learn lessons from the same events both symbolically and practically. Just as dreams can be interpreted on a symbolic level to illustrate lessons we need to learn, we can often see symbolic arrangements in our physical situations, teaching us multiple layers of lessons.

Interconnected functioning of vibrational energies indicate ultimate intent and purpose working within the universe, just as an automobile indicates intent and purpose in its design and manufacture:

> *The various working parts of an automobile all indicate an ultimate purpose. The engine, the wheels, the axles, the trunk, the steering wheel, the seats, the doors, etc., all have their part in contributing to the ultimate working purpose of its operation: allowing a human being to drive from one location to another while carrying family, friends and belongings as needed.*

In the same way, the various features of the universe are all inter-related for a purpose. Events are connected to other events for a particular objective. It is a web of connectivity, in which each part is interconnected in coordinated functionality and interwoven with freedoms to make decisions and choices. This functionality indicates purpose and an overall intention.

Theoretical physics seems to have yet to focus on any intended purpose of this inter-connected energy and structure. The expression *'not distinguishing the forest from the trees'* may be applicable here. Thus far, theoretical physics has considered only one assumption of reality: that the universe stems from an accidental combination of lifeless chemistry, membranes, or whatever. As a result, energy has been related to lifeless factors such as mass, speed, and heat. These formulae only scratch one surface of the energetic intent flowing within the universe. They ignore all the living characteristics of energy flow. We can certainly *relate* various characteristics of energy flow, such as force and mass (F=ma). We can say that force and energy are related in other ways as well, deriving other formulae—some even extremely long and complex. These relationships are only a small part of the multi-dimensional characteristics of these intentional energies however. They are like looking at the scoreboard during a baseball game instead of watching the game. We can certainly get a bunch of statistics about the game but we are not capturing the live events of the game from the scoreboard. In the same way, limited relationships coming from physical observation simply will not *reach* the complete picture of the universe because they do not reach the *consciousness,* which cannot be measured physically:

> *Consider looking down from a low-flying plane or helicopter at the movement of umbrellas in a city during a rainstorm (not realizing they were umbrellas). We would see many circles moving around. Some might move together in the same direction while some move in different directions. From this view we could count how many circles go one way and how many go the other way. This relationship could be expressed as a formula between direction, speed, and time of the circle movement. Once we discovered that the round circles were actually people walking to work holding umbrellas rather than simply round inanimate objects, and we discovered it was rush hour, we would be able to understand from another perspective what was going on. Before we knew they were people with umbrellas, it might seem fantastic that there were relationships between these seemingly random moving circles. Once we knew there was a reason people were walking in one direction or another, the equation would not seem so fantastic. The equation would only reflect the fact that people have to walk to work, and a lot of people work in the city's business district.*

If there is measured force in a particular direction, there must be a source of energy being applied in that direction. Further, if the force was not only measured, but it was in fact directed or customized for a *particular* journey, then this would indicate more than a simple accidental force—it would indicate an intentional force. In order to provide just the right mix of force and direction to exactly steer something to a *specific* conclusion out of a choice of millions of other possible conclusions, there must be intentional forces at work. In other words, a force precisely directing something to a specific conclusion must have intention. Without intention there would be no rational explanation for complexly consistent direction. Without a purpose there is no explanation for customized, consistent functionality. Chaos cannot accidentally result in *consistent* precision and measurement. This would not make sense. Further, the forces required to push things toward constructive and intentional results must have *consciousness* behind them in order to be intentional. Since all of nature can be applied to several layers of measurable precision, from the one-dimensional mathematics to the multi-dimensional grand scheme of migrations, harmonic rhythm, etc., we can understand that the energy pushing these forces must have guidance through *conscious intention*.

The universe pulses from a superior source.

Every atom and molecule; every living organism; and every universe is charged with the personal energy of the Supreme Person. The Supreme Being disburses His Personal Energies through the physical universe through two basic facilities: He expands though reflective energy vibrating His conscious intelligence throughout matter from the universal aspect down through the atomic level. Every atom is charged with His organizing, bonding and directive energies. This means that every molecule, every structure, and every function are all guided by His conscious energies from a microcosmic basis. Nothing moves without His knowledge and sanction: not even one grain of sand.

Each and every universe is pulsing to the energies of the Supreme Being: From the Supreme Being generates the conscious vibrations which pulse through the universe. Through these personal energies, the creative and maintenance processes are initiated. All the galaxies, solar systems, and planets float within the medium of space, all moving to the rhythm of His pulse.

His conscious energies are thus vibrating harmoniously, reflecting throughout every portion of each universe. This is the feature of a perfect hologram: each part reflects the whole. While each physical living organism is charged with a vibrating living being of transcendental identity, the universe is charged with the vibrating Supreme Being. While the transcendental living being is connected through the false ego to the symphony of experience acting upon the physical body, the Transcendental Supreme Being drives the physical universe with an orchestral arrangement of intentional learning experiences. While the living being is tuned to the physical body, the physical body's functions are tuned to the universal body reflected from the Supreme Being. The arrangement is beautiful and precise, as would be expected from a Superior Conscious Being with intelligence and capabilities beyond our comprehension.

Superior intentional transmissions are interactive.

As we have discussed, within every living organism is a unique living being, driving that body according to the living being's desires and consciousness. Within each living organism, alongside of the living being, the Supreme Being transmits a personal reflection of Himself. This transmission would be compared to the broadcasting of a television program from one source into millions of televisions in so many homes (except His transmission is independently interactive). Through this expansion, the Supreme Being observes and provides guidance to each living being in a distinct manner.

Using this facility, the Supreme Being provides direct support and stability to each of us as needed. He personally monitors our progress as we learn lessons He sets up for us. He oversees the functionality of the physical body within the harmonics of the inferior physical world. At the same time, He is always there personally for us when needed. Through this facility, He is our Constant Companion. Though we may choose to ignore Him, like a faithful friend, He never leaves our side.

Having the supernatural powers only the Supreme Being could maintain, these pervasive intentional and personal energies do not detract from His separate existence in His transcendental world. The transcendental dimension, several times larger than the physical dimension, defines His personal existence. The Supreme Person has personal residential zones on various planets of this transcendental realm, where He partakes in many activities. He remains aloof yet still involved in the physical dimension:

> *As the sun stays in the sky, yet is reflected throughout the earth, so the Supreme Person stays within His kingdom while vibrating His energies through all things.*

The personal forces of the Supreme Being are spread through His manifested creations from within and without: the physical world is His reflective energy and the transcendental world is His direct energy. Nothing within either dimension is impersonal, however. The nature of the reflective physical universe is holographic. Each physical body reflects the whole of the universe, which reflects the Supreme Being. Every atom, every universe, and every living organism is synchronized, harmonizing to His personal intentional vibrations. Everything hums to His conscious direction, guided by His personal motives and intentions. Still, within His intention lies flexibility and choice for each of us individual living beings—His separated expansions. The magic and beauty of this universe is that though He has charged it with mechanical precision, we each have complete freedom to make decisions which can affect dramatic change all around us. He has set everything up with the ultimate combination of precision and flexibility, providing a fair and just, yet seamlessly responsive feedback system to promote our individual learning experiences.

A purpose pervades organized complexity.

A better course than to try to comprehend the vastness of these energies with our tiny minds would be to understand what the larger purpose is: What is the purpose of all this organized complexity?

These are the key questions of life common to all humans. Everyone at some point asks themselves these questions about the meaning of life. Many see connectedness and synchronicity within their own lives and wonder what the reason is. Others may ask only when things get rough or they feel physically or mentally threatened by those interconnected events: *"Why did all this happen to me?"*

Some wonder specifically why there is pain and suffering in the world, while some just want to know why they themselves are not happy. The very raising of these questions is one of the purposes for these conditions. Looking at our existence from an objective viewpoint reveals an overall coded system allowing for fairness and purpose:

> *A basketball team will have players on each side, each having particular positions to play and numbered jerseys in order to provide respective identification. The rules of the game are established and written in a codebook, and the game is monitored by a referee. Still within these rules, each player can freely choose how to play.*

Like players in a game, we each have a temporary physical existence with strict rules of engagement, and positions to play. The rules of the game are necessary to give us ethical guidance. The goal of the game is to learn something in particular. Within all these rules we can make decisions that choose our ultimate direction. The game will accommodate each choice we make with perfect harmony, responding with various results that help us grow.

A moral is a conscious learning experience.

A camera and recorder are required to record a scene, but any interesting movie must have a moral. Without a moral to the story there is no purpose to watch. Who would want to watch disconnected random scenes? Certainly the most successful movies and television programs are those which communicate a moral the viewer is interested to learn. A moral is a lesson about life. A story with a moral worth learning requires a conscious effort from the writers and producers to communicate that lesson in a way the viewer can experience it. Conscious effort is required to bring forth a meaningful story or movie that dispatches a moral: the learning experience.

In the same way, the Supreme Being is consciously conveying a moral through life's arrangements. This moral is taught through the passage of various learning experiences. If we look around us we can quite easily see life as a series of lessons. We can see events taking place which teach us in smaller ways and larger ways the same lessons. Because of the conscious intent of these teaching energies around us, events teach us how some decisions have one result, while other decisions have other results. Each decision has a particular result and we are thus challenged to make decisions that have positive results. While we are doing this, we may at any time connect the rational reasoning behind the array of positive results.

True learning heightens consciousness.

In other words, as we learn from the results of our decisions, we become more conscious of the things life was designed to teach us. We begin to see a reason behind the things that take place in our lives, many resulting from our decisions, and some resulting from the decisions of others. These lessons are *intelligent.* They teach things that we need to learn at that particular moment, to guide us to the next lesson. These lessons are also persistent. Should we not learn a necessary lesson; that lesson will be continuously taught until we choose to learn it. We will not *graduate* through that lesson until we learn it. Consider the perfection of the design of this system. Also consider that such a system must have a flexible design, responding perfectly to our choices to learn from an experience or not. Should we not learn, then we will be faced with that same perplexing issue until we do. If we do learn from it, we can then progress to the next level.

Once we understand that we are being taught lessons and life does have meaning, we may be able to enter those lessons consciously to see their intent. Seeing the conscious intent within the lesson itself can be a tremendous realization. By seeing this conscious intention through our experiences, we begin to understand that there is *consciousness* behind the teaching of these lessons: i.e., they were personally designed for our particular situation and issues. We can still learn without being aware that we are learning, however. Being conscious of our learning will serve to accelerate our ability to learn because we can more easily sort out learning experiences from situations we are put into. We experience that life is arranged to teach us lessons, and these lessons are intended by a conscious Being who is in control of both the lessons and their purpose. By learning these lessons, our consciousness is raised.

The questions now become: Why are we being taught lessons to increase our consciousness? What or who are we supposed to become conscious of? What is the overall moral?

The lessons of the various energies moving around and through our physical bodies have their root in the purpose of the Conscious Energy Source. Just as the broadcasting of television has an underlying reason or motive reflecting the underlying purpose of the station's ownership, the conscious energy transmissions throughout the universe reflect the purpose of the transmission Source:

> *While one television station's motive and mission may be fixed upon making a profit, another station may be nonprofit*

and may be driven by an overall motive to educate people. The programming of each station will reflect the ultimate motive of the station's ownership. Therefore each broadcast will directly or indirectly reflect those overall motives.

This universe is like one gigantic television, and the signal is the transcendental vibrational energies of the Supreme Being. Each (interactive) show from this signal delivers a particular lesson to each of us. Each of us walks through our own personal, unique series of learning experiences as these lessons are being broadcast through our personal lives. Each of our decisions and actions has a resulting reaction. Some reactions are positive while some are negative. Each of us thus learns a unique and personal range of lessons, arranged upon our particular situation and choices. What are we ultimately supposed to learn?

Intentional purpose is broadcast through love.

As we closely listen to the sounds of living organisms, we find that most are connected to relationships. While some cries are based on survival, most other animal communications are related to finding a mate, calling a mate, defending ones mate or family, or communicating to ones mate or potential mate. In human life we find love songs pervading our radio airwaves, relationship stories crowding our television shows and movies, and a constant focus upon our various relationships (or our intentions of finding them) within our personal lives.

We are surrounded by relationships. Each of us seeks a loving relationship and someone to love us. We thus spend much of our lives seeking the perfect loving relationship, and we seek to lovingly serve someone. The larger lessons of life relate to these loving relationships. Suffering is related to loneliness and an absence of love. All of us are all ultimately affected by love and loneliness as we seek out meaningful relationships.

As we travel through life, we learn that some actions increase our ability to have relationships while other actions decrease our relationships. We learn that actions that harm others cause us sadness and future pain while decisions that help others bring us immediate joy. We learn that giving love freely brings us love, while greedily demanding attention usually brings us loneliness. We learn that a life of loving without demands returns love, while a life of greed returns emptiness. More importantly, we learn that we each need a loving friend and companion. We each need to serve someone. We each need to love someone: not just anyone, but the Greatest One: The Supreme Being.

A vibration is an intentional communication: a song or a message. The vibrations pulsing through the various functions of physical existence are essentially orchestrated intentional communications of a particular beautiful song, echoing over and over in different melodies and harmonies. What is this song being vibrated throughout our universe? It is the love song of a Personal Supreme Being, requesting each of us to return to our natural state of exchanging a loving relationship with Him.

***

Conclusion: *Contrary to lifeless theories of random particles, quantum mechanics, membranes, quarks, or strings, the universe reveals an orchestration of vibrational energies pulsed from an Intelligent Being. The Supreme Being, originating from a dimension transcendental to the physical world, transmits conscious vibrational energy through our environment to communicate lessons of love and identity, all in an effort to call us back home to resume our lost loving relationship with Him.*

References and Bibliography

Ackerman D. *A Natural History of the Senses*. New York: Vintage, 1991.

Aissa J, Harran H, Rabeau M, Boucherie S, Brouilhet H, Benveniste J. Tissue levels of histamine, PAF-acether and lysopaf-acether in carrageenan-induced granuloma in rats. *Int Arch Allergy Immunol*. 1996 Jun;110(2):182-6.

Aïssa J, Jurgens P, Litime M, Béhar I, Benveniste J. Electronic transmission of the cholinergic signal. *FASEB Jnl*. 1995;9: A683.

Aïssa J, Litime M, Attias E, Allal A, Benveniste J. Transfer of molecular signals via electronic circuitry. *FASEB Jnl*. 1993;7: A602.

Aïssa J, Litime M, Attias E, Benveniste J. Molecular signaling at high dilution or by means of electronic circuitry. *Jnl Immun*. 1993;150: 146A.

Aïssa J, Nathan N, Arnoux B, Benveniste J. Biochemical and cellular effects of heparin-protamine injection in rabbits are partially inhibited by a PAF-acether receptor antagonist. *Eur J Pharmacol*. 1996 Apr 29;302(1-3):123-8.

Appleman P ed. *Darwin: A Norton Critical Edition*. New York: Norton, 1970.

Asch, S.E. Effects of Group Pressure upon the Modification and Distortion of Judgment. In Guetzkow J, ed., *Groups, Leadership and Men*. Pittsburgh: Carnegie, 1951. Petiot JF, Sainte-Laudy J, Benveniste J. Interpretation of results on a human basophil degranulation test. *Ann Biol Clin (Paris)*. 1981;39(6):355-9.

Avanzini G, Lopez L, Koelsch S, Majno M. The Neurosciences and Music II: From Perception to Performance. *Annals of the New York Academy of Sciences*. 2006 Mar;1060.

Bache C. *Lifecycles: Reincarnation and the Web of Life*. New York: Paragon House, 1994.

Bannerjee H. *Americans Who Have Been Reincarnated.* New York: Macmillan, 1980.

Baranauskas G, Nistri A. Sensitization of pain pathways in the spinal cord: cellular mechanisms. *Prog Neurobiol.* 1998 Feb;54(3):349-65.

Barker A. *Scientific Method in Ptolemy's Harmonics.* Cambridge: Cambridge Univ Press, 2000.

Bastide M, Daurat V, Doucet-Jaboeuf M, Pélegrin A, Dorfman P. Immunomodulator activity of very low doses of thymulin in mice, *Int J Immunotherapy.* 1987;3:191-200.

Bastide M, Doucet-Jaboeuf M, Daurat V. Activity and chronopharmacology of very low doses of physiological immune inducers. *Immun Today.* 1985;6: 234-235.

Bastide M. Immunological examples on ultra high dilution research. In: Endler P, Schulte J (eds.): *Ultra High Dilution. Physiology and Physics.* Dordrech: Kluwer Academic Publishers, 1994:27-34.

Beauvais F, Bidet B, Descours B, Hieblot C, Burtin C, Benveniste J. Regulation of human basophil activation. I. Dissociation of cationic dye binding from histamine release in activated human basophils. *J Allergy Clin Immunol.* 1991 May;87(5):1020-8.

Beauvais F, Burtin C, Benveniste J. Voltage-dependent ion channels on human basophils: do they exist? *Immunol Lett.* 1995 May;46(1-2):81-3.

Beauvais F, Echasserieau K, Burtin C, Benveniste J. Regulation of human basophil activation; the role of Na+ and Ca2+ in IL-3-induced potentiation of IgE-mediated histamine release from human basophils. *Clin Exp Immunol.* 1994 Jan;95(1):191-4.

Beauvais F, Shimahara T, Inoue I, Hieblot C, Burtin C, Benveniste J. Regulation of human basophil activation. II. Histamine release is potentiated by K+ efflux and inhibited by Na+ influx. *J Immunol.* 1992 Jan 1;148(1):149-54.

Becker R. *The Body Electric.* New York: Morrow, 1985.

Bensky D, Gable A, Kaptchuk T (transl.). *Chinese Herbal Medicine Materia Medica.* Seattle: Eastland Press, 1986.

Benveniste J, Aïssa J, Guillonnet D. A simple and fast method for *in vivo* demonstration of electromagnetic molecular signaling (EMS) via high dilution or computer recording. *FASEB Jnl.* 1999;13: A163.

Benveniste J, Aïssa J, Guillonnet D. Digital biology : Specificity of the digitized molecular signal. *FASEB Jnl.* 1998;12: A412.

Benveniste J, Aïssa J, Guillonnet D. The molecular signal is not functional in the absence of "informed" water. *FASEB Jnl.* 1999;13: A163.

Benveniste J, Aissa J, Litime MH, Tsaegaca GT, Thomas Y. Transfer of the molecular signal by electronic amplification. *FASEB J.* 1994; 8:A398.

Benveniste J, Arnoux B, Hadji L. Highly dilute antigen increases coronary flow of isolated heart from immunized guinea-pigs. *FASEB Jnl.* 1992;6: A1610.

Benveniste J, Davenas E, Ducot B, Cornillet B, Poitevin B, Spira A. L'agitation de solutions hautement diluées n'induit pas d'activité biologique spécifique. *Comptes-Rendus de l'Académie des Sciences de Paris.* 1991;312 :461-466.

Benveniste J, Davenas E, Ducot B, Spira A. Basophil achromasia by dilute ligand: a reappraisal. *FASEB Jnl.* 1991;5: A1008.

Benveniste J, Ducot B, Spira A. Memory of water revisited. *Nature.* 1994 Aug 4;370(6488):322.

Benveniste J, Guillonnet D. QED and digital biology. *Riv Biol.* 2004 Jan-Apr; 97(1):169-72.

Benveniste J, Jurgens P, Aïssa J. Digital recording/transmission of the cholinergic signal. *FASEB Jnl.* 1996;10: A1479.

Benveniste J, Jurgens P, Hsueh W, Aïssa J. Transatlantic transfer of digitized antigen signal by telephone link. *Jnl Aller Clin Immun.* 1997;99: S175.

Benveniste J, Kahhak L, Guillonnet D. Specific remote detection of bacteria using an electromagnetic / digital procedure. *FASEB Jnl.* 1999;13: A852.

Benveniste J. Benveniste on Nature investigation. *Science.* 1988 Aug 26;241(4869):1028.

Benveniste J. Benveniste on the Benveniste affair. *Nature.* 1988 Oct 27;335(6193):759.

Benveniste J. Diagnosis of allergic diseases by basophil count and in vitro degranulation using manual and automated tests. Nouv Presse Med. 1981 Jan 24;10(3):165-9.

Benveniste J. Meta-analysis of homoeopathy trials. *Lancet.* 1998 Jan 31;351 (9099):367.

Berk M, Dodd S, Henry M. Do ambient electromagnetic fields affect behaviour? A demonstration of the relationship between geomagnetic storm activity and suicide. *Bioelectromagnetics.* 2006 Feb;27(2):151-5.

Bitbol M, Luisi PL. Autopoiesis with or without cognition: defining life at its edge. *J R Soc Interface.* 2004 Nov 22;1(1):99-107.

Bjerregaard C. Plato and the Greeks on Music as an Element in Education. *The Word.* 1913 Feb.

Blackmore SJ. Near-death experiences. *J R Soc Med.* 1996 Feb;89(2):73-6.

Bourgine P, Stewart J. Autopoiesis and cognition. *Artif Life.* 2004 Summer;10(3):327-45.

Bowler PJ. *The Eclipse of Darwinism: Antievolutionary Theories in the Decades Around 1900.* Baltimore: Johns Hopkins, 1983.

Braunstein G, Labat C, Brunelleschi S, Benveniste J, Marsac J, Brink C. Evidence that the histamine sensitivity and responsiveness of guinea-pig isolated trachea are modulated by epithelial prostaglandin E2 production. *Br J Pharmacol.* 1988 Sep;95(1):300-8.

Burr H, Smith G, Strong L. Bio-electric Properties of Cancer-Resistant and Cancer-Susceptible Mice. *American Journal of Cancer.* 1938;32:240-248

Burr H. *The Fields of Life*. New York: Ballantine, 1972.

Calvin W. *The Handbook of Brain Theory and Neural Networks.* Boston: MIT Press, 1995.

Churchill G, Doerge R. Empirical threshold values for quantitative trait mapping. *Genetics* 1994;138:963-971.

Chwirot WB, Popp F. White-light-induced luminescence and mitotic activity of yeast cells. *Folia Histochemica et Cytobiologica.* 1991;29(4):155.

Citro M, Endler PC, Pongratz W, Vinattieri C, Smith CW, Schulte J. Hormone effects by electronic transmission. *FASEB J.* 1995:Abstract 12161.

Citro M, Smith CW, Scott-Morley A, Pongratz W, Endler PC. Transfer of information from molecules by means of electronic amplification, in P.C. Endler, J. Schulte (eds.): *Ultra High Dilution. Physiology and Physics.* Dordrecht: Kluwer Academic Publishers. 1994;209-214.

Cohen S, Popp F. Biophoton emission of the human body. *J Photochem & Photobio.* 1997;B 40:187-189.

Cohen S, Popp F. Low-level luminescence of the human skin. *Skin Res Tech.* 1997;3:177-180.

Crick F. *Life Itself: Its Origin and Nature.* New York: Simon and Schuster, 1981.

Davenas E, Beauvais F, Amara J, Oberbaum M, Robinzon B, Miadonna B, Tedeschi A, Pomeranz B, Fortner P, Belon P, Sainte-Laudy J, Poitevin B, Benveniste J. Human basophil degranulation triggered by very dilute antiserum against IgE. *Nature.* 1988;333: 816-818.

Davenas E, Poitevin B, Benveniste J. Effect on mouse peritoneal macrophages of orally administered very high dilutions of silica. *European Journal of Pharmacology.* 1987;135: 313-319.

Davis GE Jr, Lowell WE. Chaotic solar cycles modulate the incidence and severity of mental illness. *Med Hypotheses.* 2004;62(2):207-14.

Davis GE Jr, Lowell WE. Solar cycles and their relationship to human disease and adaptability. *Med Hypotheses.* 2006;67(3):447-61.

Davis GE Jr, Lowell WE. The Sun determines human longevity: teratogenic effects of chaotic solar radiation. *Med Hypotheses.* 2004;63(4):574-81.

Dawkins R. *Climbing Mount Improbable.* New York: Viking Press, 1996.

Dawkins R. *The Selfish Gene.* Oxford: Oxford UP, 1977 (1989 edition).

Dennett D. *Brainstorms: Philosophical Essays on Mind & Psychology.* Cambridge: MIT Press., 1980.

Dennett,D. *Consciousness Explained.* London: Little, Brown and Co., 1991.

Depue BE, Banich MT, Curran T. Suppression of emotional and nonemotional content in memory: effects of repetition on cognitive control. *Psychol Sci.* 2006 May;17(5):441-7.

Dere E, Kart-Teke E, Huston JP, De Souza Silva MA. The case for episodic memory in animals. *Neurosci Biobehav Rev.* 2006;30(8):1206-24.

Dunne B, Jahn R, Nelson R. Precognitive Remote Perception. *Princeton Engineering Anomalies Research Laboratory Report.* Princeton. 1983 Aug.

Egon G, Chartier-Kastler E, Denys P, Ruffion A. Spinal cord injury patient and Brindley neurostimulation. *Prog Urol.* 2007 May;17(3):535-9.

Einstein In Need Of Update? Calculations Show The Speed Of Light Might Change. Science Daily. 2001 Feb 12. www.sciencedaily.com/releases/2001/02/010212075309.htm. Acc. 2007 Oct.

Electronic Evidence of Auras, Chakras in UCLA Study. *Brain/Mind Bulletin.* 1978;3:9 Mar 20.

Endler P, Pongratz W, van Wijk R, Waltl K, Hilgers H, Brandmaier R. Transmission of hormone information by non-molecular means. *FASEB Jnl.* 1994;8: A400.

Endler PC, Pongratz W, Kastberger G, Wiegant F, Schulte J. The effect of highly diluted agitated thyroxine on the climbing activity of frogs, *J Vet Hum Tox.* 1994;36:56-59.

Endler PC, Pongratz W, Smith CW, Schulte J. Non-molecular information transfer from thyroxine to frogs with regard to 'homoeopathic' toxicology, *J Vet Hum Tox.* 1995:37:259-260.

Endler PC, Pongratz W, Van Wijk R, Kastberger G, Haidvogl M. Effects of highly diluted sucussed thyroxine on metamorphosis of highland frogs, *Berlin J Res Hom.* 1991;1:151-160.

Endler PC, Pongratz W, Van Wijk R, Waltl K, Hilgers H, Brandmaier R. Transmission of hormone information by non-molecular means, *FASEB J.* 1994;8:A400.

Endler PC, Pongratz W, Van Wijk R, Wiegant F, Waltl K, Gehrer M, Hilgers H. A zoological example on ultra high dilution research. In: Endler PC, Schulte J (eds.): *Ultra High Dilution. Physiology and Physics.* Dordrecht: Kluwer Academic Publishers. 1994:39-68.

Endler PC, Pongratz W. *On effects of agitated highly diluted thyroxine (E-30).* Comprehensive report, available at the Institute for Zoology. University of Graz, Universitätsplatz 2, A-8010 Graz, 1994.

Endler PC, Schulte, J. *Ultra High Dilution. Physiology and Physics.* Dordrecht: Kluwer Academic Publ, 1994.

Fiore E. *You Have Been Here Before.* New York: Ballantine, 1978.

Forget-Dubois N, Boivin M, Dionne G, Pierce T, Tremblay RE, Perusse D. A longitudinal twin study of the genetic and environmental etiology of maternal hostile-reactive behavior during infancy and toddlerhood. *Infant Behav Dev.* 2007 Aug;30(3):453-65.

Gerber R. *Vibrational Healing.* Sante Fe: Bear, 1988.

Goldberg B. *Past Lives, Future Lives.* New York: Ballantine, 1982.

Gould SJ. *Wonderful Life: The Burgess Shale and the nature of history.* New York: Penguin Books, 1989.

Grad B. A Telekinetic Effect on Plant Growth. *Intl Jnl Parapsy.* 1964;6:473.

Grad B. The 'Laying on of Hands': Implications for Psychotherapy, Gentling, and the Placebo Effect. *Jnl Amer Soc for Psych Res.* 1967 Oct;61(4):286-305.

Grad, B. A telekinetic effect on plant growth II. Experiments involving treatment of saline in stoppered bottles. *Internl J Parapsychol.* 1964;6:473-478, 484-488.

Grasso F, Grillo C, Musumeci F, Triglia A, Rodolico G, Cammisuli F, Rinzivillo C, Fragati G, Santuccio A, Rodolico M. Photon emission from normal and tumour human tissues. *Experientia.* 1992;48:10-13.

Grasso F, Musumeci F, Triglia A, Rodolico G, Cammisuli F, Rinzivillo C, Fragati G, Santuccio A, Rodolico M. In Stanley P, Kricka L (ed). *Ultraweak Luminescence from Cancer Tissues. In Bioluminescence and Chemiluminescence - Current Status.* New York: Wiley, 1991:277-280.

Grasso F, Musumeci F, Triglia A. Yanbastiev M. Borisova, S. Self-irradiation effect on yeast cells. *Photochemistry and Photobiology.* 1991;54(1):147-149.

Hadji L, Arnoux B, Benveniste J. Effect of dilute histamine on coronary flow of guinea-pig isolated heart. *FASEB J.* 1991;5:A1583.

Hagins WA, Penn RD, Yoshikami S. Dark current and photocurrent in retinal rods. *Biophys J.* 1970 May;10(5):380-412.

Hagins WA, Robinson WE, Yoshikami S. Ionic aspects of excitation in rod outer segments.

Hagins WA, Yoshikami S. Ionic mechanisms in excitation of photoreceptors. Ann N Y Acad Sci. 1975 Dec 30;264:314-25.

Hahnemann S. *Oreganon of Homeopathic Medicine.* New York: W. Radde, 1843.

Halpern S. *Tuning the Human Instrument.* Palo Alto, CA: Spectrum Research Institute, 1978.

Hamel P. *Through Music to the Self: How to Appreciate and Experience Music.* Boulder: Shambala, 1979.

Hameroff SR, Kaszniak A, Scott AC (eds.): *Toward a Science of Consciousness - The First Tucson Discussions and Debates.* Cambridge: MIT Press, 1996.

Hameroff SR, Penrose R. Conscious events as orchestrated spacetime selections. *J Consc Studies.* 1996;3(1):36-53.

Hameroff SR, Smith, S, Watt.R. Nonlinear electrodynamics in cytoskeletal protein lattices. In: Adey W, Lawrence A (eds.), *Nonlinear Electrodynamics in Biological Systems.* 1984:567-583.

Hameroff SR, Watt, R. Information processing in microtubules. *J Theor Biology.* 1982;98:549-561.

Hameroff SR. Coherence in the cytoskeleton: Implications for biological information processing. In: Fröhlich H. (ed.): *Biological Coherence and Response to External Stimuli.* Springer, Berlin-New York 1988, pp.242-264.

Hameroff SR. Light is heavy: Wave mechanics in proteins - A microtubule hologram model of consciousness. *Proceedings 2nd. International Congress on Psychotronic Research.* Monte Carlo, 1975:168-169.

Hameroff SR. *Ultimate Biocomputing - Biomolecular Consciousness and Nanotechnology.* Amsterdam: Elsevier, 1987.

Hameroff, SR. Ch'i: A neural hologram? Microtubules, bioholography and acupuncture. *Am J. Chin Med.* 1974;2(2): 163-170.

Hardin P. Transcription regulation within the circadian clock: the E-box and beyond. *J Biol Rhythms.* 2004 Oct;19(5):348-60.

Harlow HF, Dodsworth RO, Harlow MK. Total social isolation in monkeys. *Proc Natl Acad Sci U S A.* 1965.

Harlow HF. Development of affection in primates. In Bliss E (ed): *Roots of Behavior*. New York: Harper, 1962: 157-166.

Harlow HF. Early social deprivation and later behavior in the monkey. In: Abrams A, Gurner H, Tomal J (eds): *Unfinished tasks in the behavioral sciences*. Baltimore: Williams & Wilkins. 1964: 154-173.

Haye-Legrand I, Norel X, Labat C, Benveniste J, Brink C. Antigenic contraction of guinea pig tracheal preparations passively sensitized with monoclonal IgE: pharmacological modulation. *Int Arch Allergy Appl Immunol.* 1988;87(4):342-8.

Hoyle F. *Evolution from Space.* Londong: JM Dent, 1981 Huffman C. Archytas of Tarentum: *Pythagorean, philosopher and Mathematician King.* Cambridge: Cambridge University Press, 2005.

Hur YM, Rushton JP. Genetic and environmental contributions to prosocial behaviour in 2- to 9-year-old South Korean twins. *Biol Lett.* 2007 Aug 28.

Inaba H. INABA Biophoton. Exploratory Research for Advanced Technology. *Japan Science and Technology Agency.* 1991. http://www.jst.go.jp/erato/project/isf_P/isf_P.html. Acc. 2006 Nov.

Ivanovic-Zuvic F, de la Vega R, Ivanovic-Zuvic N, Renteria P. Affective disorders and solar activity. *Actas Esp Psiquiatr.* 2005 Jan-Feb;33(1):7-12.

Jahn R, Dunne, B. *Margins of Reality: the Role of Consciousness in the Physical World.* New York: Harcourt Brace Jovanovich, 1987.

Jahn R, Dunne B. Science of the subjective. *J Sci Expl.* 1997;11(2):201-224.

Jahn R, Dunne B, Nelson R. Engineering anomalies research. *J Sci Expl.* 1987;1(1):21-50.

Jahn R, Dunne B, Nelson R, Dobyns Y, Bradish G. Correlations of random binary sequences with pre-stated operator intention: A review of a 12-year program. *J Sci Expl.* 1997; 11(3):345-368.

Jahn R, Nelson R, Dunne B. *Variance Effects in REG Series Score Distributions, Technical Note PEAR 85001*. Princeton Engineering Anomalies Research, Princeton Univ. 1985 June.

Johari H. *Ayurvedic Massage: Traditional Indian Techniques for Balancing Body and Mind*. Rochester, VT: Healing Arts, 1996.

Johari H. *Chakras*. Rochester, VT: Destiny, 1987.

Johnston A. A spatial property of the retino-cortical mapping. *Spatial Vision*. 1986;1(4):319-331.

Karnstedt J. Ions and Consciousness. *Whole Self*. 1991 Spring.

Keil J, Stevenson I. Do cases of the reincarnation type show similar features over many years? A study of Turkish cases. *J. Sci. Exploration*. 1999;13(2) 189-198.Pasricha S. *Claims of reincarnation: An Empirical Study of Cases in India*. New Delhi: Harman, 1990.

Kinoshameg SA, Persinger MA. Suppression of experimental allergic encephalomyelitis in rats by 50-nT, 7-Hz amplitude-modulated nocturnal magnetic fields depends on when after inoculation the fields are applied. *J Neulet*. 2004;08:18.

Kubler-Ross E. *On Life After Death*. Berkeley, CA: Celestial Arts, 1991.

Lafrenière, G. The material Universe is made purely out of Aether. *Matter is made of Waves*. 2002: http://www.glafreniere.com/matter.htm. Acc. 2007 June.

Langhinrichsen-Rohling J, Palarea RE, Cohen J, Rohling ML. Breaking up is hard to do: unwanted pursuit behaviors following the dissolution of a romantic relationship. *Violence Vict*. 2000 Spring;15(1):73-90.

Litime M, Aïssa J, Benveniste J. Antigen signaling at high dilution. *FASEB Jnl*. 1993;7: A602.

Lovelock, J. *Gaia: A New Look at Life on Earth*. Oxford: Oxford Press, 1979.

Lucas A, Morley R, Cole T, Lister G, Leeson-Payne C. Breast milk and subsequent intelligence quotient in children born premature. *Lancet*. 1992;339:261-264.

Lucas WB (ed). *Regression Therapy: A Handbook for Professionals. Past-Life Therapy.* Crest Park, CA: Deep Forest Press, 1993.

MacKay D. *Science, Chance, and Providence.* Oxford: Oxford Univ Press, 1978.

Maes HH, Silberg JL, Neale MC, Eaves LJ. Genetic and cultural transmission of antisocial behavior: an extended twin parent model. *Twin Res Hum Genet.* 2007 Feb;10(1):136-50.

Marasanov SB, Matveev II. Correlation between protracted premedication and complication in cancer patients operated on during intense solar activity. *Vopr Onkol.* 2007;53(1):96-9.

Marks C. *Commissurotomy, Consciousness, and Unity of Mind.* Cambridge: MIT Press, 1981.

Marks L. *The Unity of the Senses: Interrelations among the Modalities.* New York: Academic Press, 1978.

Mayr E. *Toward a New Philosophy of Biology: Observations of an evolutionist.* Boston: Belknap Press, 1988.

Melzack R, Wall P. Pain Mechanisms: A New Theory. *Science.* 1965;150:171-179.

Melzack R. Evolution of the neuromatrix theory of pain. The prithvi raj lecture: presented at the third world congress of world institute of pain, barcelona 2004. *Pain Pract.* 2005 Jun;5(2):85-94.

Melzack R. Pain: past, present and future. *Can J Exp Psychol.* 1993 Dec;47(4):615-29.

Melzack R. Pain—an overview. *Acta Anaesthesiol Scand.* 1999 Oct;43(9):880-4.

Milgram S. *Obedience to Authority: An Experimental View.* New York: Harper, 1974.

Mills A. A replication study: Three cases of children in northern India who are said to remember a previous life," *J. Sci. Exploration* 3, No. 2 (1989) pp. 133-184Mills A. Moslem cases of the reincarnation type in northern India: A test of the hypothesis of imposed identification, Part I: Analysis of 26 cases. *J. Sci. Exploration.* 1990;4(2): 171-188.

Mishkin M, Appenzeller T. The Anatomy of Memory. *Sci. Am.* 1987 June.

Mishkin M. Memory in monkeys severely impaired by combined but not by separate removal of amygdala and hippocampus. *Nature*. 1978;273: 297-298.

Mitchell JL. *Out-of-Body Experiences: A Handbook.* New York: Ballantine Books, 1981.

Monod J. *Chance and Necessity.* New York: Vintage, 1972.

Monroe R. *Far Journeys.* Garden City, NY: Doubleday & Co., 1985.

Monroe R. *Journeys Out of the Body.* Garden City, NY: Anchor Press, 1977.

Moody R. *Coming Back: A Psychiatrist Explores Past-Life Journeys.* New York: Bantam Books, 1991.

Moody, R. *Life After Life: The Investigation of a Phenomenon - Survival of Bodily Death.* New York: Bantam, 1975.

Moody, R. *Reflections on Life After Life: More Important Discoveries In The Ongoing Investigation Of Survival Of Life After Bodily Death.* New York: Bantam, 1977.

Moore RY. Circadian Rhythms: A Clock for the Ages. *Science* 1999 June 25;284(5423):2102 – 2103.

Moore RY. Neural control of the pineal gland. Behav Brain Res. 1996;73(1-2):125-30.

Moore RY. Organization and function of a central nervous system circadian oscillator: the suprachiasmatic hypothalamic nucleus. Fed Proc. 1983 Aug;42(11):2783-9.

Morse M. *Closer to the Light.* New York: Ivy Books, 1990.

Mumby DG, Wood ER, Pinel J. Object-recognition memory is only mildly impaired in rats with lesions of the hippocampus and amygdala. *Psychobio.* 1992;20: 18-27.

Murchie G. *The Seven Mysteries of Life.* Boston: Houghton Mifflin Company, 1978.

Murphy R. *Organon Philosophy Workbook.* Blacksburg, VA: HANA, 1994.

Musaev AV, Nasrullaeva SN, Zeinalov RG. Effects of solar activity on some demographic indices and morbidity in Azerbaijan with reference to A. L. Chizhevsky's theory. *Vopr Kurortol Fizioter Lech Fiz Kult.* 2007 May-Jun;(3):38-42.

Netheron M. *Past Lives Therapy.* New York: Morrow, 1978.

Ostrander S, Schroeder L, Ostrander N. *Super-Learning.* New York: Delta, 1979.

Otani S. Memory trace in prefrontal cortex: theory for the cognitive switch. *Biol Rev Camb Philos Soc.* 2002 Nov;77(4):563-77.

Otsu A, Chinami M, Morgenthale S, Kaneko Y, Fujita D, Shirakawa T. Correlations for number of sunspots, unemployment rate, and suicide mortality in Japan. *Percept Mot Skills.* 2006 Apr;102(2):603-8.

Ott J. Color and Light: Their Effects on Plants, Animals, and People (Series of seven articles in seven issues). *International Journal for Biosocial Research.* 1985-1991.

Palmer J. Hit-contingent response biases in Helmut Schmidt's automated precognition experiments. J Parapsy. 1997:61; 135-141.

Partonen T, Haukka J, Nevanlinna H, Lonnqvist J. Analysis of the seasonal pattern in suicide. *J Affect Disord.* 2004 Aug;81(2):133-9.

Petiot JF, Sainte-Laudy J, Benveniste J. Interpretation of results on a human basophil degranulation test. *Ann Biol Clin (Paris).* 1981;39(6):355-9.

Pittalwala I. Research Shows Earth's Earliest Animal Ecosystem Was Complex and included Sexual Reproduction. *UC Riverside Newsroom.* 2008 Mar 20.

Plotkin H. *Darwin Machines and the Nature of Knowledge: Concerning adaptations, instinct and the evolution of intelligence.* New York: Penguin, 1994.

Poitevin B, Davenas E, Benveniste J. In vitro immunological degranulation of human basophils is modulated by lung histamine and Apis mellifica. *Br J Clin Pharmacol.* 1988 Apr;25(4):439-44.

Poitevin B, Davenas E, Benveniste J. In vitro immunological degranulation of human basophils is modulated by Lung histamine and Apis mellifica. *British Journal of Clinical Pharmacology*. 1988;25: 439-444.

Polkinghorne J. *Science and Providence.* Boston: Shambhala Publications, 1989.

Pongratz W, Endler PC, Poitevin B, Kartnig T. Effect of extremely diluted plant hormone on cell culture, *Proc. 1995 AAAS Ann. Meeting*, Atlanta, 1995.

Popp F Chang J. Mechanism of interaction between electromagnetic fields and living organisms. *Science in China.* 2000 Series C;43(5):507-518.

Popp F, Chang J, Herzog A, Yan Z, Yan Y. Evidence of non-classical (squeezed) light in biological systems. *Physics Lett.* 2002;293:98-102.

Popp F, Yan Y. Delayed luminescence of biological systems in terms of coherent states. *Phys.Lett.* 2000;293:91-97.

Popp F. Properties of biophotons and their theoretical implications. *Indian J Exper Biology*. 2003 May;41:391-402.

Popp F. Molecular Aspects of Carcinogenesis. In Deutsch E, Moser K, Rainer H, Stacher A (eds.). *Molecular Base of Malignancy.* Stuttgart: G.Thieme, 1976:47-55.

Protheroe WM, Captiotti ER, Newsom GH. *Exploring the Universe.* Columbus, OH: Merrill, 1989.

Puthoff H, Targ R, May E. Experimental Psi Research: Implication for Physics. *AAAS Proceedings of the 1979 Symposium on the Role of Consciousness in the Physical World.* 1981.

Puthoff H, Targ R. A Perceptual Channel for Information Transfer Over Kilometer distances: Historical Perspective and Recent Research. *Proc. IEEE.* 1976;64(3):329-254.

Radin D. *The Conscious Universe.* San Francisco: HarperEdge, 1997.

Reilly D, Taylor M, Beattie N, Campbell J, McSharry C, Aitchison T, Carter R, Stevenson R. Is evidence for homoeopathy reproducible? *Lancet,* 1994;344: 1601-1606.

Reilly D. The puzzle of homeopathy. *J Altern Complement Med.* 2001;7 Suppl 1:S103-9.

Rieder M. *Mission to Millboro.* Nevada City, CA: Blue Dolphin, 1995.

Rieder M. *Return to Millboro: The Reincarnation Drama Continues.* Nevada City, CA: Blue Dolphin, 1995.

Ring K. *Life at Death: A Scientific Investigation of the Near-Death Experience.* New York: Quill, 1982.

Sabom M. *Light and Death: One Doctor's Fascinating Account of Near Death Experiences.* Grand Rapids, MI: Zondervan Publishing, 1998.

Sabom, M. *Recollections of Death: A Medical Investigation.* New York: Simon & Schuster, 1982.

Sanders R. Slow brain waves play key role in coordinating complex activity. *UC Berkeley News.* 2006 Sep 14.

Schlebusch KP, Maric-Oehler W, Popp FA. Biophotonics in the infrared spectral range reveal acupuncture meridian structure of the body. *J Altern Complement Med.* 2005 Feb;11(1):171-3.

Schlebusch KP, Maric-Oehler W, Popp FA. Biophotonics in the infrared spectral range reveal acupuncture meridian structure of the body. *J Altern Complement Med.* 2005 Feb;11(1):171-3.

Schmidt H, Quantum processes predicted? *New Sci.* 1969 Oct 16.

Serway R. *Physics For Scientists & Engineers.* Philadelphia: Harcourt Brace, 1992.

Shaffer D. *Developmental Psychology: Theory, Research and Applications.* Monterey, CA: Brooks/Cole, 1985.

Sharp KC. *After the Light*. New York: William Morrow & Co., 1995.

Shui-Yin Lo. Anomalous State of Ice. *Mod Phys Lttrs*. 1996;10(19): 909-919.

Shupak NM, Prato FS, Thomas AW. Human exposure to a specific pulsed magnetic field: effects on thermal sensory and pain thresholds. *Neurosci Lett*. 2004 Jun 10;363(2):157-62.

Sicher F, Targ E, Moore D, Smith H. A Randomized Double-Blind Study of the Effect of Distant Healing in a Population With Advanced AIDS. Targ R, Katra J, Brown D, Wiegand W. Viewing the future: A pilot study with an error-detecting protocol. *J Sci Explo, 9:3*, pp. 367-380, 1995.

Simpson G. *The Major Features of Evolution*. New York: Columbia Univ Press, 1953.

Smith CW. Coherence in living biological systems. *Neural Network World*. 1994:4(3):379-388.

Smith MJ. *The Influence on Enzyme Growth By the 'Laying on of Hands: Dimenensions of Healing*. Los Altos, California: Academy of Parapsychology and Medicine, 1973.

Soul Has Weight, Physician Thinks. *New York Times*. 1907 March 11:5.

Speed Of Light May Not Be Constant, Physicist Suggests. *Sci Dly*. 1999 Oct 6.

Spence A. *Basic Human Anatomy*. Menlo Park, CA: Benjamin/Commings, 1986.

Spetner L. *Not By Chance! -Shattering The Modern Theory of Evolution*. New York: The Judaica Press, 1997.

Spillane M. Good Vibrations, A Sound 'Diet' for Plants. *The Growing Edge*. 1991 Spring.

Squire LR, Zola-Morgan S. The medial temporal lobe memory system. *Science*. 1991;253(5026):1380-1386.

Stanford, C. B. The hunting ecology of wild chimpanzees: Implications for the evolutionary ecology of Pliocene hominids. *American Anthropologist*. 1996;98: 96-113.

Steck B. Effects of optical radiation on man. *Light Resch Techn.* 1982;14:130-141.

Stevenson I, Samararatne G. Three new cases of the reincarnation type in Sri Lanka with written records made before verification. *J. Sci. Exploration.* 1988;2(2): 217-238.

Stevenson I. *Cases of the Reincarnation Type.* Charlottesville, VA: Univ. of Virginia Press. Vol. 1 *Ten Cases in India* (1975) Vol. 2 *Ten Cases in Sri Lanka,* 1977. Vol. 3 *Twelve Cases in Lebanon and Turkey,* 1980. Vol. 4 *Twelve Cases in Thailand and Burma,* 1983.

Stevenson I. *Children Who Remember Previous Lives: A Question of Reincarnation.* Charlottesville, VA: University of Virginia Press, 1987.Stevenson I. American children who claim to remember previous lives. *J. Nervous and Mental Disease.* 1983;171: 742-748.

Stevenson I. *European Cases of the Reincarnation Type.* Jefferson, NC: McFarland and Co., 2003.

Stevenson I. *Reincarnation and Biology: A Contribution to the Etiology of Birthmarks and Birth Defects.* (2 volumes). Westport: Praeger Publishers, 1997.

Stevenson I. *Twenty Cases Suggestive of Reincarnation.* New York: American Society for Psychical Research, 1967.

Stevenson I.*Where Reincarnation and Biology Intersect.* Westport: Praeger, 1997.

Stoupel E, Babyev E, Mustafa F, Abramson E, Israelevich P, Sulkes J. Acute myocardial infarction occurrence: Environmental links - Baku 2003-2005 data. *Med Sci Monit.* 2007 Aug;13(8):BR175-179.

Stoupel E, Kalediene R, Petrauskiene J, Gaizauskiene A, Israelevich P, Abramson E, Sulkes J. Monthly number of newborns and environmental physical activity. *Medicina Kaunas.* 2006;42(3):238-41.

Stoupel E, Monselise Y, Lahav J. Changes in autoimmune markers of the anti-cardiolipin syndrome on days of extreme geomamagnetic activity. *J Basic Clin Physiol Pharmacol.* 2006;17(4):269-78.

Stoupel EG, Frimer H, Appelman Z, Ben-Neriah Z, Dar H, Fejgin MD, Gershoni-Baruch R, Manor E, Barkai G, Shalev S, Gelman-Kohan Z, Reish O, Lev D, Davidov B, Goldman B, Shohat M. Chromosome aberration and environmental physical activity: Down syndrome and solar and cosmic ray activity, Israel, 1990-2000. *Int J Biometeorol.* 2005 Sep;50(1):1-5.

Strange BA, Dolan RJ. Anterior medial temporal lobe in human cognition: memory for fear and the unexpected. *Cognit Neuropsychiatry.* 2006 May;11(3):198-218.

Suppes P, Han B, Epelboim J, Lu ZL. Invariance of brain-wave representations of simple visual images and their names. Proceedings of the National Academy of Sciences Psychology-BS. 1999;96(25):14658-14663.

Targ R, Puthoff H. Information transfer under conditions of sensory shielding. *Nature.* 1975;251:602-607.

Thakur CP, Sharma D. Full moon and crime. *Br Med J.* 1984 December 22; 289(6460): 1789-1791.

Thomas Y, Litime H, Benveniste J. Modulation of human neutrophil activation by "electronic" phorbol myristate acetate (PMA). *FASEB Jnl.* 1996;10: A1479.

Thomas Y, Schiff M, Belkadi L, Jurgens P, Kahhak L, Benveniste J. Activation of human neutrophils by electronically transmitted phorbol-myristate acetate. *Med Hypoth.* 2000; 54: 33-39.

Thomas Y, Schiff M, Litime M, Belkadi L, Benveniste J. Direct transmission to cells of a molecular signal (phorbol myristate acetate, PMA) via an electronic device. *FASEB Jnl.* 1995;9: A227.

Thomas-Anterion C, Jacquin K, Laurent B. Differential mechanisms of impairment of remote memory in Alzheimer's and frontotemporal dementia. *Dement Geriatr Cogn Disord.* 2000 Mar-Apr;11(2):100-6.

Thompson D. *On Growth and Form.* Cambridge: Cambridge Univ Press, 1992.

Tompkins, P, Bird C. *The Secret Life of Plants.* New York: Harper & Row, 1973.

Triglia A, La Malfa G, Musumeci F, Leonardi C, Scordino A. Delayed luminsecence as an indicator of tomato fruit quality. *J Food Sci.* 1998;63:512-515.

Tsuei JJ, Lam Jr. F, Zhao Z. Studies in Bioenergetic Correlations—Bioenergetic Regulatory Measurement Instruments and Devices. *Am J Acupunct.* 1988;16:345-9.

Tucker J. *Life Before Life: A Scientific Investigation of Children's Memories of Previous Lives.* New York: St. Martin's, 2005.

Vaquero JM, Gallego MC. Sunspot numbers can detect pandemic influenza A: the use of different sunspot numbers. *Med Hypotheses.* 2007;68(5):1189-90.

Vargha-Khadem F, Polkey CE. A review of cognitive outcome after hemidecortication in humans. *Adv Exp Med Biol.* 1992;325:137-51.

Vyasadeva S. *Srimad Bhagavatam.* Approx rec 4000 BCE.

Wagenaar, W. Generation of random sequences by human subjects: A critical survey of literature. *Psych Bulletin.* 1972:77(1):65-72.

Wambach H. *Reliving Past Lives.* New York: Bantam, 1978.Fiore E. *You Have Been Here Before.* New York: Ballantine, 1978.

Weiss B. *Many Lives, Many Masters.* New York: Simon & Schuster, 1988.

White J, Krippner S (eds). *Future Science: Life Energies & the Physics of Paranormal Phenomena.* Garden City: Anchor, 1977.

Whitfield KE, King G, Moller S, Edwards CL, Nelson T, Vandenbergh D. Concordance rates for smoking among African-American twins. *J Natl Med Assoc.* 2007 Mar;99(3):213-7.

Whittaker E. *History of the Theories of Aether and Electricity*. New York: Nelson LTD, 1953.

Whitton J. *Life Between Life.* New York: Warner, 1986.

Winchester AM. *Biology and its Relation to Mankind.* New York: Van Nostrand Reinhold, 1969.

Wixted JT. A Theory About Why We Forget What We Once Knew. *CurrDir Psychol Sci.* 2005;14(1):6-9.

Wolf, M. Beyond the Point Particle - *A Wave Structure for the Electron. Galilean Electrodynamics.* 1995 Oct;6(5): 83-91.

Wood M. *The Book of Herbal Wisdom.* Berkeley, CA: North Atlantic, 1997.

Woolger R. *Other Lives, Other Selves.* New York: Bantam, 1988.

Youbicier-Simo BJ, Boudard F, Meckaouche M, Bastide M, Baylé JD. The effects of embryonic bursectomy and in ovo administration of highly diluted bursin on adrenocorticotropic and immune response of chicken, *Int. J. Immunother.* 1993;9:169-190.

Zhang C, Popp, F., Bischof, M.(eds.). *Electromagnetic standing waves as background of acupuncture system. Current Development in Biophysics - the Stage from an Ugly Duckling to a Beautiful Swan.* Hangzhou: Hangzhou University Press, 1996.

Index

accidental, 42, 47, 92, 102, 105, 106, 107, 108, 109, 111, 113, 117, 123, 132, 141, 143, 144, 147, 148, 153, 156, 158, 159, 160, 161, 164, 165, 167, 169, 171, 172, 175, 177, 178, 179, 180, 183, 185, 186, 187, 188, 189, 197, 206, 214, 216, 239, 241, 252, 255, 258, 260
acetylcholine, 25, 239
Adrenaline, 27
adrenocorticotropic, 25, 30
airwaves, 266
amygdala, 22
antiquarks, 225
aquariums, 181
astronomers, 235, 244, 246
astrophysicist, 229
atmosphere, 57, 62, 66, 78, 167, 172, 231, 232, 244, 245
Atoms, 20, 21, 71, 110, 111, 114, 116, 117, 118, 120, 121, 122, 124, 125, 126, 150, 172, 218, 219, 220, 228, 250
awareness, 19, 47, 135, 162, 190, 191, 193, 194, 199, 202, 203, 204, 205, 206, 208, 213, 245, 246
bacterium, 18
Beauty, 6, 113, 118, 187, 213, 262
behavior, 1, 2, 26, 28, 33, 34, 41, 43, 44, 60, 114, 124, 176, 177, 181, 183, 184, 185, 195, 199, 206, 226, 246, 247, 250, 251, 252
biochemicals, 25, 27, 30, 31, 32, 160, 239
biochemistry, 31, 32, 33
biofeedback, 32, 35
Body, 1, 13, 14, 15, 16, 17, 18, 20, 21, 23, 24, 25, 26, 27, 28, 29, 30, 31, 32, 33, 34, 35, 36, 37, 40, 41, 43, 45, 46, 47, 48, 68, 70, 85, 88, 100, 108, 126, 129, 130, 138, 142, 143, 145, 146, 147, 148, 149, 154, 158, 159, 160, 169, 176, 178, 181, 182, 184, 185, 188, 189, 190, 191, 192, 193, 194, 196, 197, 198, 199, 200, 204, 207, 212, 214, 236, 237, 240, 241, 242, 244, 251, 253, 254, 255, 256, 261, 262
bonding, 118, 120, 122, 260
Boson, 225, 228
brain, 15, 20, 21, 22, 23, 29, 33, 34, 37, 38, 62, 63, 67, 68, 176, 233, 241, 256
brainwaves, 29, 32, 46, 236
broadcasting, 154, 232, 233, 234, 261, 265
Butane, 119
butterflies, 135
cadaver, 15, 16
cell, 18, 20, 21, 25, 126, 138, 143, 145, 146, 149, 176, 184, 236, 237, 240, 251
change, 3, 5, 6, 14, 21, 23, 24, 32, 40, 42, 119, 123, 136, 140, 145, 146, 165, 173, 176, 177, 184,

186, 187, 188, 194, 199, 203, 206, 213, 220, 252, 262
chaotic, 47, 111, 112, 113, 114, 117, 123, 131, 135, 143, 175, 251, 252
chemical, 15, 24, 25, 27, 30, 34, 110, 111, 112, 120, 126, 141, 142, 143, 144, 147, 149, 159, 163, 164, 183, 186, 187, 234, 239, 240, 244
chemicals, 24, 25, 27, 100, 106, 141, 143, 144, 147, 160, 161, 162, 163, 164, 178, 179, 190, 191, 235
chemiluminescence, 236
chemistry, viii, 33, 99, 110, 118, 147, 148, 160, 162, 177, 190, 191, 258
chloroplasts, 239
chromatography, 73, 235
chromium, 70
circulation, 15, 129, 231, 244
clockworks, 173, 255, 256
codons, 42
coin-toss, 131, 132
complexity, 42, 76, 92, 98, 140, 147, 148, 152, 158, 166, 175, 179, 217, 222, 245, 254, 263
consciousness, 19, 20, 43, 47, 55, 79, 99, 133, 134, 145, 151, 182, 183, 184, 185, 186, 188, 189, 190, 191, 193, 194, 195, 197, 198, 199, 202, 203, 204, 206, 210, 212, 213, 214, 231, 243, 244, 250, 252, 254, 259, 260, 261, 264, 265
cortisol, 25, 256
deoxyribonucleic, 142
dogs, 15, 180, 181, 185, 189, 195, 196, 197, 233
dolphins, 194, 195, 233
dominos, 139, 140
double-helix, 142, 144
earth, 66, 95, 99, 109, 114, 116, 141, 147, 159, 167, 168, 172, 179, 180, 231, 232, 244, 245, 262
earthquake, 68, 216
electroencephalograph, 29
electromagnetic, 71, 72, 115, 116, 120, 122, 219, 227, 228, 229, 233, 250
electromagnetism, 115, 222
endocrine, 241, 256
energy, 14, 16, 35, 45, 62, 100, 110, 111, 112, 113, 120, 124, 126, 140, 149, 154, 190, 191, 217, 219, 220, 231, 234, 235, 241, 243, 244, 250, 251, 252, 253, 254, 255, 257, 258, 259, 260, 262, 265, 267
environment, 44, 53, 58, 59, 100, 101, 141, 168, 173, 174, 182, 183, 188, 194, 199, 200, 205, 207, 232, 267
evolution, 14, 47, 50, 158, 159, 160, 161, 163, 164, 165, 167, 169, 175, 185, 186, 187, 188, 189, 190, 191, 192, 193, 194, 205, 206, 207, 208, 209, 210, 211, 213, 214
existence, vii, viii, ix, x, 4, 5, 7, 10, 11, 14, 38, 40, 41, 45, 46, 47, 48, 50, 51, 60, 64, 75, 78, 91, 92, 94, 95, 96, 97, 98, 99, 101, 102, 103, 105, 108, 109,

110, 112, 113, 115, 120, 136, 147, 151, 152, 153, 155, 159, 160, 164, 183, 189, 191, 198, 200, 205, 206, 208, 211, 213, 224, 225, 226, 229, 231, 232, 235, 237, 239, 241, 243, 244, 255, 262, 263, 267
eyeball, 62, 244
faith, vii, viii, 50, 79, 92, 93, 95, 96, 97, 98, 99, 102, 103
feedback-response, 33
flea, 68, 244
force, 16, 28, 40, 43, 82, 102, 108, 111, 114, 115, 116, 123, 124, 126, 140, 146, 152, 156, 160, 213, 223, 225, 226, 250, 259
fossil, 158, 159, 165, 166, 167, 168, 172, 179
frequencies, 29, 67, 69, 128, 233, 234, 235, 236, 237, 239, 241, 242
functionality, 117, 148, 149, 150, 153, 176, 177, 230, 250, 251, 253, 258, 260, 261
galaxies, 66, 107, 110, 150, 261
galaxy, 66, 78, 107
gamma, 69, 72, 113, 235
gatekeeper, 75
gender, 24
genes, 42, 43, 145, 146, 197
genetic, 42, 43, 44, 100, 143, 146, 158, 159, 163, 164, 178, 181, 183, 186, 197, 221, 248, 249
genetics, 43, 44, 45, 96, 106, 146, 180
geology, 231
geomagnetic, 247, 248, 249
geometric, 117, 127, 150, 152
geophysiology, 231
ghosts, 48
gluon, 225, 226, 228
gluons, 225
growth, 30, 83, 127, 145, 194, 202, 207, 232, 236, 237, 238, 256
hadon, 225
haplotypes, 42
happiness, 6, 7, 187, 192, 193, 206
harmonies, 257, 267
harmony, 243, 255, 256, 257, 263
headaches, 32, 58
health, 4, 58, 184, 186, 242, 247
heart, ix, 17, 25, 28, 32, 33, 130, 154, 176, 184, 241, 255, 256
heartbeat, 149, 236, 255
hearts, viii, 17
Helix, 142, 143, 179
Herbs, 129
hexane, 119
hippocampus, 22
hologram, 63, 149, 261
holographic, 41, 63, 68, 149, 150, 151, 152, 153, 235, 262
holography, 146, 222
homeopathy, 122, 239
homeostasis, 231
homosexuality, 24
hormones, 24, 25, 30, 142, 182, 256
humankind, 39, 77, 115, 129, 168, 170, 171
humans, xi, 8, 19, 21, 42, 55, 58, 60, 68, 69, 75, 106, 127, 128, 134, 152, 168, 170, 171, 180, 181, 182, 183, 185, 187, 192,

194, 195, 196, 204, 206, 222, 232, 233, 241, 244, 248, 255, 263
hydrocarbon, 119
hydrogen, 117, 119, 126, 142
hypnotherapists, 201
hypnotist, 201
hypothalamic, 25
hypothalamus, 25, 30, 34
hypothesis, 51, 52, 55, 56, 59, 80, 81, 82, 88, 90, 91, 106, 113
identity, 10, 11, 13, 14, 16, 17, 20, 21, 23, 24, 27, 35, 42, 44, 46, 48, 73, 74, 159, 192, 261, 267
illusion, 6, 62, 87, 102, 208, 224, 230
individual, 4, 10, 14, 42, 44, 45, 46, 47, 48, 53, 80, 81, 83, 84, 85, 91, 92, 98, 135, 152, 155, 160, 168, 176, 177, 186, 192, 262
information, vii, x, xiii, 4, 9, 11, 14, 29, 30, 39, 41, 42, 63, 65, 67, 73, 75, 76, 77, 78, 79, 80, 91, 93, 94, 95, 97, 98, 103, 107, 108, 109, 126, 169, 175, 183, 201, 210, 213, 221, 227, 246, 250
instruments, 15, 39, 51, 52, 59, 60, 61, 63, 69, 72, 73, 74, 76, 77, 78, 83, 91, 92, 103, 216, 219, 222, 234, 235, 242, 245, 256, 257
intention, 18, 19, 29, 30, 32, 33, 40, 108, 141, 149, 152, 153, 155, 162, 190, 243, 257, 258, 260, 262, 265
interpretations, viii, 9, 52, 65, 68, 168
isotopes, 110, 172, 174, 242
lattice, 118, 119, 138
learning, ix, 7, 14, 19, 95, 97, 154, 155, 185, 190, 193, 194, 196, 202, 203, 204, 208, 209, 210, 212, 257, 261, 262, 263, 264, 265, 266
leptons, 225
lesions, 22
lifespan, 20, 249
light, viii, x, 36, 46, 61, 62, 63, 66, 70, 73, 74, 96, 113, 132, 161, 175, 215, 217, 219, 220, 221, 236, 237, 238
logic, xii, 17, 27, 30, 141, 143, 180
magnetism, 96, 219, 247
memory, 19, 22, 23, 27, 28, 38, 105, 121, 122, 123, 124, 135, 148, 185, 212, 239
messengers, 27, 31, 97, 99, 241
molecules, 20, 38, 43, 66, 70, 73, 110, 111, 114, 117, 118, 119, 120, 121, 122, 123, 125, 126, 142, 143, 145, 147, 172, 192, 218, 239, 240, 250, 254
mortality, 81
motive, xii, 53, 90, 94, 265
movie, 40, 41, 136, 141, 195, 263
muscle, 25, 32, 240, 241
music, 6, 8, 41, 43, 256
mystery, 3, 102, 213, 221, 223, 232
near-death, 37
neuro-chemicals, 26
neuromatrix, 26
neurotransmitter, 31, 182

neurotransmitters, 24
neutrino, 221, 226
neutrons, 110, 172, 221, 224, 225, 228
non-life, 105, 164, 191
nutrients, 33, 126, 145, 147, 231
observations, xi, 3, 9, 29, 37, 38, 51, 52, 64, 65, 75, 78, 111, 116, 120, 123, 131, 136, 158, 185, 188, 189, 195, 219, 224, 225, 226, 227, 228, 235, 240, 245, 246
ocean, 47, 50, 113, 128, 232
octahedral, 118
octaves, 257
offspring, 163, 164, 181, 186
operators, 13, 18, 54, 55, 57, 58
orchestra, 256, 257
organ, 17, 24, 25, 125, 176, 177, 189, 251
organism, 14, 18, 19, 27, 43, 48, 109, 124, 125, 142, 143, 144, 145, 146, 147, 148, 149, 150, 154, 158, 159, 162, 163, 164, 166, 168, 172, 182, 183, 185, 187, 188, 189, 190, 191, 192, 194, 222, 231, 232, 237, 243, 244, 250, 251, 253, 257, 260, 261, 262
organs, 15, 17, 30, 39, 127, 158, 175, 176, 179, 181, 240, 241
origin, 11, 13, 101, 106, 107, 108, 109, 113, 114, 121, 123, 135, 148, 159, 168, 169, 170, 174, 175, 230, 236, 243
oscillation, 67, 114, 219
pain, 18, 19, 26, 34, 68, 164, 185, 192, 197, 201, 202, 203, 204, 211, 216, 263, 266
pancreas, 25
parents, 43, 65, 186, 204, 207
particle, 71, 110, 111, 115, 116, 117, 119, 120, 121, 124, 150, 154, 217, 219, 221, 222, 223, 224, 225, 227, 228, 229
particles, 71, 109, 110, 114, 116, 117, 120, 121, 123, 124, 126, 161, 217, 218, 219, 220, 221, 223, 224, 225, 226, 227, 228, 229, 230, 250, 267
peer-acceptance, 85
peer-control, 85
peer-pressure, 65
perception, 9, 18, 26, 39, 59, 61, 63, 65, 69, 74, 75, 78, 80, 83, 91, 94, 106, 107, 116, 117, 121, 125, 126, 127, 128, 136, 137, 138, 139, 144, 146, 148, 149, 152, 154, 175, 219, 227, 232, 235, 240, 241, 244, 245, 246
perhaps, 50, 56, 167, 177
personality, 14, 16, 17, 22, 24, 27, 33, 36, 43, 45, 46, 47, 48, 102, 105, 151, 152, 160, 190, 191, 196
pharmaceuticals, 56, 129
physicist, 2, 132, 161, 218, 224, 226, 230
physics, viii, 96, 99, 111, 112, 121, 122, 146, 217, 219, 221, 223, 227, 228, 230, 258
plants, 22, 70, 127, 128, 129, 130, 192, 194, 195, 239

primordial, 106, 109, 141, 147, 161
propane, 119
protons, 219, 224, 225, 228
psychosomatic, 26
pulse, 114, 235, 241, 243, 250, 251, 255, 256, 261
purpose, 5, 8, 10, 11, 14, 47, 48, 53, 96, 102, 105, 108, 109, 138, 141, 146, 148, 149, 150, 152, 155, 156, 179, 180, 191, 207, 208, 213, 225, 230, 243, 250, 252, 254, 258, 260, 263, 264, 265, 266
pyrimidine, 142
quadriplegic, 17
quantum, 96, 111, 115, 219, 221, 222, 223, 224, 226, 227, 228, 230, 267
receptors, 25, 28, 29, 34, 240
relativity, 95, 96, 115, 153, 228
religion, vii, 97
rennin, 256
researchers, vii, xi, 14, 15, 24, 25, 26, 35, 37, 44, 45, 51, 53, 54, 55, 58, 60, 63, 65, 70, 71, 76, 80, 83, 84, 85, 86, 87, 88, 90, 91, 92, 93, 96, 122, 129, 131, 132, 134, 135, 166, 173, 174, 183, 185, 200, 232, 236, 237, 247, 248
resonance, 72, 73, 227, 241, 242
rhythms, 20, 114, 176, 236, 237, 246, 250, 256
scientists, vii, xi, xii, 19, 30, 47, 51, 56, 59, 78, 82, 85, 86, 90, 92, 94, 95, 97, 99, 102, 105, 107, 109, 111, 115, 118, 119, 121, 123, 131, 141, 143, 146, 147, 148, 158, 159, 169, 172, 173, 178, 195, 216, 217, 221, 222, 235, 240, 243, 252, 255
self-awareness, 211
self-consciousness, 212
self-distinction, 162
selfishness, 187
semi-helix, 142
senses, 6, 8, 38, 39, 41, 42, 47, 61, 62, 63, 65, 67, 68, 69, 70, 74, 75, 77, 78, 83, 91, 92, 98, 102, 108,[1] 109, 148, 192, 193, 196, 245, 246, 253
serotonin, 25, 30, 34, 35, 182
sonar, 67, 76, 233, 241
space-time, 115
species, 47, 63, 67, 100, 105, 129, 130, 158, 159, 161, 163, 164, 165, 166, 167, 170, 172, 173, 178, 179, 183, 185, 186, 187, 188, 189, 191, 192, 193, 194, 195, 199, 202, 203, 205, 207, 211, 213, 231, 232, 244, 245
spectroscopy, 72, 74, 235
spectrum, 39, 59, 61, 69, 70, 72, 96
speed, 35, 36, 62, 82, 85, 139, 236, 240, 258, 259
spirit, 14, 47
stress, 7, 29, 31, 32, 103, 187, 188, 240
struggle, 23, 24, 94, 121, 162, 163, 203, 207
subatomic, 110, 111, 116, 117, 120, 121, 124, 125, 150, 217, 250

1

suprachiasmatic, 255
survival, 4, 18, 19, 57, 83, 100, 105, 158, 162, 163, 164, 165, 167, 179, 182, 183, 185, 186, 187, 188, 189, 190, 191, 194, 195, 203, 207, 211, 232, 266
synchronicity, 114, 149, 176, 241, 250, 251, 256, 263
tomatoes, 238
transcendental, 39, 45, 47, 48, 50, 51, 78, 103, 108, 109, 148, 149, 153, 191, 192, 202, 203, 204, 205, 207, 213, 214, 251, 261, 262, 266, 267
transcription, 43, 126
trust, 50, 60, 79, 80, 92, 93, 94, 97, 98, 102, 103, 195, 207, 213
truth, x, 7, 50, 53, 90, 91, 92, 94, 95, 190, 214, 243
universe, ix, xiii, 2, 40, 61, 66, 69, 70, 78, 92, 98, 99, 102, 105, 106, 107, 108, 109, 113, 114, 116, 124, 127, 135, 140, 148, 149, 150, 151, 152, 153, 154, 155, 156, 168, 172, 176, 216, 217, 220, 221, 222, 223, 229, 230, 231, 235, 243, 245, 250, 251, 252, 253, 255, 256, 257, 258, 260, 261, 262, 265, 266, 267
vibration, 114, 233, 234, 235, 242, 243, 254, 255, 257, 267
vibrational, 62, 234, 235, 239, 240, 241, 243, 250, 251, 252, 253, 254, 255, 257, 258, 266, 267
waterfall, 21, 49, 50
wave, 20, 29, 71, 116, 117, 118, 122, 128, 219, 220, 222, 224, 226, 227, 229, 230, 242
waveform, 30, 34, 41, 73, 219, 224
wavelengths, 39, 60, 61, 62, 67, 70, 236, 237
wave-particle, 116, 117, 118, 122, 220, 222, 224, 229, 230
zebras, 165